12/19/2019

ENDORSEMENTS

Those from Reformed circles are sometimes critiqued for being "brains on a stick," making faith all about head knowledge and insulating hearts from the warm embrace of the gospel. That's just one reason to celebrate this devotional founded on the core standards of our faith that unites deep understanding of doctrinal essentials with profound reflections on the personal implications of those truths.

Bryan Chapell, senior pastor, Grace Presbyterian Church, Peoria, Illinois

I'm thankful for Pastor Bob Flayhart and his team at Oak Mountain Presbyterian Church for providing this devotional on the *Westminster Shorter Catechism*. The shorter catechism ought to be more widely used and appreciated than it is in our circles, and this tool aims to make it accessible for use in personal and family settings by supplying accompanying memory verses, Scripture readings, stories, and short reflections. In addition, preachers and teachers may benefit from reading the personal stories included. There is good material for sermon/lesson illustrations to be gleaned from them.

J. Ligon Duncan, John E. Richards professor of Systematic and Historical Theology, chancellor and CEO of Reformed Theological Seminary

For me, two trustworthy and well-anchored voices merge together in this volume. The first is *The Westminster Shorter Catechism*, the abbreviated, memorable version of the rich, historic *Confession* by the same name, which so many of us lean upon as a theological compass. The second voice is that of Oak Mountain Presbyterian Church, led by my good friend Bob Flayhart. This combination of voices results in a refreshing dance between two essentials that must undergird every mention of the person and work of Jesus Christ, namely, *grace* and *truth*. Take this resource up, use it, and by all means share it. Both you and your faith community will be much the richer if you do.

Scott Sauls, senior pastor of Christ Presbyterian Church in Nashville, Tennessee, and author of *Befriend* and *Irresistible Faith*

A big thank you to Oak Mountain Presbyterian Church for utilizing the framework of the Westminster Shorter Catechism and the gifts of their own congregation to give us *A Good Confession*. This devotional plan will be a great adventure for individuals, families, and churches who want to pass the richness and relevance of the Reformed faith to the next generation. I plan to give a copy to our children and grandchildren so we can journey through it together.

Susan Hunt, author of *Spiritual Mothering* and former coordinator of women's ministries for the Presbyterian Church in America

As the mother of three young children, a realistic plan can make or break whether or not I carry out my heartfelt desires. Through catechism questions and answers, relevant quotations, and relatable storytelling, this weekly devotional points our family toward the foundational doctrines of the Christian faith in an accessible way. It is an invaluable resource for parents, pastors, and teachers who desire to both teach and grow in their theology.

Hunter Beless, founder of Journeywomen and host of The Journeywomen Podcast

Does the image of a kaleidoscope of grace, a fountain of encouragement, and a tapestry of truth sound inviting to you? Then, by all means, grab this new devotional by my dear friends at Oak Mountain Presbyterian Church. With the *Westminster Shorter Catechism* as the heartbeat, Bob Flayhart and his staff have woven scriptures, quotes, and stories together to reveal the beauty of Jesus and the riches of the gospel. What a gift!

Scotty Smith, pastor emeritus of Christ Community Church and teacher in residence at West End Community Church, Nashville, Tennessee

A Good Confession is a much needed resource for Christians today. With warmth, wit, and wisdom, the authors give insight that will encourage, strengthen, and edify. The book offers Scripture verses to memorize, questions and answers from the *Westminster Shorter Catechism*, and short reflections with Scripture readings. If you are looking for a book to help you learn old truths in new ways, connect the dots between what you know and how you live, and fall more deeply in love with your Savior, this is the book for you!

Courtney Doctor, coordinator of Women's Training and Content,
The Gospel Coalition speaker, Bible teacher, and author of
From Garden to Glory: A Bible Study on the Bible's Story

I picked up this devotional guide and before I blinked, it had swept me through weeks of readings. What treasure is this book: Scripture readings and delightful quotations that guide the reader through the central doctrines of the faith and the practices of the faithful, in one year. The stories and quotations bring joy, even delight, in God's truths and ways, day after day. Whether you have read morning devotionals for decades, you will enjoy this book like no other. And if you are giving devotionals a first thought, start here.

Dr. Dan Doriani, professor and vice president, Covenant Seminary, St. Louis, Missouri

A Good Confession brings head and heart together around theological substance and engaging stories. This accessible devotional encourages the church to live out the content of what they believe in the context of community.

Karen Hodge, women's ministry coordinator, Presbyterian Church in America,
and author of *Transformed: Life-taker to Life-giver* and *Life-giving Leadership*.

With its theologically rich stories, practical devotional format, and integrated Bible reading and memorization plans, *A Good Confession* brings the *Westminster Shorter Catechism* to life. This resource is a gift for both the individual and the family who wants to regularly and systematically set their hearts and minds on the elemental and critical truths of God's Word.

Katie Orr, author and Bible teacher

Practicing a plan for daily communion with God is one of the most frequent challenges I and my congregation face. The Oak Mountain Presbyterian staff team has done the church a tremendous service by compiling scriptures, catechisms, prayers, quotes, and stories—access to which would normally require a small library—into one, easy-to-use devotional. The material is theologically rich, enjoyable to read, and focused on growing in the gospel. I'm looking forward to recommending this to others and seeing the fruit that is produced in their lives as a result.

Ray Cortese, pastor, Seven Rivers Presbyterian Church, Lecanto, Florida

A Good Confession is an excellent devotional book that brings to life timeless truths from the *Westminster Shorter Catechism*. I so appreciate this work, which feeds the soul and equips the saints for kingdom service.

Lloyd Kim, coordinator, Mission to the World

Through prayers, Scripture readings, quotes, and stories, *A Good Confession* ignites the heart and challenges the mind so we can all do what we were created to do: glorify God and enjoy him forever.

Christina Fox, speaker, writer, and author of *A Heart Set Free*,
Closer Than a Sister, and *Idols of a Mother's Heart*

A Good Confession

DAILY REFLECTIONS ON THE

WESTMINSTER SHORTER CATECHISM

....

*Written and collected
by the members and affiliates of
Oak Mountain Presbyterian Church,
Birmingham, AL*

GREG POOLE, editor
HOLLY MACKLE, managing editor
LISA STILWELL, associate editor
CARA JOHNSON, associate editor
ELISABETH WELTY, associate and quotes editor
MATT REDMOND, quotes editor

©2019 Oak Mountain Presbyterian Church

Published by:

Committee on Discipleship Ministries
1700 North Brown Road, Suite 102
Lawrenceville, Georgia 30043

PCA Bookstore: 1-800-283-1357
678-825-1100
www.pcacdm.org/bookstore

ISBN: 978-1-944964-40-5

TABLE OF CONTENTS

FOREWORD

GRACE IS: *the only hope we have for growing in intimacy with God.*

THE MEANS OF GRACE: *the sustaining part of growing in intimacy with God, including spiritual practices such as reading and memorizing the Word of God, spending time in prayer, having fellowship, lifting our hearts in worship, giving generously, and fasting regularly, as well as participating in the sacraments of baptism and the Lord's Supper.*

After almost forty years of ministry, I've never met anyone actively growing in intimacy with God who is not regularly taking advantage of the means of grace. This means they are particularly exemplified in the Word of God, focused in prayer, devoted in worship, and soaked in fellowship. These practices that draw us close to the Father began in the first century church (Acts 2:42–47) and are as timeless and integral to our faith today as they were then.

I had the privilege of planting Oak Mountain Presbyterian Church in 1989 and have served as its senior pastor for almost thirty years. I've experienced the power of the means of grace in my own life and have also seen the life-changing grace of those means in the lives of others. However, I've also witnessed the struggle that many in the church experience to spend regular, meaningful time with Jesus. It seems that most Christians *know* they need to have regular devotional times and even *desire* to have that time, but they struggle to follow through.

Part of discipleship in the local church is helping God's people with the how-to's. Several years ago, our pastoral staff discovered that many in our congregation were not spending quality time with God on a daily basis, including many of our leaders. As we discussed how to create an atmosphere for changing that pattern, we landed on finding a devotional for the entire congregation to participate in together—one that would give a daily reading plan that would engage our thoughts, feelings, desires, and choices.

After implementing this plan, we soon discovered a dramatic increase in the number of people having a meaningful devotional time. We also learned that a congregation-wide devotional was a great motivator and provided weekly accountability for the body as we entered into the same scriptures and texts together. Furthermore, congregants had a common experience that manifested itself during various small group gatherings at lunches, Bible studies, fellowship groups, and brief encounters throughout the week. In thirty years of ministry at Oak Mountain, few practices have had the spiritual growth impact that a church-wide devotional experience has given us.

We have a saying around Oak Mountain: "Small things done slowly over a long period of time change the world." It has been incredible to see what God has done in our congregation throughout years of emphasizing the grace of God as the motivation for enabling greater faith and obedience.

It has been so fulfilling for me as a pastor to see the gospel fruit of grace expressed through the many contributors to *A Good Confession*. These contributors are not super-saints, and many of them are not church staff, elders, or deacons. They are fellow journeymen and women walking side by side on the path of sanctification, still in the process of becoming who God created and called them to be. They are people who realize that grace doesn't fix us. Rather, they understand that grace is simply how broken people with broken lives live in a broken world, yet continually wait with hope and expectancy for redemption, both present and future, as we long for Christ's return.

Our prayer and hope is that you would use this devotional to grow in the grace and knowledge of our Lord and Savior, Jesus Christ (2 Peter 3:18). Perhaps God might lead you and your faith community to begin an annual congregational devotional. But even if he doesn't do that, we hope you find yourself personally growing in intimacy with the Father, and with his Son, through the Spirit. Begin now. Remember that small things done slowly over a long period of time change the world . . . beginning with your own heart.

Enjoy.
Dr. Bob Flayhart,
Senior Pastor, Oak Mountain Presbyterian Church

INTRODUCTION

I'm a runner. I enjoy the simple pleasure of running. The experience is mentally grounding and settling for me. It's the feel of the wind on my face, the sense of stepping away from the pressure and weight of life, and the space to let my mind roam from one thought to another without distraction. Because of my love for the sport, I'm even willing to experience pain and discomfort in order to run faster or farther, and to see what my body can do. In other words, I like to grow as a runner. But over time, I've learned I need a plan as well as an understanding of the nuances of the sport to create one that works. I need to know how to schedule the right mix of fast runs, easy runs, and long runs. I need to know my dietary requirements and the needs of my body in regard to rest.

Obviously, there is a lot to know about running if one is to do it well. How did I learn so much? I observed those who went before me, read running magazines, and simply ran—sometimes poorly and slowly—but I ran. Without a plan, I'd still be a runner, but I would miss out on so much delight. I am a runner because it's something I was made to be.

So it goes with being a follower of Jesus. When it comes to a growing spiritual life, we need the desire, the plan, and the know-how. A healthy aim requires both the reality of the gift of grace as well as its persevering disciplines.

We see this most plainly stated in the first question and answer of the subject of this devotional, the *Westminster Shorter Catechism*:

Q: What is man's chief end?
A: Man's chief end is to glorify God and enjoy him forever.

The catechism authors recognized that the spiritual life is not a split between head and heart, but rather an integration of the two, resulting in gratitude to the Father and grace to others and ourselves. Both the intentional glorification of God with one's will and the enjoyment of God with one's heart combine to connect us to the Father on a personal and intimate level. Yet, so often, believers miss this and fall heavy-handed on one side or the other.

After over thirty years of pastoral work, I've become increasingly aware of my own tendency to falter in both my desire and discipline when it comes to my spiritual life. I don't think I'm alone. Many Christians say they believe great things about God, but their lives say something else. Because our actions flow out of our beliefs, how do we foster an atmosphere of daily devotional study that connects us to deep and lasting communion with God and moves outward in our practical daily living? Our wish is that *A Good Confession: Daily Reflections on the Westminster Shorter Catechism* will do just that: connect our confessions of faith from the mouth with our doing of faith from a wellspring of love and devotion to God and neighbor.

Throughout this devotional you will find a theological framework, key passages of scripture, modeled prayers, and spiritual insights from true life stories and powerful quotes. The hope is that these elements will open a new space in your heart and mind in which to welcome the Holy Spirit to engage you with God at more than just a rational level, but in a deep, multifaceted, whole-hearted way.

Why the *Westminster Shorter Catechism*?

The theological framework for this book is provided by the *Westminster Shorter Catechism*, which was written over 350 years ago for the purpose of clarifying doctrinal standards and offering a broad theological understanding of what the Bible teaches. In 1643, the British Parliament convened a gathering of pastors and biblical scholars, known as the Westminster Assembly, with the charge to develop a statement of faith and tools for instruction for the church in Britain. One of those tools was the *Shorter Catechism*, published in 1646, which was originally written for use with children, but is used today with all ages in a variety of denominations around the world. Designed in a question and answer format, the *Shorter Catechism* is composed of 107 questions and answers, fifty-two of which we've chosen as a devotional focus for each week of the year.

God has been, and will continue to be, faithful to believers across time and space. His promises apply to his people regardless of era, location, birthright, or any other qualifying factors man has placed on himself. With grateful hearts, Oak Mountain Presbyterian Church celebrates the work of the Westminster Assembly and its adherence to the truth of the Bible in creating a succinct, doctrinally clarifying document to aid even us, as modern-day believers, as we seek to know Jesus.

HOW TO USE THIS DEVOTIONAL

This devotional is designed for use individually. However, because God made us to live in community, you might consider using it as a family, a small group, or even as a church body. Several of each week's elements could be used in corporate worship and could give friends, couples, or congregations a common vocabulary, just as the Westminster Assembly intended.

Below lists the variety of components offered to help enrich your time with the Lord each day.

Weekly and Daily Elements

Each week begins with an introductory story to prepare your heart and mind for the theme of the week. There are six daily elements which include a memory verse (to be learned incrementally during the week), a prayer, a psalm, and the catechism question and answer. Also, there is a unique Scripture passage plus reflective readings for each of the five days.

Personal Story

Real-life stories, each from a different person, are given on the first day of the week to demonstrate how someone has experienced the broader topic of the week's catechism question theme in everyday life. We hope these stories will give practicality to theological concepts you study, helping you remember and connect with them in a personal way.

Catechism Question and Answer

For churches using this devotional congregationally, we encourage you to incorporate the question and answer as a responsive reading during your worship service each week. For individual study, seek to find the spiritual truth they provide and meditate on it throughout the week.

Prayer

All prayers included in this text are from *Valley of Vision*, and are used with the kind permission of Banner of Truth Trust. The full book, *Valley of Vision*, is available from banneroftruth.org. Our hope is that this prayer will awaken and direct your heart as you approach the Lord each day.

Memory Verse

The week starts with a short memory verse (intended for daily practice) to complement the catechism question. The discipline of storing up God's word in your mind produces readily available fruit to meditate on and recall when you are faced with doubts, struggles and temptation. The verse is broken down into brief phrases, so you can memorize a small piece of the verse on Monday, add another phrase Tuesday, and so forth, so that by the end of the week it is familiar and easy to recall.

Scripture Reading

Each day provides a brief passage of scripture that ties in with that week's question and answer. By providing five days of material instead of seven, we hope you experience freedom to spend extra time on certain readings but that you won't feel as though you're falling behind if you miss a day.

Reflections

Each day ends with one or two reflections from a variety of authors—past and present, male and female, theological and secular—selected because they bring understanding, insight, and creative reflection on the catechism question at hand.

I've been a runner for many years now. I've learned that whenever I stop following a plan, I get hurt more easily, lose motivation, and don't make progress. It's been the same way in my devotional life. Whenever I've taken the "wing it" approach, I've wound up spiritually limping, losing delight in and enjoyment of God, and not experiencing the growth God desires. But reading the Bible is about more than just building spiritual muscles. Although it certainly does strengthen our hearts, it's ultimately about understanding why we would want to build those muscles at all and to see that we must look at Who it is that's asking us to run. Devotion is delight because of the deep goodness and unwavering heart of the One asking for it. That's the kind of invitation that draws our hearts near to his own and brings us into true and sincere worship.

We invite you to join with us on this devotional journey as we seek to reach back to take the torch from the Westminster Assembly and confess with them as the communion of saints: yes, we were created to both glorify God and enjoy him forever. Because the torch doesn't ultimately stay with us—it was created to be passed along. Lord, equip us to do so.

Soli Deo Gloria.
Greg Poole
Associate Pastor, Oak Mountain Presbyterian Church
with Cara Johnson, Holly Mackle, Matt Redmond,
and Elisabeth Welty

··

How To Use This Devotional

QUICK START GUIDE

EACH DAY OF THE WEEK

- First, read and recite the catechism question and answer.
- Pray the weekly prayer.
- Worship God as you read the Psalm selection for the week.
- Reflect on the memory verse, and practice the portion of that day's memory work.
- For the first day of the week, read the story that introduces the theological truth.
- Read the specific daily Scripture reading.
- Read the daily reflections from various writers.

WEEK 1

OUR CHIEF END

WESTMINSTER SHORTER CATECHISM QUESTION 1

Q | What is the chief end of man?

A | Man's chief end is to glorify God and to enjoy him forever.

PRAY *O Father, thou has made man for the glory of thyself, and when not an instrument of that glory, he is a thing of nought. Amen.*

WORSHIP GOD BY MEDITATING ON PSALM 5

COMMIT GOD'S WORD TO MEMORY | ROMANS 11:33

DAY 1 | Oh, the depth
DAY 2 | of the riches
DAY 3 | and wisdom and knowledge of God!
DAY 4 | How unsearchable are his judgments
DAY 5 | and how inscrutable his ways!

INDIA

The giant wheels tuck into the underbelly of the plane as it ascends into the sky, and I find myself praying for God's eyes, ears, and heart to help me embrace the country to where I am heading yet never desired to visit. After eighteen hours of in-flight meals, naps, and movies, every preconceived notion of safety, cleanliness, and order I have of the third world country is challenged the moment the wheels touch down.

As I deboard the plane, I welcome myself to the city of Bangalore. I immediately notice the irony of contrast all around. Beautiful buildings rise from torn and pot-holed streets by the efforts of laborers standing on bamboo scaffolding. The streets are swept clear, yet they're lined with roadside mounds that garbage wallahs compile nightly. Stray dogs dart collarless down dirty streets while owners walk leashed ones on makeshift sidewalks. The smell of garbage disgusts the senses on one corner while the delicious aromas of curries tantalize on the next. A crippled beggar in tattered clothes sits crosslegged at a temple while a dark-skinned beauty in aristocratic colors drops him a coin. A man ogles a western-dressed woman as another chivalrously holds the door for his bride.

And then there's the traffic. The constant flow of cars, scooters, buses, motorbikes, and vans rush down rivers of concrete with no mind to rules or regulations. The constant cacophony of beeping horns sound off messages of "On your left," "I'm passing," "Move!" Attempting to cross over through the chaos seems futile at best, suicidal at worst. Surprisingly, drivers instinctively know when and how to dodge one another and the persistent push of pedestrians.

After moments of soaking it all in, I pause to listen and find there is an unexpected rhythm to the madness. It's a joyous chord hidden in the chorus composed by the Conductor for his creation to hear. And I catch a strain of that joyful melody as I find myself in the very flow of the river. Fear and prejudice had blinded me to this continent, culture, and people. Until that moment, I had sadly missed their part in the orchestra of God's symphony—a music of contrasts and disarray more beautiful than the small ensemble of my tiny spot back home across the globe.

I'm anxiously ready to join Indians from this city, Americans from across the U.S., and people from around the world in worship of the One who sees each of us, the One who unites us as one people of many nations, the One who gives all of our differences the rhythm of his Son. It is in and through his Son that "different" is diffused into prisms of glory mirroring the Creator in his creation. And I find myself wanting to twirl, spin, dip and sway to his rhythm of joy.

DAY 1

READ ROMANS 11:33-36

" Once you become aware that the main business that you are here for is to know God, most of life's problems fall into place of their own accord.

J. I. PACKER

" One of the strategies for dealing with worry is to be overtaken by something more important than the object of your worries.

EDWARD T. WELCH

DAY 2

READ ISAIAH 12:1-6

> We don't have a lot of time on this earth. We weren't meant to spend it this way. Human beings were not meant to sit in little cubicles staring at computer screens all day, filling out useless forms and listening to eight different bosses drone on about mission statements.
>
> PETER GIBBONS

> Man was originally made that he might glorify God. "The chief end of man is to glorify God and enjoy him forever," as the Shorter Catechism reminds us; and the heinous character of sin is that it is a failure to glorify God. In the same way, when we are thinking of salvation, we must not think of it in the first instance in terms of our deliverance from particular sins, or even from condemnation. It includes that, of course, but the chief thing about it is that the glory of God has been revealed to us through it, the glory of his love and grace, has embraced us where we were. Our thinking about salvation should always, primarily, be in terms of the glory of God.
>
> D. MARTYN LLOYD-JONES

DAY 3

READ REVELATION 4:1-11

66 Because the face of God is so lovely, my brothers and sisters, so beautiful, once you have seen it, nothing else can give you pleasure. It will give insatiable satisfaction of which we will never tire. We shall always be hungry and always have our fill.

AUGUSTINE

66 I think we delight to praise what we enjoy because the praise not merely expresses but completes the enjoyment; it is its appointed consummation. It is frustrating to have discovered a new author and not to be able to tell anyone how good he is; to come suddenly, at the turn of the road, upon some mountain valley of unexpected grandeur and then to have to keep silent because the people with you care for it no more than for a tin can in the ditch; to hear a good joke and find no one to share it with. . . . The Scotch catechism says that man's chief end is "to glorify God and enjoy him forever." But we shall then know that these are the same thing. Fully to enjoy is to glorify. In commanding us to glorify him, God is inviting us to enjoy him.

C. S. LEWIS

DAY 4

READ PSALM 86:1-13

    God formed us for his pleasure, and so formed us that we as well as he can in divine communion enjoy the sweet and mysterious mingling of kindred personalities. He meant us to see him and live with him and draw our life from his smile.

A. W. TOZER

    Let a man who is thirsty be brought to an ocean of pure water, and he has enough. . . . God is a satisfying good—the soul cries out, "I have enough." God is the chief good. That which is the chief good must ravish the soul with pleasure! There must be in it rapturous delight and quintessence of joy! God is the chief good. Therefore the enjoyment of him is the highest felicity.

THOMAS WATSON

DAY 5

READ ISAIAH 60:1-22

" The most influential Christian authors of the twentieth century believed that every human soul was caught up in a very great story: a fearsome war against a Shadow of Evil that has invaded the world to enslave the sons and daughters of Adam. Yet those who resist the Shadow are assured that they will not be left alone; they will be given the gift of friendship amid their struggle and grief. Even more, they will find the grace and strength to persevere, to play their part in the story, however long it endures and wherever it may lead them.

JOE LOCONTE

" With God at the center of your universe of worship, with the gospel at the center of your life, all other good gifts—people and pleasures, thoughts and things—take their proper place and proportion in our lives. They are more pleasing and enjoyable because they give the pleasures they are designed to give, and no more.

JARED C. WILSON

WEEK 2

THE WORD OF GOD

WESTMINSTER SHORTER CATECHISM QUESTION 2

Q | What rule has God given to direct us how we should glorify and enjoy him?

A | The Word of God, which is contained in the Scriptures of the Old and New Testaments, is the only rule to direct us how we may glorify and enjoy him.

PRAY *O thou who hast the hearts of all men in thine hand, form my heart according to the Word, according to the image of thy Son, so shall Christ the Word, and his Word be my strength and comfort. Amen.*

WORSHIP GOD BY MEDITATING ON PSALM 19

COMMIT GOD'S WORD TO MEMORY | PSALM 19:7

DAY 1 | The law of the Lord is perfect,
DAY 2 | reviving the soul;
DAY 3 | the testimony of the Lord is sure,
DAY 4 | rejoicing the heart.

GETTING READY FOR SCHOOL

t was one of those days—one of those tedious, aggravating, death-by-a-thousand-paper-cuts days where I could almost *feel* individual hairs on my head turning gray.

My husband and I had overslept, which resulted in a frenzy of strategic damage control, especially considering our current car-sharing situation. With only thirty minutes to get five people fed, dressed, and out the door, our home turned into the War Room. We both needed showers! The kids' clothes weren't ready! Why didn't we make school snacks the night before? Oh, right, because we'd been so tired we couldn't see straight. We flew around the house searching for shoes, digging clean socks out of the ever-growing pile of unfolded laundry, and shouting about jackets.

Thanks to the chaos, our daughters—three angelic creatures ages seven, five, and two—went into what I like to call "velociraptor mode." Talons popped, fangs glistened, and the scent of fragile emotions hung in the air. As my husband and I tore the house apart looking for the keys to the van, our little cherubs amused themselves by shredding each other's feelings until *all* of them were crying.

By the time we finally stuffed them into their car seats, I was ready to cry too. And it was only 7:30 a.m.

On our way to the younger ones' preschool, other stressors began to pile on top of the morning's turbulent start: our bank account wasn't where it should be; the van was making a funny noise; we had a million projects around the house that needed doing, but no money or time to do them. And then there were the *really* serious concerns: health problems in our extended family and multiple friends enduring unbelievably difficult circumstances.

Fear began to burn through my brain like molten lava.

As my children raged about things that didn't even make sense, much less matter, I fired a prayer toward the sky:

Lord, I'm having a hard time believing—that you love me, that you care about my stress, that you see my loved ones' pain. How can I believe when things are like this?

In the next instant, truth came tumbling forth: *he is the God of my unbelief.*

The God of my unbelief? What did that mean?

I needed truth—and there was only one place to find it.

That morning, God made it clear that he has already given me everything I need to find rest. He has given me his Word which contains all the affirmation, wisdom, reassurance, and compassion I could ever need. In short, it contains truth—for the easy days, for the hard days, and for everything in between.

DAY 1

> **READ** 2 PETER 3:1-18

> " Happiness can be found, even in the darkest of times, if one only remembers to turn on the light.
>
> J. K. ROWLING

> " By the reading of scripture I am so renewed that all nature seems renewed around me and with me. The sky seems to be a pure, a cooler blue, the trees a deeper green, light is sharper on the outlines of the forest and the hills and the whole world is charged with the glory of God and I feel fire and music in the earth under my feet.
>
> THOMAS MERTON

DAY 2

READ 1 JOHN 1:1-4

> Our aim in studying the Godhead must be to know God himself the better. Our concern must be to enlarge our acquaintance, not simply with the doctrine of God's attributes, but with the living God whose attributes they are. As he is the subject of our study, and our helper in it, so he must himself be the end of it. We must seek, in studying God, to be led to God. It was for this purpose that revelation was given, and it is to this use we must put it.

J. I. PACKER

> I like good strong words that mean something.

LOUISA MAY ALCOTT

DAY 3

READ JOHN 15:1-17

> Just as I would reveal something of myself through a work of art, so God reveals something of himself through nature. Just as I might reveal my character through a personal visit, so Jesus reveals the character of God. And just as a letter might reveal the heart of the sender, so scripture is a window into the heart of God. . . . It is a written document of intentional communication from one living person (God is personal) to another.

JAMES WILHOIT & EVAN HOWARD

> For me, the Bible is the Book. I cannot see how anybody can live without it.

GABRIELA MISTRAL

DAY 4

READ DEUTERONOMY 4:1-9

> I had to lean and lean hard on the full weight of scripture, on the fullness of the Word of God . . . I had a pastor and friends in the Lord who asked nothing less of me than that I die to myself. Biblical orthodoxy can offer real compassion, because in our struggle against sin, we cannot undermine God's power to change lives.

ROSARIA BUTTERFIELD

> I have found in the Bible words for my inmost thoughts, songs for my joys, utterances for my hidden griefs, and pleadings for my shame and feebleness.

SAMUEL TAYLOR COLERIDGE

DAY 5

> **READ** 2 TIMOTHY 3:10-17

"" If you look for truth, you may find comfort in the end: if you look for comfort, you will not get either comfort or truth—only soft soap and wishful thinking to begin with and, in the end, despair.

C. S. LEWIS

"" If we come to scripture with our minds made up, expecting to hear from it only an echo of our own thoughts and never the thunderclap of God's, then indeed he will not speak to us and we shall only be confirmed in our own prejudices. We must allow the Word of God to confront us, to disturb our security, to undermine our complacency and to overthrow our patterns of thought and behavior.

JOHN STOTT

WEEK 3

WHAT THE SCRIPTURES TEACH

WESTMINSTER SHORTER CATECHISM QUESTION 3

Q | What do the Scriptures principally teach?

A | The Scriptures principally teach, what man is to believe concerning God, and what duty God requires of man.

PRAY *I thank thee for the Holy Scriptures, their precepts, promises, directions, light. In them may I learn more of Christ, be enabled to retain his truth and have grace to follow it. Amen.*

WORSHIP GOD BY MEDITATING ON PSALM 119:97-112

COMMIT GOD'S WORD TO MEMORY | PSALM 119:105

DAY 1 | Your word
DAY 2 | is a lamp
DAY 3 | to my feet
DAY 4 | and a light
DAY 5 | to my path.

POLICE OFFICERS

As a kid, I remember my pastor quoting Charles Spurgeon who said, "The Word of God is like a lion. You don't have to defend a lion. All you have to do is let the lion loose, and the lion will defend itself." Almost nothing has proven more true in my life.

When I met my former co-worker Kevin, a young professional in his mid-twenties, he was completely engaged in his occupation as a police officer and enjoying his life at full speed. He didn't seem interested in spiritual things or in attending church. Yet, during our years together, I witnessed this young man accept Christ for the sole reason that he was fully convinced in his own heart that Jesus was the only way to heaven (John 14:6). The Holy Spirit immediately and perfectly taught his heart and mind what to believe and so he believed. No apologetics, no specific prayer in any specific order, no teaching from any certain pastor—just reading out loud the Word of God to him and briefly explaining the verse of Acts 4:12 was all that was necessary. The Lion of the Word prevailed in procuring eternal life for him as he put his faith alone in Christ.

Since knowing Kevin at the force, I've transitioned from full-time police duty to the counseling office. As a result, I've had the privilege of seeing many people change their entire life's direction after being confronted with Matthew 6:33: "Seek first the kingdom of God and his righteousness, and all these things will be added to you." As the people under my counsel started putting first the kingdom of God in their planning, it utterly transformed their lives' focus.

One elderly woman named Sarah was dealing with large amounts of stress and regret over the passing of time. She knew that most of her life was behind her and had been deep in thought about what impact she wanted her remaining years to have for others. All of these thoughts overwhelmed her and made her depressed. As we were talking, she stopped to meditate on the call of Jesus to "seek first the kingdom," and without me having to say the first word, she then looked at me and said, "I am having a God moment because he is totally rearranging my priorities."

What other book has such power to totally change people's thoughts and behaviors in an instant of time? Certainly no novel, poem, or biography has such power. Wise King Solomon explains that God's words are "like nails firmly fixed" so our beliefs are steady and also like "goads" in order to continually move our actions toward the will of God (Eccl. 12:11). Solomon classically sums up this twin effect of the Word with Ecclesiastes 12:13, "The end of the matter; all has been heard. Fear God and keep his commandments, for this is the whole duty of man."

DAY 1

READ JOHN 20:30-31

> We should note the grand end and object for which this and all the books of the New Testament were written. They were written to glorify Christ, to make us believe on him as the only Saviour of sinners, and to lead us to eternal life through faith in his name.
>
> J. C. RYLE

> Wouldn't it be amazing to learn to be a disciple by actually walking along with Jesus, as those first disciples did? We could hear him speak, watch him in action, and speak to him whenever we wanted. On the one hand, it is true that we don't have that exact experience, but on the other hand, we can hear the words of Jesus and see him in action and speak to him whenever we want to—this is because we have the Bible.
>
> STEPHEN SMALLMAN

DAY 2

> **READ** PSALM 119:1-16

> " Many a night I woke to the murmur of paper and knew (Dad) was up, sitting in the kitchen with frayed King James—oh, but he worked that book; he held to it like a rope ladder.
>
> LEIF ENGER

> " We are like Moses. The Bible is our burning bush—a faithful declaration of the presence and holiness of God. We ask it to tell us about ourselves, and all the while it is telling us about "I AM." We think that if it would just tell us who we are and what we should do, then our insecurities, fears, and doubts would vanish. But our insecurities, fears, and doubts can never be banished by the knowledge of who we are. They can only be banished by the knowledge of "I AM." We must read and study the Bible with our ears trained on hearing God's declaration of himself.
>
> JEN WILKIN

DAY 3

READ ACTS 10:34-43

> If you look at God through the lens of your human experience, you do so at your peril. To those who will listen, the Holy Spirit speaks through the Word to reinterpret our life experiences. This truth then goes on to shape our perceptions of future experience.
>
> DAVID POWLISON

> Counsel that contradicts the written Word is ungodly counsel.
>
> ELISABETH ELLIOTT

DAY 4

READ LUKE 24:13-35

> The Bible tells a true tale from God's perspective through the individual voices of the human authors. The Bible is God's story, his declaration of the way the world really is. The Bible is not an exhaustive history of the world, but it narrates, in a progressive way over time, the story of God's actions and what they mean for the people of God. . . . God reveals himself to restore relationship with his people. He enters history to rescue his creation and then proclaims that fact through the many writers of Scripture.
>
> MICHAEL EMLET

> There is an old jingle which is certainly simple and verges on the simplistic, but our forebears were fundamentally right when they taught that: the Old Testament is Jesus predicted; the Gospels are Jesus revealed; Acts is Jesus preached; the Epistles, Jesus explained; and the Revelation, Jesus expected. He is the climax as well as the substance and centre of the whole. In him all God's promises are yea and amen.
>
> J. A. MOTYER

DAY 5

READ JOSHUA 1:1-9

❝ Lisping our syllables, we scramble next
Through moral narrative, or sacred text;
And learn with wonder how this world began,
Who made, who marr'd, and who has ransomed man.

WILLIAM COWPER

❝ In both its diagnoses and its descriptions, the Bible is honest about life in a fallen world. This honesty is a sign of God's love. He is the wise and gentle father preparing his child for that walk through a tough neighborhood on the first day of school. He is a faithful friend praying with you before you face an unusual challenge. He is the caring physician informing you of what to expect from the disease he has just diagnosed.

PAUL DAVID TRIPP

WEEK 4

WHAT IS GOD

WESTMINSTER SHORTER CATECHISM QUESTION QUESTION 4

Q | What is God?

A | God is a Spirit, infinite, eternal, and unchangeable, in his being, wisdom, power, holiness, justice, goodness, and truth.

PRAY *Thou art the blessed God, happy in thyself, source of happiness in thy creatures. . . . Thou hast produced and sustained me . . . saved and kept me; thou art in every situation able to meet my needs and miseries. Amen.*

WORSHIP GOD BY MEDITATING ON PSALM 139:1–12

COMMIT GOD'S WORD TO MEMORY | 1 TIMOTHY 1:17

DAY 1 | To the King of the ages,
DAY 2 | immortal, invisible,
DAY 3 | the only God,
DAY 4 | be honor and glory
DAY 5 | forever and ever. Amen.

TEENAGE QUESTIONS

When you're in a room full of teenagers, it's rare to hear silence or have stillness. I would know, since I spend my days teaching them. One day, as I talked with a group of about twenty, I asked the question "What is God?" Students were quick to offer a variety of answers: "He is love," or "He is everything." But in the middle of all the answers, one girl shouted, "He is not us!" And everyone settled, quieted, and wondered.

I asked if she could explain her answer a little more, and she began to describe a distant, divine being, untouchable because of our sin and his absolute holiness. He was over us, better than us. She had a solid understanding that God was wise, powerful, just, good, infinite, and eternal, but I wondered how that understanding of God impacted her, so I pressed again, "What does your answer about God say about *you*?"

Before she could answer, others started in, and several came to the same conclusion: "We don't feel like we can get close to God because we know ourselves and how limited and sinful we are."

There it was. God without Jesus. Sin without a rescue plan.

We then discussed how head knowledge about God as spirit, infinite and eternal, wise and holy, demonstrates how set apart God is from us—and how different we are from him. And the gap between his goodness and our depravity further reveals how desperately we need him. But that gap was intended to lead us to a place of awe that a God so holy and "other" would shed glory and put on skin to become a person . . . that in Christ he would draw near when he had every reason to be distant.

God's nearness was a much easier truth to teach my students that day than it was to learn myself. I thought I understood the beautiful reality of both his complete control over all things and his intimate nearness to me . . . until two of my children left the country to go to life-threatening places to help those who couldn't defend themselves.

In the span of a month, my daughter, drawn to the plight of abused women and children, decided to help combat sex slavery in Bulgaria.

Then my son, ever the quiet defender of his family and friends, headed off to Afghanistan with his Marine battalion. And for three nights in a row I woke up in a cold sweat thinking of all the things that could go wrong for them both. Fear and anxiety gripped me to such a degree, I had to seek help. I met with a wise friend who listened before turning a question on me: "Whose hands are your children safer in? Yours or God's?" Before I could catch myself, "Mine" slipped out.

And there it was, the same question I'd asked my students: What does your answer say about you? And a similar answer: God isn't near.

God used my friend to remind me of the truth that there is no longer any gap between God and man; that the whisper that he isn't near is, in fact, a lie; that Jesus put on flesh and died to give me access to God—such close access, he lives inside me now through the Holy Spirit. He's so close, he says he will make his dwelling with me in the world to come (Rev. 21:3).

DAY 1

READ 1 TIMOTHY 1:12-17

> Let a man who is thirsty be brought to an ocean of pure water, and he has enough. If there is enough in God to satisfy the angels, then surely there is enough to satisfy us. The soul is but finite, but God is infinite.

THOMAS WATSON

> A God you understood would be less than yourself.

FLANNERY O'CONNOR

DAY 2

READ MICAH 7:1-20

On the whole, I do not find Christians, outside of the catacombs, sufficiently sensible of conditions. Does anyone have the foggiest idea what sort of power we so blithely invoke? Or, as I suspect, does no one believe a word of it? The churches are children playing on the floor with their chemistry sets, mixing up a batch of TNT to kill a Sunday morning. It is madness to wear ladies' straw hats and velvet hats to church; we should all be wearing crash helmets. Ushers should issue life preservers and signal flares; they should lash us to our pews. For the sleeping god may wake someday and take offense, or the waking god may draw us out to where we can never return.

ANNIE DILLARD

At these words I was utterly stupefied and terror-stricken. I thought to myself, "With what tongue shall I address such majesty, seeing that all men ought to tremble in the presence of even an earthly prince? Who am I, that I should lift up mine eyes or raise my hands to the divine Majesty? The angels surround him. At his nod the earth trembles. And shall I, a miserable little pygmy, say 'I want this, I ask for that?' For I am dust and ashes and full of sin and I am speaking to the living, eternal and the true God."

MARTIN LUTHER

DAY 3

READ PSALM 145:1-21

No doubt we will spend eternity enjoying an ever-increasing revelation of the things we do not yet know about God. Because he is infinitely good, the things that we do not know about God are only good things. . . . The secret attributes of God, should we come to learn them, would bring us nothing but pleasure and assurance. The infinite unknown of God holds no faith-shattering duplicity, just a multiplicity of perfections waiting to be discovered across eternity.

JEN WILKIN

Here, and in all our meditations upon the qualities and content of God we pass beyond our power of fit conception, nor can human eloquence put forth a power commensurate with his greatness. At a contemplation and utterance of his majesty all eloquence is rightly dumb, all mental effort is feeble. For God is greater than mind itself. His greatness cannot be conceived.

A. W. TOZER

DAY 4

READ JEREMIAH 32:16-44

" Your days, whether easy or difficult, should be filled with thanksgiving because while life changes drastically, your God remains the same forever. He is constant—constantly good, loving, and faithful.

JOE THORN

" In this world where men forget us, change their attitude toward us as their private interests dictate, and revise their opinion of us for the slightest cause, is it not a source of wondrous strength to know that the God with whom we have to do changes not? That his attitude towards us now is the same as it was in eternity past and will be in eternity to come?

A. W. TOZER

DAY 5

> **READ** DEUTERONOMY 33:26-29

> When you're in a dark place, when lions surround you, when you need strong help to rescue you from impossibility, you don't want "sweet." You don't want faded pastels and honeyed softness. You want mighty. You want the strong arm and unshakable grip of God who will not let you go—no matter what.

JONI EARECKSON TADA

> When the Bible calls God holy it means primarily that God is transcendentally separate. He is so far above and beyond us that he seems almost totally foreign to us. To be holy is to be "other," to be different in a special way.

R. C. SPROUL

> The perfection of learning is to know God in such a way that, though you realize he is knowable, yet you know him as indescribable.

HILARY OF POITIERS

WEEK 5

ONLY ONE GOD

WESTMINSTER SHORTER CATECHISM QUESTION 5

Q | Are there more gods than one?

A | There is but one only, the living and true God.

....

PRAY *Help me to adore thee by lips and life. O that my every breath might be ecstatic praise, my every step buoyant with delight. Amen.*

....

WORSHIP GOD BY MEDITATING ON PSALM 97

....

COMMIT GOD'S WORD TO MEMORY | DEUTERONOMY 6:4

DAY 1 | Hear,
DAY 2 | O Israel:
DAY 3 | The Lord our God,
DAY 4 | the Lord is one.

THE TEACHER

I've been told I was born to teach. I received the birthright from my father who served as my high school principal and track coach. His tender legacy mentored me through the dark, musky hallways of adolescence and into the wide space of adulthood where, through teaching, I would give back the gifts of language and story to those who thirsted for them like I did. For those who didn't, well, that brings me to the lesson *they* taught *me*.

My husband's job change caused me to leave a job and students I loved. I was faced with a bittersweet return to my hometown, where, many thanks to my father's reputable recommendation, I was offered and accepted a junior high-level English position at my once-rival high school. Even though I had five years of experience teaching seventh graders under my belt, I felt a new challenge and determination to meet above normal standards with the next grade up. So, on that first day of school, I wore my tallest heels and my sternest look, took a deep breath, and faced the eyes of twenty-five eighth graders.

I set high expectations and drew a hard line, but they danced around those expectations with quiet bitterness and resentment that I didn't detect until March, when teacher surveys were conducted. My reputation was placed in the hands of hormonal thirteen year olds, so the day slowly passed with higher anxiety than I cared to admit. My pulse finally slowed during sixth period, and as my last student, whom I adored, was leaving the room, she turned to me with a troubled face and hesitantly asked how important the surveys were. I replied, "Ah, they just help us learn how to be better teachers, that's all." My heart stopped. *I must have gotten some bad reviews from my difficult kids.* The truth would prove far worse.

For the first time in my life, I was called to the principal's office for correctional reasons. She handed me a copy of the survey, and I never knew black numbers on a white page could shatter my identity as a successful educator so quickly. The results were overwhelmingly negative. *I thought I was challenging them, but clearly I built an image that was unapproachable, even lacking in love. Now I look like a monster who hates kids. And I've tarnished my father's name.*

My cheeks burned as my trembling hands found the chair arms across from my boss's desk. "How do you feel about the results?" she asked steadily.

I buried my face in my hands and said, "I've lost their trust in pursuit of my own respect." She replied, "I'd be worried if you weren't upset. I've known you since you ran track against us in high school. But your students haven't, and neither has our superintendent. Still, I will tell them that I'd hire you again because I know you, and you know your mistake." She was right, I did. I'd wanted the approval and respect of pubescent teenagers and thought that tall heels and five-star reviews could get me there. It was my principal's grace that saw through to my heart, unlike I had done with my students, and it changed my teaching from that day forward. The fall I had to take began my uphill journey to redemption.

DAY 1

> **READ** 1 JOHN 5:13-21

❝ Whatever your heart clings to and confides in, that is really your God.

MARTIN LUTHER

❝ A man's god is that for which he lives, for which he is prepared to give his time, his energy, his money, that which stimulates him and rouses him, excites, and enthuses him.

D. MARTYN LLOYD-JONES

DAY 2

READ PSALM 18:2-36

" The natural man is a sinner because and only because he challenges God's selfhood in relation to his own. In all else he may willingly accept the sovereignty of God; in his own life he rejects it. For him, God's dominion ends where his begins. For him, self becomes Self, and in this he unconsciously imitates Lucifer, that fallen son of the morning who said in his heart, "I will ascend into heaven, I will exalt my throne above the stars of God . . . I will be like the Most High."

A. W. TOZER

" Thus does the world forget you, its Creator, and falls in love with what you have created instead of with you.

AUGUSTINE

DAY 3

READ ISAIAH 44:1-8

> There is something exceedingly improving to the mind in a contemplation of the Divinity. It is a subject so vast, that all our thoughts are lost in its immensity; so deep, that our pride is drowned in its infinity. . . . No subject of contemplation will tend more to humble the mind, than thoughts of God.
>
> J. I. PACKER

> If our thinking about God is not correct then every other doctrine we apply our minds to will also be incorrect. This is the most important doctrine yet people seem to think they are free to make up their minds as to what God is like.
>
> PETER JEFFERY

DAY 4

READ JEREMIAH 10:1-16

Knowledge of ourselves through the knowledge of God is humbling. We are not God nor are we like him. He is holy; we are unholy. He is good; we are not good. He is wise; we are foolish. He is strong; we are weak. He is loving and gracious; we are filled with hate and with selfish affectations. Therefore to know God is to see ourselves as Isaiah did: "Woe is me! For I am lost; for I am a man of unclean lips, and I dwell in the midst of a people of unclean lips; for my eyes have seen the King, the Lord of Hosts!" (Is. 6:5). . . . On the other hand, such knowledge of ourselves through the knowledge of God is also reassuring and satisfying. For in spite of what we have become we are still God's creation and are loved by him.

JAMES M. BOICE

DAY 5

READ DEUTERONOMY 6:1-15

> He who knows the answer to this knows all things. He is alone. His name is God.
>
> VICTOR HUGO

> Whatever a man seeks, honors, or exalts more than God is the god of his idolatry. . . . Whatever is preferred in mind and heart to God, whatever is chosen as the chief end of man's pursuit in place of God, constitutes the idolatry of these times.
>
> WILLIAM B. ULLATHORNE

WEEK 6

THE TRINITY

WESTMINSTER SHORTER CATECHISM QUESTION 6

Q | How many persons are there in the Godhead?

A | There are three persons in the Godhead: the Father, the Son, and the Holy Spirit; and these three are one God, the same in substance, equal in power and glory.

PRAY *O Holy Father, thou hast freely given thy Son, O Divine Son, thou has freely paid my debt, O Eternal Spirit, thou dost freely bid me come, O Triune God, thou dost freely grace me with salvation. Amen.*

WORSHIP GOD BY MEDITATING ON PSALM 143

COMMIT GOD'S WORD TO MEMORY | 2 CORINTHIANS 3:17

DAY 1 | Now the Lord
DAY 2 | is the Spirit,
DAY 3 | and where the Spirit
DAY 4 | of the Lord is,
DAY 5 | there is freedom.

MORNING WALK

t was a sunny, summer day when I left for my usual morning walk. But I returned to an unfamiliar black sedan in my driveway. The driver, an officer dressed in a dark suit, stepped out and showed me his badge. I glanced up as clouds began to block the sun.

We walked inside and sat at my breakfast table where the officer asked me a series of questions, and fears shot like cannons through my mind. Finally, he said, "Ma'am, I hate to be the one to tell you, but your husband committed suicide this morning."

I don't remember much said after that because my mind and emotions were a swirl of past, present, and future thoughts, stirred up at an incomprehensible rate. Sadness and anger pummeled me as I grieved that my husband's pain had taken him to such depths. Satan had won . . . But in the days and weeks to follow, I fought to believe in God's good purposes and plans, and he comforted me through his Word.

"Because, if you confess with your mouth that Jesus is Lord and believe in your heart that God

raised him from the dead, you will be saved." (Romans 10:9)

God reminded me that my husband was now with his Abba and Savior.

"I will instruct you and teach you in the way you should go; I will counsel you with my eye upon you" (Psalm 32:8).

I knew that Jesus, living in me through his Spirit, would give me comfort, guidance, and power for the journey ahead. Satan had not won— the story was not over.

Resting in the promises of scripture, I had the courage to move forward. At least I think I was moving, but in some ways, it seemed I was being carried. Before long the house was full of people who seemed to know what to do, as if it was a great theatrical play and all the actors stepped right into their parts. All the actors except me. I realized I had been chosen to play a leading role but didn't know the first thing about my part. I had not rehearsed for this and certainly was not prepared, and fear multiplied fast. How would I make it through without falling flat on my face? But then, before I could even express my inadequacy to those around me, my fellow actors began to give me my lines, one by one: "Have you thought about what time you'd like to have the service?" "Would you like me to call any relatives?" "Let me help you with the flowers."

Somehow, in the midst of this dark, dark place, a sliver of light began to pierce the clouds. It was inexplicable. All I know is that even though my heart was still weighted with grief and that there would be a hard road ahead, I also was experiencing something sweet and tender that I had never experienced before. I was confident that even in this, I was going to be met by the power and perfection of the three in one—Father, Son, and Holy Spirit—who were at work in the believers around me as much as they were at work in me.

DAY 1

READ 2 CORINTHIANS 3:17-4:5

> Emmanuel. God with us. He who resided in heaven, co-equal and co-eternal with the Father and the Spirit, willingly descended into our world. He breathed our air, felt our pain, knew our sorrows, and died for our sins. He didn't come to frighten us, but to show us the way to warmth and safety.
>
> CHARLES R. SWINDOLL

> Augustine, while puzzling over the doctrine of the Trinity, was walking along the beach one day when he observed a young boy with a bucket, running back and forth to pour water into a little hole. Augustine asked, "What are you doing?" The boy replied, "I'm trying to put the ocean into this hole." Then Augustine realized that he had been trying to put an infinite God into his finite mind.
>
> MICHAEL GREEN

DAY 2

READ MATTHEW 3:13-4:11

> Behold the Spirit of the Lord, who first of all moved upon chaos and brought forth order, who now visits the chaos of your soul and creates the order of holiness. Behold him as the Lord and Giver of spiritual life, the Illuminator, the Instructor, the Comforter, and the Sanctifier. Behold him as he descends upon the head of Jesus, and then as he rests upon you. Such an intelligent, scriptural, and experiential belief in the Trinity is yours if you truly know God; and such knowledge brings peace indeed.

CHARLES SPURGEON

> The Christian God is a relational God. He exists relationally within his Triune self—as Father, Spirit, and Son—but God's actions in the world are also driven by a mission to reconcile his relationship with humanity. He was so intent on this mission that he emptied himself by becoming the "other"—a human being.

DAVID KINNAMAN

DAY 3

READ JOHN 1:1-18

"Now the Christian account of God involves just the same principle. The human level is a simple and rather empty level. On the human level one person is one being, and any two persons are two separate beings—just as, in two dimensions (say on a flat sheet of paper) one square is one figure, and any two squares are two separate figures. On the Divine level you still find personalities; but up there you find them combined in new ways which we, who do not live on that level, cannot imagine. In God's dimension, so to speak, you find a being who is three Persons while remaining one Being, just as a cube is six squares while remaining one cube. Of course we cannot fully conceive a Being like that: just as, if we were so made that we perceived only two dimensions in space we could never properly imagine a cube, but can get a sort of faint notion of it. And when we do, we are then, for the first time in our lives, getting some positive idea, however faint, of something super-personal—something more than a person. It is something we could never have guessed, and yet, once we have been told, one almost feels one ought to have been able to guess it because it fits in so well with all the things we know already.

C. S. LEWIS

DAY 4

READ HEBREWS 9:11-14

" You have a God who hears you, the power of love behind you, the Holy Spirit within you, and all of heaven ahead of you. If you have the Shepherd, you have grace for every sin, direction for every turn, a candle for every corner and an anchor for every storm. You have everything you need.

MAX LUCADO

" All sorts of people are fond of repeating the Christian statement that "God is love." But they seem not to notice that the words "God is love" have no real meaning unless God contains at least two persons. Love is something that one person has for another person. If God was a single person, then before the world was made, he was not love.

C. S. LEWIS

DAY 5

READ EPHESIANS 4:1-6

> It is commonly said that the Trinity is a mystery. And it certainly is
> .... But it is not a mystery veiled in darkness in which we can only
> grope and guess. It is a mystery in which we are given to under-
> stand that we will never know all there is of God. ... It is not a mys-
> tery that keeps us in the dark, but a mystery in which we are taken
> by the hand and gradually led into the light.
>
> EUGENE PETERSON

> There is mystery here. But it is the mystery in the light of which
> clarity is brought to all of our thinking about God, creation, prov-
> idence, and redemption. Like the light of the sun we cannot gaze
> into it without danger; and yet it is the light in which we are able to
> see everything else more clearly. As Augustine wrote: "In no other
> subject is error more dangerous, or inquiry more laborious, or the
> discovery of truth more profitable."
>
> SINCLAIR FERGUSON

WEEK 7

GOD'S ETERNAL PURPOSE

WESTMINSTER SHORTER CATECHISM QUESTION 7

Q | What are the decrees of God?

A | The decrees of God are, his eternal purpose, according to
the counsel of his will, whereby, for his own glory, he has
foreordained whatsoever comes to pass.

PRAY *Help me to see how good thy will is
in all, and even when it crosses mine teach
me to be pleased with it. Amen.*

WORSHIP GOD BY MEDITATING ON PSALM 33

COMMIT GOD'S WORD TO MEMORY | PSALM 33:11

DAY 1 | The counsel of the Lord
DAY 2 | stands forever,
DAY 3 | the plans
DAY 4 | of his heart
DAY 5 | to all generations.

KIDNEYS

The nephrologist called, and a pulse surged in my neck. The kidney surgery would be scheduled for the following month. Most twenty-two-year-olds dream of trips overseas or jobs with benefits—definitely not having surgery. But that's where I found myself several years ago. It was hydronephrosis, a condition that caused swelling and significant damage to my right kidney. I had never had any procedure in my life, much less a major operation. I hung up the phone and felt the pinpricks of terror on the back of my neck. But it wasn't long after the diagnosis that the real fear started, and I began to question God's purposes for me. Some days I couldn't even get out of bed because of the pain. I would cry out to him, "How could you say you love me and put me through so much suffering?"

For much of the two years leading up to my diagnosis and surgery I had been detached from the Lord and swept up by the world. I was so disconnected from him that one evening I walked out of the house without any real idea of where I was headed and found myself on a parking deck, where I began to weep at what my life had become. My excessive drinking felt as though I had wasted everything away—my testimony, intimacy with Christ, even my relationship with God—and it seemed that there was no way out of my idolatry of alcohol. I pursued my college dreams and ultimately accomplished them, but I discovered it was all vanity. Day after day, contentment played a game of hide and seek, and I could never find her. That night on the parking deck I prayed that the Lord would take the things that were distracting me from him out of my life. I wish I could say I experienced radical change with that prayer, but I didn't, and I continued down the same path.

After two years of meaninglessness, God graciously sliced through my darkness to reveal a sliver of hope—a flicker where before was only a damp soul. While on a camping trip with some close friends, I sensed how the Lord was answering my two-year cry for help—but not in the way I expected. Instead of removing the temptation to drink to excess, God physically removed my body's ability to deal with high alcohol intake. So rather than viewing my medical condition as a curse, I began to see the gift it was—not a gift I would ask for, but one I was grateful for because of how it led me back to God.

My heart was profoundly changed once I saw that God didn't answer my prayer too late—he had already written my life story, and he wasn't finished. My prayer was answered from my mother's womb, when God formed me with a condition that would be the instrument he would use to draw me back to him and reawaken me to his goodness. He answered my prayer before I even knew to pray it.

DAY 1

READ EPHESIANS 1:3-14

> God's having chosen his people to blessedness and glory long before they were born is evidence of the glory of divine grace, in that his love to them is prior to all they have or do, being influenced by any excellency of theirs.

> JONATHAN EDWARDS

> The Love of God is one of the great realities of the universe, a pillar upon which the hope of the world rests. But it is a personal, intimate thing, too. God does not love populations, he loves people. He loves not masses, but men. He loves us all with a mighty love that has no beginning and can have no end.

> A. W. TOZER

DAY 2

| READ ISAIAH 14:24–27 |

> The Christian is joyful, not because he is blind to injustice and suffering, but because he is convinced that these, in the light of the divine sovereignty, are never ultimate. The Christian can be sad, and often is perplexed, but he is never really worried, because he knows that the purpose of God is to bring all things in heaven and on earth together under one head, even Christ.
>
> ELTON TRUEBLOOD

> I learned to watch, to put my trust in other hands than mine.
>
> BERYL MARKHAM

DAY 3

READ ACTS 2:22-36

"Sometimes God allows what he hates to accomplish what he loves.

JONI EARECKSON TADA

"In the beginning God." The first four words of the Bible are more than an introduction to the creation story or to the book of Genesis. They supply the key which opens our understanding to the Bible as a whole. They tell us that the religion of the Bible is a religion of the initiative of God.

You can never take God by surprise. You can never anticipate him. He always makes the first move. He is always there "in the beginning." Before man existed, God acted. Before man stirs himself to seek God, God has sought man. In the Bible we do not see man groping after God; we see God reaching after man.

JOHN STOTT

DAY 4

READ ROMANS 9:1-26

" While we deliberate, God reigns; when we decide wisely, God reigns; when we decide foolishly, God reigns; when we serve God in humble loyalty, God reigns; when we serve God self-assertively, God reigns; when we rebel and seek to withhold our service, God reigns—the Alpha and the Omega, which is, and which was, and which is to come, the Almighty.

ARCHBISHOP WILLIAM TEMPLE

" [W]e hold that God is the disposer and ruler of all things—that from the remotest eternity, according to his own wisdom, he decreed what he was to do, and now by his power executes what he decreed. Hence, we maintain, that by his providence, not heaven and earth and inanimate creatures only, but also the counsels and wills of men are so governed as to move exactly in the course which he has destined.

JOHN CALVIN

DAY 5

READ ISAIAH 46:1-13

" If in some sense God does not ordain everything that comes to pass, then in the final analysis he is not really sovereign; and if he is not sovereign, he cannot be God.

R. C. SPROUL

" Faith in God offers no insurance against tragedy. Nor does it offer insurance against feelings of doubt and betrayal. If anything, being a Christian complicates the issue. If you believe in a world of pure chance, what difference does it make whether a bus from Yuba City or one from Salina crashes? But if you believe in a world ruled by a powerful God who loves you tenderly, then it makes an awful difference.

PHILIP YANCEY

WEEK 8

GOD'S WORK

WESTMINSTER SHORTER CATECHISM QUESTION 8

Q | How does God execute his decrees?

A | God executes his decrees in the works of creation and providence.

PRAY *Impress me deeply with a sense of thine omnipresence, that thou art about my path, my ways, my lying down, my end. Amen.*

WORSHIP GOD BY MEDITATING ON PSALM 148:1-14

COMMIT GOD'S WORD TO MEMORY | PSALM 148:5-6

DAY 1 | Let them praise the name of the Lord!
DAY 2 | For he commanded and they were created.
DAY 3 | And he established them forever and ever;
DAY 4 | he gave a decree,
DAY 5 | and it shall not pass away.

GARDENING

In college, I was a fall season athlete, which meant I had spring training—a brutal two practices a day, five days a week, in addition to games on weekends. If it were only the physical rigor of spring training, I could've handled it. But I was also experiencing relational brokenness and significant personal insecurity.

One morning after I got home from a challenging 6 o'clock workout, I leaned on the side of my car with the heels of my hands pressed onto my eyes to try and stop the flood of tears. I was broken down physically and emotionally and trying to hold myself together. Then I heard a rustling nearby, unusual for the early hour, and looked up to see my next door neighbor on hands and knees, gardening. He was pulling weeds, tilling the soil, and preparing his flower bed for the blooms that would come in a few weeks.

He had such purpose and vision with his garden. He yanked the invasive intruders from their shallow roots—he knew pulling them out would make room for something much more beautiful to come. My freshly-pruned heart could identify with his actions. I wiped sweat and tears from my cheeks, picked up my workout gear, and headed inside to get on with the day. Both my body and heart still ached, but suddenly they ached with new purpose, new promise.

It's been a decade, and I still find myself drawn to gardens and the process for making them thrive. One of my family's favorite weekend activities is to walk through our local botanical garden. In this picturesque place, each type of tree and flower blooms in its own season. We particularly love the rose garden, so we went there one weekend during the transitional periods between winter and spring. I'm not sure what I expected to see, but when we walked up to them, they were pruned down to stubs, just as my heart was that spring day long ago. They were short, bare, lifeless looking sticks in the ground. But I knew what they would become—high and wide, full of blossoms. I knew that soon the sticks would be covered with foliage, giant blooms, and bursts of color. I knew of the beautiful aromas they would grace us with in the coming season . . . and I felt at peace.

DAY 1

READ ISAIAH 40:9-31

> That which tears open our souls, those holes that splatter our sight, may actually become the thin, open places to see through the mess of this place to the heart-aching beauty beyond. To him. To the God whom we endlessly crave.

ANN VOSKAMP

> We have an excellent foundation if we understand the goodness of creation and the dignity of work. We work in a wondrous world that is designed in part for our pleasure. The author of Genesis tells us we should experience awe as we stand before the richness of the creation, for it teems with life. God seems to delight in diversity and creativity.

TIM KELLER AND KATHERINE ALSDORF

DAY 2

READ ACTS 4:23-31

> It is not allowable to love the Creation according to the purposes one has for it, any more than it is allowable to love one's neighbor in order to borrow his tools.

> EUGENE PETERSON

> Nothing in all the vast universe can come to pass otherwise than God has eternally purposed. Here is a foundation of faith. Here is a resting place for the intellect. Here is an anchor for the soul, both sure and steadfast. It is not blind fate, unbridled evil, man or Devil, but the Lord Almighty who is ruling the world, ruling it according to his own good pleasure and for his own eternal glory.

> A. W. PINK

DAY 3

READ DANIEL 4:1-36

> Predestination does not always offer a straight road to the predestined; there are many twists and turns, forks, and crossroads.
>
> VICTOR HUGO

> All of the testimonies that I had heard up to this point were egocentric and filled with pride. *Aren't I the smarty-pants for choosing Christ! I made a decision for Christ, aren't I great? I committed my life to Christ, aren't I better than those heathens who haven't?* This whole line of thinking is both pervasive among evangelical Christians and absurd. My whole body recoiled against this line of thinking. I'm proof of the pudding. I didn't choose Christ. Nobody chooses Christ. Christ chooses you or you're dead. After Christ chooses you, you respond because you must. Period. It's not a pretty story.
>
> ROSARIA BUTTERFIELD

DAY 4

READ PSALM 135:1-21

How we understand the person and character of God the Father affects every aspect of our lives. It affects far more than what we normally call the "religious" aspects of our lives. If God is the Creator of the entire universe, then it must follow that he is the Lord of the whole universe. There is no part of the world that is outside of his Lordship. That means that there must be no part of my life that is outside of his Lordship. His holy character has something to say about economics, politics, athletics, romance—everything that we are involved with.

R. C. SPROUL

[I]t is God's manner, in the great works of his power and mercy which he works for his people, to order things so as to make his hand visible, and his power conspicuous, and men's dependence on him most evident, that no flesh should glory in his presence . . . that God alone might be exalted, and that the excellency of the power might be of God and not of man, and that Christ's power might be manifested in our weakness, and none might say, mine own hand hath saved me.

JONATHAN EDWARDS

DAY 5

READ 1 CHRONICLES 16:8-36

> His kingdom is not merely drab and functional; somehow the kingdom he is announcing is a kingdom of beauty. The Beautiful One is King, and his children are and will be reflections of his beauty.
>
> EDWARD T. WELCH

> Every day is important for us because it is a day ordained by God. If we are bored with life there is something wrong with our concept of God and his involvement in our daily lives. Even the most dull and tedious days of our lives are ordained by God and ought to be used by us to glorify him.
>
> JERRY BRIDGES

WEEK 9

THE WORK OF CREATION

WESTMINSTER SHORTER CATECHISM QUESTION 9

Q | What is the work of creation?

A | The work of creation is, God's making all things of nothing, by the word of his power in the space of six days, and all very good.

....

PRAY *Teach me to behold my Creator, his ability to save, his arms outstretched, his heart big for me. Amen.*

....

WORSHIP GOD BY MEDITATING ON PSALM 104:1-35

....

COMMIT GOD'S WORD TO MEMORY | COLOSSIANS 1:15-16

DAY 1 | He is the image of the invisible God, the firstborn of all creation.
DAY 2 | For by him all things were created,
DAY 3 | in heaven and on earth, visible and invisible,
DAY 4 | whether thrones or dominions or rulers or authorities—
DAY 5 | all things were created through him and for him.

THE GRAND CANYON

I n 1976, I added seeing the Grand Canyon to my bucket list in all caps. Despite the seeming urgency then, it took me thirty long years to finally get there. I knew I had high and possibly unattainable expectations, but I still hoped against hope that it wouldn't disappoint. It didn't.

Its grandeur was something bigger and more spectacular than I had imagined. Arriving arm-in-arm with my best friend and two siblings, I carried a well-worn map with marks, arrows and notes written all over it. One morning we would watch the sunrise *here*. Later, we would hike *this* trail. Then, we'd watch the sunset *there*. If we expected a thunderstorm, we'd go to *this* lookout point to watch the lightning flash over the canyon. I read reviews, books, and insider's guides to learn how to experience my time there the best possible way, but even with all my planning and researching, I still wasn't fully prepared for the breathtaking panoramas that stirred my soul. The heights were dizzying, the depths unfathomable, the colors more brilliant, and vistas more breathtaking . . . At one point or another each day, I would turn a corner of a trail and be seized by the vastness and unmatched beauty surrounding me. It literally took my breath away—I was readily moved to tears. It was more than just a gigantic crevice created by a river flowing over thousands of years. It was glorious splendor that made me come alive more than ever.

But nothing compared to the first night we arrived. We didn't want to miss our first sunset, so we hustled to park the car and searched for a place to watch that big orange ball slowly descend behind the edge of the canyon. We raced the sun from cliff to cliff around the edge of different lookout points, trying to experience as much as we could in the remnant daylight. There were other tourists, but we quickly weaved through them like running backs looking for the end zone.

With every hurried step, I cried more and smiled bigger. The beauty of something so incredible, so majestic, so strong, so elusive, so good, was almost overwhelming. I felt so small yet, at the same time, so loved, uttering under my breath again and again, "Lord, have mercy."

Eventually, we found a place to pause and sit. We weren't alone long. As the sunset came closer and closer to its grand finale, our secret spot became quite crowded.

Typically, this would bother me, but for some reason, as the sun began to disappear, everyone grew quiet. Even children sat silently, eager faces turned due west. I snapped picture after picture, hoping to capture the scene just right, but found myself missing the experience, so instead, I stopped, took a few deep, slow breaths and simply observed.

The spectacular light filled the sky and illuminated colors I'd never before seen upon the rocky faces of a canyon. For a moment, mankind was speechless. Then slowly, it left us, as if to take a rest from the day's work. And all of us broke into a thunderous applause.

DAY 1

READ GENESIS 1:1-31

It is remarkable that in Chapter 1 of the book of Genesis, God not only works but finds delight in it. . . . God finds what he has done beautiful. He stands back, takes in "all that he has made," and says, in effect, "That's good!" Like all good and satisfying work, the worker sees himself in it.

TIM KELLER AND KATHERINE ALSDORF

Seven times in the book of Genesis, God steps back from the canvas of his creation and admires his handiwork and sees that it is good. It is the Almighty's first reaction to his creation. It's the first recorded emotion that God expresses. The word good comes from the Hebrew word "tob," it's joy unspeakable. It's pure delight.

MARK BATTERSON

DAY 2

READ HEBREWS 1:1-14

" The creation of the universe not only attests to the supreme omnip-
otence of God, it also displays his creativity in all its glory, for God
is the author of beauty as well as truth. In traveling the world, you
cannot escape being struck by its natural beauty. We sing of purple
mountains' majesty profiled against the beautiful blue spacious
skies that stretch from sea to shining sea. We capture its essence in
others ways as well: the gurgle of the cold, frothy, mountain brook;
the dramatic burst of yellow forsythia emerging from the drab
bleakness of winter; the translucent beauty of a rainbow perched
in the sky; the magnificent grandeur of a colossal waterfall; or the
winter wonderland created by a fresh snowfall. Add to that the
graceful glide of a deer through dappled woods, the proud strut
of a prairie partridge, or the cute antics of a playful, young puppy.
Then close your eyes and listen to the rhythmic pounding of the
surf or the whisper of the wind in the palms. What a magnificent
creation—the work of the quintessential artist!

LUDER G. WHITLOCK

DAY 3

READ COLOSSIANS 1:15-20

> Here is where I got an Excedrin headache in my philosophy class. Before the world began there was nothing. But what in the world is "nothing"? Have you ever tried to think about nothing? Where can we find it? Obviously nowhere. Why? Because it is nothing and nothing doesn't exist. It can't exist, because if it did, then it would be something and nothing. Are you starting to get a headache like mine? Think about it for a second. Nuts! I can't tell you to think about "it" because nothing isn't an "it." I can only say "nothing isn't."
>
> R. C. SPROUL

> For until men recognize that they owe everything to God, that they are nourished by his fatherly care, that he is the Author of their every good, that they should seek nothing beyond him—they will never yield him willing service.
>
> JOHN CALVIN

DAY 4

READ ACTS 17:22-34

> The world is to God as wine and chocolate are to us. Creation isn't something God needs; it's something he likes. He doesn't say, "I need the world." That's a statement that would get him off the train of delight many stops short of "I love the world." Therefore, the world is not something God has to have; it's the overflow of the totally unnecessary love of the Trinity as they tell each other how delicious they find things. And it's precisely that deliciousness of things in the sight of God that's the taproot of our existence. We're all fine wines in God's cellar. He has all of eternity to give us the aging we deserve.
>
> ROBERT FARRAR CAPON

> Earth's crammed with heaven
> And every common bush afire with God.
> But only he who sees takes off his shoes.
>
> ELIZABETH BARRETT BROWNING

DAY 5

READ JOB 38:1-41

> Gazing on beautiful things acts on my soul.
>
> MICHELANGELO

> There is not one blade of grass, there is no color in this world that is not intended to make us rejoice.
>
> JOHN CALVIN

> God enjoys his creation. The apostle John says frankly that God's purpose in creation was his own pleasure. God is happy in his love for all that he has made. We cannot miss the feeling of pleasure in God's delighted references to his handiwork. Psalm 104 is a divinely inspired nature poem almost rhapsodic in its happiness, and the delight of God is felt throughout it. "The glory of the Lord shall endure forever: the Lord shall rejoice in his works."
>
> A. W. TOZER

WEEK 10

THE CREATION OF MAN

WESTMINSTER SHORTER CATECHISM QUESTION 10

Q | How did God create man?

A | God created man male and female, after his own image, in knowledge, righteousness, and holiness, with dominion over the creatures.

PRAY *Plough deep in me, great Lord . . . that my being may be a tilled field, the roots of grace spreading far and wide, until thou alone art seen in me, thy beauty golden like summer harvest, thy fruitfulness as autumn plenty. Amen.*

WORSHIP GOD BY MEDITATING ON PSALM 8:1–9

COMMIT GOD'S WORD TO MEMORY | GENESIS 1:27

DAY 1 | So God created man
DAY 2 | in his own image,
DAY 3 | in the image of God
DAY 4 | he created him;
DAY 5 | male and female he created them.

MICHELANGELO

Florence, Italy is known for many things—sumptuous food, some of the world's oldest museums, breathtaking art—but it is Michelangelo's famous *David* statue at the Accademia Gallery Museum that stands in a category all its own. Prior to my first visit to Florence in high school, I had seen a few pictures of it online and in books, so I knew what it looked like: a large marble carving of the biblical icon, just before he threw the stone to deal Goliath his fatal blow. I'd done my homework and felt prepared for what I was about to see.

But nothing could have prepared me to experience the reality and beauty of the sculpture when I saw it for the first time.

The museum itself is larger than life, with columns the size of tree trunks greeting you at the entrance. Once inside, I turned a corner to walk down a hallway lined with other statues and, there at the end, surrounded by arched ceilings on all sides and a skylight that made him glow, was the *David*. My head barely grazed the top of the platform he was standing on, which elevated him seventeen feet in the air. Even though the ceiling above him was three stories tall, he filled the space with strong authority.

I circled the statue in what can only be described as a trance, admiring from every angle the sizeable and seemingly impossible task that Michelangelo completed. Although no artist myself, I imagined the unspeakable effort, focus, and time that making this piece demanded, noting the careful curves and lines, the definition in the muscles, the smooth perfection of the stone, and the determined expression on David's face. *How did he take such a large block of stone and create the masterpiece before me? How did he create something so lifelike and beautiful?* I wondered.

The feeling that kept bubbling up more than any other was that of feeling so small—not only compared to the giant statue before me but also compared to the extraordinary talent and dedication of the artist who created such a work of perfection.

Michelangelo was himself an imperfect person, and yet was able to create a flawless piece of art. His masterpiece reflected who he was as an artist: a creator of beauty and someone who paid attention to every detail. Over five centuries later, it continues to possess great value not only because of its beauty, but because of the artist who fashioned it. Michelangelo's work and name have remained the pinnacle of artistic skill and talent through the ages. Because I was able to see the beauty that Michelangelo created, I could understand more deeply the beauty that God sees in me, his creation.

DAY 1

READ EPHESIANS 4:17-32

❝ We cannot deal with people like human beings, we cannot deal with them on the high level of true humanity, unless we really know their origin—who they are. God tells man who he is. God tells us that he created man in his image. So man is something wonderful.

FRANCIS A. SCHAEFFER

❝ A man should carry two stones in his pocket. On one should be inscribed, "I am but dust and ashes." On the other, "For my sake was the world created." And he should use each stone as he needs it.

JEWISH RABBI, AS QUOTED BY PHILIP YANCEY

DAY 2

READ GENESIS 2:4-24

" In ancient Egypt and Mesopotamia . . . the phrase ["image of god"] had a specific meaning: the king was the "image of God" and no one else. The king was thought to be god's representative on earth. So if you wanted to honor god, or the gods, you had better honor the king, the "image of god." . . . Also in those ancient cultures, the king was often considered to be the sole mediator between the god(s) and the people. He had access. He was the priest. So the early readers would hear Genesis 1 saying not only are you royalty, you are royalty and you are a priest. You were created to represent God and have access to God. You are a royal priest.

RANKIN WILBOURNE

" God calls his image-bearers to join him in saving the world. This is the Blessed Alliance . . . God's image bearers—male and female— serving God together. Each of them has a major contribution to make, and the entire cause will suffer severely and the other two will be seriously hampered in their own call to obedience, if one of them backs away.

CAROLYN CUSTIS JAMES

DAY 3

READ COLOSSIANS 3:5-17

> Remember that God has created us voluntarily, he gave mankind the highest privilege of being his image bearers. He made us but a little lower than the angels. He freely gave us dominion over all the earth. We are not turtles. We are not fireflies. We are not caterpillars or coyotes. We are people. We are the image-bearers of the holy and majestic King of the cosmos.
>
> R. C. SPROUL

> "You come of the Lord Adam and the Lady Eve," said Aslan. "And that is both honour enough to erect the head of the poorest beggar, and shame enough to bow the shoulders of the greatest emperor on earth. Be content."
>
> C. S. LEWIS

> The Christian position is that man is made in the image of God and even though he is now a sinner, he can do things that are tremendous—he can influence history for this life and the life to come, for himself and for others. . . . From the biblical viewpoint, man is lost, but great.
>
> FRANCIS SCHAEFFER

DAY 4

READ PSALM 103

> He made the stars and ocean blue, but says that none compare to you. You are his treasure and great prize! He knows your name. He made your eyes. He is your Shepherd, little lamb. The King of Heaven, the Great I am.

SALLY LLOYD-JONES

> Take another look at yourself. God has declared that the person in your mirror is his regal image. You are not perfect—that should be plain enough. But you are still valuable because you are God's image. In God's eyes, you are as important as any king and as valuable as any nobleman who ever walked on this earth. Discard the lies of the world and joyfully acknowledge the dignity God has lavished on you.

RICHARD L. PRATT

DAY 5

READ PSALM 139:13-16

> David asks that question with a holy wonder, "What is man that God is so mindful of him?" But I may have his leave, and the Holy Ghost's, to say, since God is so mindful of him, since God hath set his mind upon him, What is not man? Man is all.
>
> Since we consider men in the place that they hold, and value them according to those places, and ask not how they go thither, when we see man made The Love of the Father, The Price of the Son, The Temple of the Holy Ghost, The Signet upon God's hand, The Apple of God's eye . . . For man is not only a contributory Creature, but a total Creature; he does not only make one, but he is all; he is not a piece of the world, but the world itself; and next to the glory of God, the reason why there is a world.

JOHN DONNE

WEEK 11
THE WORK OF PROVIDENCE

WESTMINSTER SHORTER CATECHISM QUESTION 11

Q | What are God's works of providence?

A | God's works of providence are, his most holy, wise, and powerful preserving and governing all his creatures, and all their actions.

....

PRAY *O Love beyond compare, thou art good when thou givest, when thou takest away, when the sun shines upon me, when night gathers over me. Amen.*

....

WORSHIP GOD BY MEDITATING ON PSALM 145:1–21

....

COMMIT GOD'S WORD TO MEMORY | PROVERBS 16:33

DAY 1 | The lot is cast
DAY 2 | into the lap,
DAY 3 | but its every decision
DAY 4 | is from the Lord.

THE SKI LESSON

t's funny how hard it is to let dreams die. Even when you're seventy. Snow has always brought out a childlike wonder and delight for me, maybe because I saw so little of it growing up in the South.

Since I was a young girl I'd dreamed of skiing, and I finally got my chance at age fifty. Feeling the wind on my face and beholding beauty from a pristine atmosphere made my heart sing along with the psalmist, "O Lord, our Lord, how majestic is Your name in all the earth!"

Last December brought another opportunity to ski, and though I felt a bit foolish at my age now, I was determined to take a lesson. Perhaps I could relive that mountaintop experience from decades ago. Bundled against the cold and taking in the frigid air, I was a child again, nervous but excited.

My instructor—a charming young man who quickly put me at ease with questions about me and my life—asked where I was from. Laughing, I said, "Alabama," waiting for the usual jokes and thinking that would be the end of it. He pursued, "Where?" When I said, "Birmingham," he told me he lives in Birmingham during the off season and works in a restaurant there.

In between lessons on starting and stopping on the bunny slope, we chatted about Birmingham neighborhoods and favorite restaurants. I learned he has an apartment in an exciting area of town, and we discovered we like some of the same kind of music. He even plays one of my favorite instruments: the cello! We seemed to have a genuine connection.

I wondered aloud if he had a church home, and with an air of finality, he told me he was "raised religious."

"So, you're kind of over that?" I replied, and he affirmed that he was. I told him I had been raised religious too but that something had changed when I was in my thirties and my life had never been the same. I asked if he would be interested in exploring some topics he might have issues with regarding the church. He said sure and that when we finished our lesson we could exchange contact information.

The ski lesson was pretty disappointing. I didn't get to experience the wind in my face or the view from the mountaintop. But when we were done we exchanged email addresses and said we'd keep in touch and get together in the summer.

So far, we've swapped some emails and I am praying this door stays open. Perhaps there is another kind of wind blowing from one heart to another—one with eternal possibilities.

. . . .

DAY 1

READ MATTHEW 10:26-33

> Real life, the real world, is a vast theater of salvation, directed by our wise and totally involved God.
>
> EUGENE PETERSON

> This doctrine is full of excellent comfort. For thereby we understand, that by the power of our God, the rage of that hungry lion is abated and bridled, and that God will never suffer him to do anything against his children, which shall not be to their good and profit, as the apostle tells us (Rom. 8:28) and also teaches us by his own example (2 Cor. 12:17).
>
> THEODORE BEZA

DAY 2

READ GENESIS 45:4–15

> Providence is the almighty and ever present power of God by which he upholds, as with his hand, heaven and earth and all creatures, and so rules them that leaf and blade, rain and drought, fruitful and lean years, food and drink, health and sickness, prosperity and poverty—all things, in fact, come to us not by chance but from his fatherly hand.
>
> We can be patient when things go against us, thankful when things go well, and for the future we can have good confidence in our faithful God and Father that nothing will separate us from his love. All creatures are so completely in his hand that without his will they can neither move nor be moved.
>
> ANSWERS TO HEIDELBERG CATECHISM 27 & 28

DAY 3

READ PROVERBS 16:1-33

> Surely you don't disbelieve the prophecies, because you had a hand in bringing them about yourself? You don't really suppose, do you, that all your adventures and escapes were managed by mere luck, just for your sole benefit? You are a fine person, Mr. Baggins, and I am very fond of you; but you are only quite a little fellow in a wide world after all!
>
> J. R. R. TOLKIEN

> You can plant the healthiest seeds available, but if God doesn't send the rain your plants will die. You are dependent on God for your very life and breath. If he would withdraw his hand, this orderly world would explode into chaos. Look how a drought or a flood can bring a region to its knees. Look at all the examples of how the goods of one part of the world are desperately needed by another part of the world. The more you consider the interdependent operation of the various elements of creation, the clearer it is that no aspect of God's creation is truly self-sufficient, including you. *Especially* you.
>
> PAUL DAVID TRIPP

DAY 4

> **READ** PROVERBS 21:1-31

" Events appear to fly at random like the dust in the whirlwind; but it is not so. The rule of the Omnipotent God extends over all things at all times! Nothing is left to its own chance, but in wisdom all things are governed. . . . He is reigning amid all the calamities which sweep the globe, as much as he shall be in the halcyon days of peace. Never is his throne vacant! Never is his scepter laid aside! Jehovah is always King, and shall be King forever and forever! This unconquerable King sits securely on his throne! There is no doctrine to the advanced Christian which contains such a deep sea of delight as this. The Lord reigns! The Lord is King forever and ever! Why, then all is well. Oh, happy subjects, who have such a throne to look to! Oh, blessed children, who have such a King to be your Father!

CHARLES SPURGEON

" Our lives are neither the product of blind fate nor the result of capricious chance, but every detail of them was ordained from all eternity, and is now ordered by the living and reigning God. Not a hair of our heads can be touched without his permission. "A man's heart deviseth his way: but the Lord directeth his steps" (Prov. 16:9). What assurance, what strength, what comfort this should give the real Christian!

A. W. PINK

DAY 5

READ ESTHER 4:1-17

> The truth of the matter is, Satan and God may want the exact same event to take place—but for different reasons. Satan's motive in Jesus' crucifixion was rebellion; God's motive was love and mercy. Satan was a secondary cause behind the Crucifixion, but it was God who ultimately wanted it, willed it, and allowed Satan to carry it out. And the same holds true for disease.
>
> JONI EARECKSON TADA

> There is something peculiarly soothing to the heart of a pious Christian; to know that he who rules over all worlds, in whose hands are the destinies of nations, and who guides the minutest concerns of families and individuals, is his Father and his Friend. The more we know of God, of his power, wisdom, love, faithfulness, and truth; the more we shall bow before his throne in humble adoration, and filial confidence and love. To know God in Christ; to know him as our God; is to possess all the sources and secrets of true peace, in the midst of surrounding storms and tempests. This knowledge will raise us above the agitated elements of the world, and place us in that pure region where the soul can breathe more freely, and expand her powers more fully. . . . Cast your care upon him who cares for you; and, under every trying event, be still, and know that he is God.
>
> THOMAS READE

WEEK 12

A SPECIAL ACT OF PROVIDENCE

> WESTMINSTER SHORTER CATECHISM QUESTION 12

Q | What special act of providence did God exercise towards man in the estate in which he was created?

A | When God had created man, he entered into a covenant of life with him, upon condition of perfect obedience; forbidding him to eat of the tree of the knowledge of good and evil, upon pain of death.

....

PRAY *I bless thee that thou hast made me capable of knowing thee, the author of all being, of resembling thee, the perfection of all excellency, of enjoying thee, the source of all happiness. Amen.*

....

WORSHIP GOD BY MEDITATING ON PSALM 15

....

COMMIT GOD'S WORD TO MEMORY | PSALM 24:3-4

DAY 1 | Who shall ascend the hill of the Lord?
DAY 2 | And who shall stand in his holy place?
DAY 3 | He who has clean hands and a pure heart,
DAY 4 | who does not lift up his soul to what is false
DAY 5 | and does not swear deceitfully.

TUBING

My wife and I were invited to lead and speak at a retreat in eastern Tennessee. Though we had three boys we only took our oldest, as the other two were too young to be toting around the Tennessee mountains. It was great quality time with our firstborn, who was almost eight years old at the time and, in typical fashion, full of life and his own way of doing things.

During a long afternoon break at the retreat, the three of us decided to go river tubing. Resist the urge to conjure up thoughts of white water rapids and death-defying tricks. This was soaking-in-the-sunshine, no-one-needs-me *glorious* kind of tubing. My wife and I each lounged back in our own inner tubes as we floated down the tranquil river. There wasn't a lot of current, but enough to keep us moving and enough to make us want to lock our tubes together as we floated down. Our son allowed us to hang onto his tube for a while, but not too long into the experience he decided he needed more independence and started pushing his tube away from ours—not *that* big of a deal since we weren't going anywhere fast, but as he was our firstborn and only eight, we still wanted to exercise a bit of caution.

We spent the next few minutes playing his game—him pushing away from us, and then us paddling back to where he was floating and trying to lock ankles or wrists again.

Then came the bend in the river.

While the current was doing its job of holding us together on the tubing path, our son was still bent on his game of independence. As we approached one section, I noticed a large mass of grass cuttings and yard junk stuck in a small bend toward the bank (likely from one of the land owners dumping cuttings). Because the pile was out of the flow of the current, it had become stagnant, motionless, smelly . . . gross.

In the midst of the distraction of his game, our son found himself drifting toward the stink. Once he realized where he was headed, he started calling out for help, and I paddled over, sticking my foot out so he could grab it and be pulled back into the current. But instead, he grinned and pushed off my foot, thinking he'd push himself further into the current. But his plan backfired, and he ended up shoving himself right into the middle of the muck.

He began to flail, calling out for help on the verge of tears and jumping out of his tube into the waist-deep water. Within seconds, he was covered in filth.

Once more, I paddled over, scooped him out of the muck and set him back in his tube. No words, no jokes, no comments. It was just the strong grasp of a father reaching into the mire to pull his son back close to him—the same strong grasp I recognize the Father making for me when I try to play my own independence game.

DAY 1

READ HOSEA 6:4-11
(SEE GENESIS 2:16-17 FOR BACKGROUND)

> Since we are dependent on the Creator for our very existence, it follows that we are morally obligated to render obedience to him, the author of our very lives. His authorship gives him authority to command whatever he will from that which he made. God's willingness to enter into a covenant (that is, an agreement, contract, or pact) with us is itself a matter of grace.
>
> R. C. SPROUL

> Where there is the tree of knowledge, there is always Paradise: so say the most ancient and the most modern serpents.
>
> FRIEDRICH W. NIETZSCHE

DAY 2

READ GALATIANS 3:1-14

" [The Serpent] used the commandment to deceive Eve about the nature of the commandment giver. This in turn produced in her a legal and bondage spirit that led to death. She saw only one law— the negative one—not the many blessings of God's commands. She saw only prohibition—not the person, full of wisdom and love, as the heavenly Father he is. Having found a landing place here in the case of Eve, Satan continues to land in the same territory in our lives too. But now he has grown from a serpent into a dragon exercising his malicious deceptive ministry. Ever since, Satan has been driving people to the law as a contract, pressing down on our failure to keep its terms, confirming our worst fears about our relationship to God, and blackmailing us into further bondage in our legalism.

SINCLAIR FERGUSON

" Sin, guilt, neurosis; they are one and the same, the fruit of the tree of knowledge.

HENRY MILLER

DAY 3

READ ROMANS 10:5-13

God places the man before a clear choice: continue in communion with God by trusting and obeying him, or break communion with God by disobeying his commandment. But disobedience will result in the penalty of death: "You shall die." The choice is an obedient life with God in Paradise or disobedience and death. The stakes are high. What will happen?

SIDNEY GREIDANUS

Our death, the tree of knowledge, grew fast by, Knowledge of good bought dear by knowing ill.

JOHN MILTON

DAY 4

READ PSALM 24

❝ As people who live by referendums and compromise, who are accustomed to being graded on a curve, we must understand that God judges his people by the standard of his own perfection.

R. C. SPROUL

❝ Sorrow is knowledge: they who know the most must mourn the deepest o'er the fatal truth, The Tree of Knowledge is not that of Life.

LORD BYRON

DAY 5

READ MATTHEW 19:16-26

> The disobedience of the first Adam was the judicial ground of our condemnation; the obedience of the last Adam is the legal ground on which God alone can justify the sinner. The substitution of Christ in the place of his people, the imputation of their sins to him and of his righteousness to them, is the cardinal fact of the Gospel. But the principle of being saved by what another has done is only possible on the ground that we are lost through what another did. The two stand or fall together. If there had been no covenant of works there could have been no death in Adam, there could have been no life in Christ.
>
> A. W. PINK

> [T]he God of the Christians is a God of love and consolation . . . a God who fills the soul and heart of those whom he possesses, a God who makes them inwardly aware of their wretchedness and his infinite mercy, who united himself with them in the depths of their soul . . . who makes them incapable of having any other end but him.
>
> BLAISE PASCAL

WEEK 13

THE FALL

WESTMINSTER SHORTER CATECHISM QUESTION 13

Q | Did our first parents continue in the estate in which they were created?

A | Our first parents, being left to the freedom of their own will, fell from the estate in which they were created, by sinning against God.

....

PRAY *O unite me to thyself with inseparable bonds, that nothing may ever draw me back from thee, my Lord, my Savior. Amen.*

....

WORSHIP GOD BY MEDITATING ON PSALM 14:1-7

....

COMMIT GOD'S WORD TO MEMORY | ROMANS 3:23-24

DAY 1 | For all have sinned

DAY 2 | and fall short of the glory of God,

DAY 3 | and are justified by his grace as a gift,

DAY 4 | through the redemption

DAY 5 | that is in Christ Jesus.

THE INTRUDER

t was around 1:00 in the morning when I reached over to my wife with one arm, like a hook, and pulled her toward me, then we both fell over the side of the bed.

"What are you doing?!" she garbled, coming out of a deep sleep. "Shhhhh, someone is in the house," I mouthed slowly and quietly.

My heart was in overdrive and not knowing what to do, I quickly considered my thoughts for next steps. *Rush attack: they will never expect me to be the aggressor. Or stay quiet: let them get close, then grab and uppercut to the gut . . . total neutralization. Or I could divert them with a noise in another room, then quickly take my wife down the hallway to safety on the opposite side of the house. I'll out sma . . .*

"Should we call the police?" she whispered back. Her cavalier tone surprised me. "Yeah," I said with a delayed obviousness.

Operator: "911 what's your emergency?"

Wife: "I'm not sure. Is this an emergency?"

Me: "I'm pretty sure this is an emergency."

Operator: "What's the emergency?"

Wife: "Honey, what's the emergency?"

Still in a daze, it occurs to me that my wife has forgotten why we were calling. Trembling with fear yet now in possession of wolf-like instincts, I assess. She wants me to explain the situation, but I've got punches to plan and an escape route to maneuver.

Devoting considerable energy not to raise my voice—a sure location giveaway—I communicate the facts. "Well, we have a person in our house that. . . is. . . a. . . stranger."

She communicates the issue to the operator and police are dispatched. Now I can wait silently and settle in to my laser-sharp focus for any more sounds.

But my bride is now fully awake and curious. Insisting on a full description of the last two and half minutes, I lose it in a Woody from *Toy Story* kind of way. I raise my eyebrows to convey frustration and start using military hand signals to walk her through my sequence of listening for the intruder and gut punching him.

A second noise occurs. I can't stand it anymore—*"I'm here and I'm ready, Bro!"* I yell with everything in me.

Standing now, I grab my trusty pitching wedge, just in time to hear a third sound. And a fourth.

It's the police knocking at the door. We run down the hallway to let them in and within a minute they find the suspect: a broken attic ceiling panel. Somehow it fell to the floor, but for the record, it was *really* loud.

Thinking back now, our story of falling out of bed reminds me of the original fall of Adam and Eve. One minute we were comfortably asleep in bed, the next, we were down on the floor in fear and confusion. Adam and Eve were enjoying the garden, then suddenly they were hiding in trepidation and shame. They believed the deception, and committed one sinful act that changed the course of everything.

DAY 1

READ GENESIS 3:1-24

> I know it may seem counterintuitive, but when we try to make hard-and-fast rules that are more far reaching and more specific than God's law, we are actually opening the door for sin and failure. Why? Because adding to God's law doesn't make it easier to obey; it makes it even more impossible to follow than it already is. We think adding to the law will make it more manageable, but we're terribly mistaken.
>
> ELYSE FITZPATRICK

> It promotes humiliation to know the whole breadth and depth of sin.
>
> RICHARD SIBBES

DAY 2

READ ROMANS 5:12-21

But the biblical account of human nature is that we are all disordered. Relationally disordered, sexually disordered, physically disordered, spiritually disordered . . . just plain disordered. We are all "born that way." The fall of Adam and Eve had consequences; distortion of God's design is one of them. Not every longing is a desire God intended us to experience. You can't find who you are simply by actualizing your desires.

DAVID KINNAMAN

Sin comes when we take a perfectly natural desire or longing or ambition and try desperately to fulfill it without God. Not only is it sin, it is a perverse distortion of the image of the Creator in us. All these good things, and all our security, are rightly found only and completely in him.

AUGUSTINE

DAY 3

READ JOB 15:8-16

> The fruit's poison has infected the whole of humanity. *Me.* I say no to what he's given. I thirst for some roborant, some elixir, to relieve the anguish of what I've believed: God isn't good. God doesn't love me. . . . And yet since we took a bite out of the fruit and tore into our own souls, that drain hole where joy seeps away, God's had this wild secretive plan. He *means to fill us with glory again.* With glory and grace.

ANN VOSKAMP

> The human mind is very fond of fetters, and is apt to forge them for itself.

CHARLES SIMEON

DAY 4

READ ROMANS 3:9-20

> Modern people and modern theology, in trying to start from man alone, are left where the brilliant German philosopher Friedrich Nietzsche found himself. Nietzsche in the 1880s was the first one who said in the modern way that God is dead, and he understood well where people end when they say this. If God is dead, then everything for which God gives an answer and meaning is dead.
>
> FRANCIS SCHAEFFER

> Humanism has led to its natural conclusion . . . starting only from man, mathematics lead us only to particulars—and particulars lead only to mechanics. Humanism had no way to find the universal in the areas of meaning and values. . . . Humanism has changed the Twenty-third Psalm:
>   They began—I am my shepherd
>   Then—Sheep are my shepherd
>   Then—Everything is my shepherd
>   Finally—Nothing is my shepherd.
>
> FRANCIS SCHAEFFER

> Keep open your own pipeline to what it was when you were lost— chief of sinners. That's the basis for deep joy in the gospel!
>
> JACK MILLER

DAY 5

READ JEREMIAH 17:1-13

> I certainly don't plan on sinning, but I don't trust myself as long as I am a mere human being. The tempter who every day tries to turn me from faith in God and the true religion is very strong—but I have dedicated myself to serve Christ my master to the bitter end. Human desires, however, are always dragging us toward death—to act out our sinful wishes.
>
> ST. PATRICK

> Sin goes in a disguise, and thence is welcome; like Judas, it kisses and kills; like Joab, it salutes and slays.
>
> GEORGE SWINNOCK

WEEK 14

WHAT IS SIN

WESTMINSTER SHORTER CATECHISM QUESTION 14

Q | What is sin?

A | Sin is any want of conformity unto, or transgression of, the law of God.

PRAY *May I always be subordinate to thee, be dependent upon thee, be found in the path where thou dost walk, and where thy Spirit moves. Amen.*

WORSHIP GOD BY MEDITATING ON PSALM 36:1-12

COMMIT GOD'S WORD TO MEMORY | JAMES 4:17

DAY 1 | So whoever knows
DAY 2 | the right thing to do
DAY 3 | and fails to do it,
DAY 4 | for him it is sin.

THE GIRL IN THE TRAILER

The beautiful little girl with picturesque golden curls and wide blue eyes approached me, and I stood immobile, paralyzed by a stabbing anguish. She took one step, then another, her little feet dragging along the carpeted floor, slowed by some invisible force as she crossed the narrow interior of the lamplit single-wide trailer. She was so young, not quite three, and yet there was something old in her eyes, the look of a wounded thing. Another jolt of emotion rocketed through me.

Hold it together, man.

She paused. I saw something clutched in her little hand, hidden shyly behind her leg. She looked to her mother who urged her on with a gentle smile and a strange mixture of sadness and hope written onto her face.

I remember the holiday trinkets on the table nearby, the smell of baked cookies, the cold outside contrasting with the warmth of the simple single parent dwelling—a home paid for with blood, sweat, and tears.

The girl looked on with earnest trepidation as one step followed the next, each bringing her closer to me. I bent to one knee, the leather of my duty belt creaking in response. Setting aside my clipboard with a State of Alabama incident/offense report titled *Sexual Abuse of a Child Less Than 12* clipped to the top, I extended open hands.

The girl held out her arms to me, her perfect, doll-like fingers clamped around a picture that she'd drawn while I'd been talking with her mother. A disjointed hodge-podge of crayon swirls and scribbles, it wouldn't have looked like much to most. To me, it was a precious gift. I gave her a hug, said my goodbyes, and gave my best reassurances, stepping back out into the cold night with a feeling of helplessness mounting inside me. I opened the door to my police cruiser and dropped into the seat. Pulling the door behind me, I fumbled with the keys, my eyes pooling with tears. Still a rookie by most standards, I sat in the driveway, concealed by the cover of my patrol car, and wept.

The perpetrator was the girl's biological father.

More than any other trial in my life, a career in police work has caused me to deliberate over the question of sin. Day in and day out, I witness the ugliness of the world and man's unending inhumanity toward fellow man. So, which was worse in the sight of God? The perverted acts of a child molester, or my hate of him, which was so strong it might've driven me to commit murder if I had him within reach? Both miss the mark of God's holy, perfect will.

In order to survive a career in law enforcement, I knew early on that I had to be resolute on one thing: that we are all affected by the sickness that is sin, and that it leads to death. There is only one cure for this lethal affliction: Christ himself.

To this day, many years later, there's still a certain picture I keep close at hand. And every so often, when I need to check my course, I pull it out to remind myself of the freedom from brokenness that is found—for us all—in Christ Jesus alone.

DAY 1

READ 1 JOHN 3:4-24

> Our culture has trivialized the word sin. Anyone worried about sin must be a hateful, self-righteous prude pointing the finger at others and saying, "Repent, you sinners!" Our culture's real attitude toward sin is seen in our candy bar commercials . . . "It's sinfully delicious." This is tragic because the word "sin" should conjure up very different images. Sin is our great problem, burden, enemy, tragedy, and disease.
>
> RON JULIAN

> Sin is fundamentally the exaltation of self at the expense of God. What someone wrote of the Englishman is true of everyman; he is "a self-made man who worships his creator."
>
> JOHN STOTT

DAY 2

READ JEREMIAH 5:1-31

" Sin is cosmic treason. Sin is treason against a perfectly pure Sovereign. It is an act of supreme ingratitude toward One to whom we owe everything, to the One who has given us life itself. Have you ever considered the deeper implications of the slightest sin, of the most minute peccadillo? What are we saying to our Creator when we disobey him at the slightest point? We are saying no to the righteousness of God. We are saying, "God, Your law is not good. My judgment is better than Yours. Your authority does not apply to me. I am above and beyond Your jurisdiction. I have the right to do what I want to do, not what You command me to do."

R. C. SPROUL

" Perversion is an ends-and-purposes disease. Most broadly understood, perversion is the turning of loyalty, energy, and desire away from God and God's project in the world: it is the diversion of construction materials for the city of God to side projects of our own, often accompanied by jerry-built ideologies that seek to justify the diversion.

CORNELIUS PLANTINGA

DAY 3

READ JAMES 4:1-17

> Just as we are not righteous simply by avoiding forbidden actions, we are not righteous simply by practicing commanded actions. Our motives must match our outward obedience. Jesus will continue to faithfully pry from his listeners' grip the desire to live a "bare minimum" faith—one in which we seek to invest as little effort as possible to enjoy as many benefits as possible as followers of Christ. Instead he will point us to an abundant faith, one that breathes righteousness into even the "secret" moments of our lives.
>
> JEN WILKIN

> Dante was the one who showed me that sin was not the breaking of the rules so much as my misdirected love. My desire was not the problem, but I desired the wrong things. For Dante, sin is loving the wrong things, or to be more precise, loving the right things in the wrong way. . . . Sin is abiding in something other than Jesus to give us significance and joy. . . . [S]in is constructing an identity around anything other than God.
>
> RANKIN WILBOURNE

DAY 4

READ ISAIAH 58:1-14

> Sin is not always expressed in conscious animosity toward God. More often it is a polite relegation of God to irrelevance. Nevertheless it is still an expression of man's cosmic rebellion against his Maker—man taking his stance in independence from anything greater than himself.

DICK KEYES

> Among the sins to which the human heart is prone, hardly any other is more hateful to God than idolatry, for idolatry is at bottom a libel on his character. The idolatrous heart assumes that God is other than he is—in itself a monstrous sin—and substitutes for the true God one made after its own likeness. Always this God will conform to the image of the one who created it and will be base or pure, cruel or kind, according to the moral state of the mind from which it emerges.

A. W. TOZER

DAY 5

READ ROMANS 2:1-16

> What is sin? It is not . . . an accident, nor an imprudence, nor a misfortune, nor a disease, nor a weakness . . . it is something beyond all these; something of a more fatal and terrible character. Sin is guilt. Sin is crime. Man's tendency is either to deny, or to extenuate sin. He either pleads not guilty, or he smoothes over the evil; giving it specious names. Or if he does not succeed in these, he casts the blame off himself; he shifts the responsibility to . . . his nature, his birth, his circumstances, his education; even to God himself!

HORATIUS BONAR

> Sin, however, is not some small aberration, some violation of inconsequential Church rules; it is the clenched fist that is raised against God.

DAVID WELLS

WEEK 15

THE FIRST SIN

WESTMINSTER SHORTER CATECHISM QUESTION 15

Q | What was the sin whereby our first parents fell from the estate in which they were created?

A | The sin whereby our first parents fell from the estate in which they were created, was their eating the forbidden fruit.

....

PRAY *Thou hast commanded me to believe in Jesus; and I would flee to no other refuge, wash in no other fountain, build on no other foundation, receive from no other fullness, rest in no other relief. Amen.*

....

WORSHIP GOD BY MEDITATING ON PSALM 10

....

COMMIT GOD'S WORD TO MEMORY | JEREMIAH 2:13

DAY 1 | For my people have committed two evils:
DAY 2 | they have forsaken me,
DAY 3 | the fountain of living waters,
DAY 4 | and hewed out cisterns for themselves,
DAY 5 | broken cisterns that can hold no water.

FLIRT BIG

Flirt big!"
It was such a strange and seemingly harmless phrase, and yet that was the phrase my parents enthusiastically shouted when dropping off their children.

I am the youngest of three. Since my older sister is nearly nine years my senior, I likely heard this mantra for the first time when she was a young teenager and I was in preschool. The send-off of "Flirt big!" was the last message I heard before the sliding door on our twilight blue Dodge Caravan thudded shut and I headed off to soccer, swim team, or even Sunday school. It seemed like a playful inside joke and nothing more. But that once-harmless phrase became deep-seated and began influencing my thought patterns. Over time, flirting became second nature—it had staked its claim on my life and actions without me even realizing it.

It started with girls in high school. Flirting big with humor, charm, and persistence usually won them over, giving me a (false) sense of success and the status I needed to feel important and complete. The charge to flirt big also flowed right into my leanings toward high achievement. Along with being student body president and captain of everything, I won the high school senior superlative for, of all things, biggest flirt. So I was good.

I was also a fraud.

I avoided any serious dating relationships because I didn't want to restrict the number of women who desired me—that would limit my sense of feeling valued. I also couldn't risk friendships with guys because they posed a threat to my endeavors. So, while my flirt big mentality won me over to the masses, I was utterly alone.

And nothing fed my time alone better than the Internet. The "Killer A's" of my budding pornography fix—affordability, availability, and anonymity—came rushing into my world giving me a new high. I could find the kind of women I wanted, when I wanted them. If I didn't like someone, or was at risk of being found out, I could click a little X on the corner of my monitor, and the mischief disappeared. Until the next time. Images couldn't reject me. I had control. But the demons of lust quickly sharpened their hooks through the glow of the computer screen. Before I knew it, I was treading water in the pool of pornography addiction.

By my freshman year of college, I stripped off the water wings and marched toward the high dive. I had my own room, a high-speed Internet connection, and a foreign language minor to help me outsmart the content filter at my Baptist university. I blew myself apart with a saturation of provocative pixels trying to fill the void I now know was meant only for God's validation.

Years later, the enemy's shrapnel still riddles my soul, tries to rob my marriage, and eats at meaningful relationships. What I thought was the way to lasting fulfillment was actually a long and lonely path to self-destruction.

DAY 1

READ JEREMIAH 2:4-29

> His [Satan's] daily study is to divide between the Son and us by breeding false opinions in us of Christ, as if there were not such tender love in him to such as we are. It was Satan's art from the beginning to discredit God with man, by calling God's love into question with our first father Adam. His success then makes him ready at that weapon still.

RICHARD SIBBES

> The first appearances of error are many times modest. There is a chain of truths; the devil taketh out a link here and a link there, that all may fall to pieces.

THOMAS MANTON

DAY 2

READ JEREMIAH 13:8-11

> I am the centre of the world I see; where the horizon is depends on where I stand. . . . Education may make my self-centeredness less disastrous by widening my horizon of interest; so far it is like climbing a tower, which widens the horizon for physical vision, while leaving me still the centre and standard of reference.
>
> WILLIAM TEMPLE

> The sin underneath all our sins is to trust the lie of the serpent that we cannot trust the love and grace of Christ and must take matters into our own hands.
>
> MARTIN LUTHER

DAY 3

READ ISAIAH 2:6-22

> The beginning of men's rebellion against God was, and is, the lack of a thankful heart.
>
> FRANCIS SCHAEFFER

> Human beings are always assigning to themselves some kind of identity. There are only two places to look. Either you will be getting your identity vertically, from who you are in Christ, or you will be shopping for it horizontally in the situations, experiences, and relationships of your daily life.
>
> PAUL DAVID TRIPP

DAY 4

READ 1 JOHN 2:15-16

One of the effects of original sin is an instinctive prejudice in favour of our own selfish desires. We see things as they are not, because we see them centered on ourselves. Fear, anxiety, greed, ambition and our hopeless need for pleasure all distort the image of reality that is reflected in our minds. Grace does not completely correct this distortion all at once: but it gives us a means of recognizing and allowing for it. And it tells us what we must do to correct it. Sincerity must be bought at a price: the humility to recognize our innumerable errors, and fidelity in tirelessly setting them right.

THOMAS MERTON

I listen and I live fully on what comes straight from his mouth. That Serpent, he's slithered with the lie that God doesn't give good but gives rocks in the mouth, leaves us to starve empty in wilderness and we'll just have to take lessons from Satan on how to take the stones of the careless God and make them into bread to feed our own hungry souls. And I hear it straight out of the speakers on a July morning breaking, the Son of God saying there is only *one* way to live full and it is "by every word that comes from the mouth of God."

ANN VOSKAMP

DAY 5

READ 1 SAMUEL 2:1-10

> The sin of egotism always takes the form of withdrawal. When personal advantage becomes paramount, the individual passes out of the community.
>
> RICHARD WEAVER

> We are line-crossers, boundary-breakers, fence-jumpers, carrying inside us a warped belief that our heavenly parent wants to withhold from us something that is needful or pleasurable. Even as we enjoy his good gifts, we feel a hyperawareness of the boundaries he has set, and we question their validity. Though he gives us nineteen gifts and warns us away from one danger, we suspect that what is withheld is not dangerous but desirable.
>
> JEN WILKIN

WEEK 16

ADAM'S SIN, OUR SIN

WESTMINSTER SHORTER CATECHISM QUESTION 16

Q | Did all mankind fall in Adam's first transgression?

A | The covenant being made with Adam, not only for himself, but for his posterity; all mankind, descending from him by ordinary generation, sinned in him, and fell with him, in his first transgression.

....

PRAY *O let me never lose sight of my need of a savior, or forget that apart from him I am nothing, and can do nothing. Amen.*

....

WORSHIP GOD BY MEDITATING ON PSALM 53

....

COMMIT GOD'S WORD TO MEMORY | GALATIANS 3:13

DAY 1 | Christ redeemed us
DAY 2 | from the curse of the law
DAY 3 | by becoming a curse for us—
DAY 4 | for it is written,
DAY 5 | "Cursed is everyone who is hanged on a tree."

FLASHBACKS

It all started when my mom picked up a paring knife from the dishwasher and flashed back to when she was three. Her soft and innocent soul was injured by the nanny who began cutting her intentionally. Soon after that first flashback, more frightening memories began to emerge, and she was terrorized at night for months. Dad said she would cry out in her sleep with a voice that trembled like a child. Physical scars addressed by a physician corroborated what her mind had suppressed for so many years: she had been horribly abused.

Being ritually violated marred Mom's soul as much as it did her body. Developing memories of the cutting compounded with lifelong remembrance of a raging father had taken an emotional toll most can't comprehend. During my early years, she unleashed her own rage toward my brothers and me. Further into my teen years, she sunk into deep depression and anxiety. And then in my young adult years, she saw a psychiatrist whose goal was to "talk about it until the pain goes away." I wonder at the extent of more damage done by reliving the trauma time and time again.

Mom would often say, "I'm such a zero," and it was clear she meant it. What she couldn't see was how she passed her self-deprecation and shame to my brothers and me. For me, the effects became most crippling when I turned thirteen. In the middle of the school year, my family moved to a new city. And it was middle school. The worst thing about my new school was lunchtime, when all the tribes gathered to eat. But I had no tribe. So I sat alone. Every day. All year.

Sitting alone at the lunch table felt like a spotlight on me and my lack of courage to make friends. In all probability, no one even noticed. But alone at the lunch table I learned to loathe myself for shyness and inability to connect with the other kids.

The legacy of my mom's soul-wounds is the last thing she would have wanted, yet shame and fear was the trajectory she unknowingly imparted. Similarly, Adam and Eve's sin-wound passed on to their children and continued for thousands of years. But God didn't abandon his people—he graciously worked his redemption and healing through his son Jesus. He provided a second Adam to redeem and heal us from all our sin and shame—healing that's shined its way right into this heart of mine. (Romans 5:18–19)

. . . .

DAY 1

READ GENESIS 6:1-8

❝ The beginning of corruption in Adam was such that it was conveyed in a perpetual stream from the ancestors into their descendants. For the contagion does not take its origin from the substance of the flesh or soul, but because it had been so ordained by God that the first man should at one and the same time have and lose, both for himself and for his descendants the gifts that God had bestowed upon him.

JOHN CALVIN

❝ You can't fight a battle you don't think exists.

JOHN ELDREDGE

DAY 2

READ ISAIAH 24:1-23

> With the Fall all became abnormal. It is not just that the individual is separated from God by his true moral guilt, but each of us is not what God made us to be. Beyond each of us as individuals, human relationships are not what God meant them to be. And beyond that, nature is abnormal—the whole cause-and-effect significant history is now abnormal. To say it another way: there is much in history now which should not be.
>
> FRANCIS SCHAEFFER

> What is in other men's practice, is in our nature. Sin in the wicked is like fire on a beacon, that flames and blazes forth; sin in the godly is like fire in the embers. Christian, though you do not break forth into a flame of scandal, yet you have no cause to boast, for there is much sin raked up in the embers of your nature. You have the root of bitterness in you, and would bear as hellish fruit as any, if God did not either curb you by his power, or change you by his grace.
>
> THOMAS WATSON

DAY 3

> **READ** GALATIANS 3:13-26

> " It was a very good thing God was always rescuing his people. Because it seemed that no matter how many times God saved his people, the Israelites were never quite safe from themselves.

> KEVIN DEYOUNG

> " We [believers] still have the presence of sin, nay, the stirrings and workings of corruption. These make us to have many a sad heart and a wet eye. Yet Christ has thus far freed us from sin; it shall not have dominion. There may be the turbulence, but not the prevalence of sin . . . [sin] may get into the throne of the heart and play the tyrant in this or that particular act of sin, but it shall never more be as a king there.

> SAMUEL BOLTON

DAY 4

READ HEBREWS 2:9-18

> "And were by nature children of wrath, even as others." This remains a plain testimony to the doctrine of original sin . . . after all the pains and art used to torture and pervert it. This doctrine is here not only plainly and fully taught, but abundantly so, if we take the words with the context; where Christians are once and again represented as being, in their first state, dead in sin, and as quickened and raised up from such a state of death, in a most marvelous display of free rich grace and love.
>
> JONATHAN EDWARDS

> This inbuilt human tendency to want to do what is wrong is well summarized in the story about a visitor to a European monastery. This visitor was shown to his room and told that he could do anything he liked—provided he didn't look out of one of the windows. Unable to control his curiosity, he eventually gave in to the desire to find out what was so wrong about looking out of this window—and was horrified to find all the monks there, waiting for him! "They always look out!" was their final word.
>
> ALISTER MCGRATH

DAY 5

READ PROVERBS 8:1-21

" The idolatry that exists in man's heart always wants to lead him away from his Savior and back to self-reliance no matter how pitiful that self-reliance is or how many times it has betrayed him.

MATT CHANDLER AND JARED WILSON

" In the beginning God fashioned us after his image (Gen. 1:27) that he might arouse our minds both to zeal for virtue and to meditation upon eternal life. Thus, in order that the great nobility of our race . . . may not be buried beneath our own dullness of wit, it behooves us to recognize that we have been endowed with reason and understanding so that, by leading a holy and upright life, we may press on to the appointed goal of blessed immortality. But that primal worthiness cannot come to mind without the sorry spectacle of our foulness and dishonor presenting itself by way of contrast, since in the person of the first man we have fallen from our original condition. From this source arise abhorrence and displeasure with ourselves, as well as true humility; and thence is kindled a new zeal to seek God in whom each of us may recover those good things which we have utterly and completely lost.

JOHN CALVIN

WEEK 17
THE PROBLEM OF SIN

WESTMINSTER SHORTER CATECHISM QUESTION 17

Q | Into what estate did the fall bring mankind?

A | The fall brought mankind into an estate of sin and misery.

....

PRAY *O Lord God, without the pardon of my sin
I cannot rest satisfied, without renovation of my
nature by grace I can never rest easy, without the
hopes of heaven I can never be at peace. Amen.*

....

WORSHIP GOD BY MEDITATING ON PSALM 58

....

COMMIT GOD'S WORD TO MEMORY | EPHESIANS 2:4–5

DAY 1 | But God, being rich in mercy,
DAY 2 | because of the great love with which he loved us,
DAY 3 | even when we were dead in our trespasses,
DAY 4 | made us alive together with Christ—
DAY 5 | by grace you have been saved.

ALMOST PERFECT

Growing up, I had an almost perfect family—on the outside, at least. We were pretty great on the inside, too, but to look at us— our family photos or lunch outings after church—you would have thought we had no problems and that all was well.

My dad was tall, good looking, brilliant, and successful. My beautiful mom stayed at home and had a smile that could light up any dark room. Then there were four of us happy, healthy, fairly popular and well-rounded kids who never wanted for a thing. Our lives really were kind of perfect.

Until one day . . .

Dad had been an athlete his entire life. He was a record-holding track star, a basketball player, a baseball player, and a football hero in high school. He was a four-year starting receiver in college and was the single greatest country club tennis player in all of Williamson County, Tennessee. He was also an avid runner. In fact, he was training for his sixth marathon when his doctor gave him a routine pre-race physical and said that he was in great shape, except . . .

"You look incredible, Bob. Blood pressure's at 110 over 70; your heart sounds great; your lungs are healthy; you've got the physique of a twenty-three year old. But you might want to get the twitching in your arm checked out."

Within a few days, several tests were run and my father sat, half-listening, to a neurologist read off a litany of sobering results.

"Okay, bottom line, doc. Can I run in the race or not?"

"I don't think you understand. This is very serious." The doctor pulled his chair closer and squeezed my father's hand. "You have a progressive neurological disorder. It's called Amyotrophic Lateral Sclerosis. I'm so sorry to tell you this, but you have Lou Gehrig's Disease."

The story goes that my dad sat blankly for a few seconds but then smiled, "Wow! Lou Gehrig, huh?" He knew what the doctor was telling him, but he also found something complimentary about whom the disease was named after. You see, Lou Gehrig, the "Iron Horse," was one of the greatest baseball players the world has ever known.

Well, eighteen months after my dad's initial meeting with his doctor—sixteen days before my sixteenth birthday—he was gone. He was only forty-one years old.

My dad loved Jesus and liked to tell people about how God had changed his life—even after he got sick. I didn't understand how he could do that then. I still don't sometimes, because *how in God's great plan is this fair? How can our gracious, merciful, loving, wonderful, powerful Creator of all things allow one of his own to suffer and die— and at such a young age?*

I don't know that I'll ever fully grasp the reasons for suffering, but just before my dad passed away, he wrote a poem that has helped give me a bit of perspective. Maybe it can do the same for you.

A SHEPHERD IN SHEEP'S CLOTHING

Why can't I walk, God?
And why can't I play?
And wrestle the kids at the end of each day?
Why can't it be like it always was before?
Why can't I play tennis, or run anymore?
I don't understand, God,
And the price is too steep.
Then the echo came back:
Just go feed my sheep.
Easy for you, you're a shepherd by trade—
A rod and a staff, and you've got it made.
You seem to forget, that I was also a sheep.
A sacrificed Lamb; the cross, too, is steep.
And all that I ask for your role to be
Is when people see you, they also see me.
Because, Bob, we're together while climbing this hill;
We're living each day, seeking God's will.
A miracle is happening, and joy follows sorrow.
But we need a perfect vantage point from which to view tomorrow.

Your weakness makes me stronger,
And my strength is all we need.
By my stripes you're healed already
So let's find a flock to feed.

DAY 1

> **READ** EPHESIANS 2:1-7

> We and the world, my children, will always be at war. Retreat is impossible. Arm yourselves.
>
> LEIF ENGER

> You cannot be more incredibly sinful than he [God] is incredibly merciful.
>
> JOHN PRESTON

DAY 2

READ PROVERBS 29:1-27

> Much that we take for granted in a "civilized" society is based upon the assumption of human sin. Nearly all legislation has grown up because human beings cannot be trusted to settle their own disputes with justice and without self-interest. A promise is not enough; we need a contract. Doors are not enough; we have to lock and bolt them. The payment of fares is not enough; tickets have to be issued, inspected and collected. Law and order are not enough; we need the police to enforce them. All this is due to man's sin. We cannot trust each other. We need protection against one another. It is a terrible indictment of the human nature.
>
> JOHN STOTT

> The idolatry that exists in man's heart always wants to lead him away from his Savior and back to self-reliance no matter how pitiful that self-reliance is or how many times it has betrayed him.
>
> MATT CHANDLER AND JARED WILSON

DAY 3

READ ISAIAH 59:1-13

> When we give anything more priority than we give to God, we commit idolatry. Thus we all commit idolatry countless times every day.
>
> BRENNAN MANNING

> Sin turns us in on ourselves. Sin causes us to be selfish, self-absorbed, and self-focused. Sin causes us to be obsessed with what we want, what we feel, and what we think we need. Sin causes us to want to exist at the center of our own universe having our feelings addressed, our wants satisfied, and our needs met. Sin makes us demanding and expectant, rather than serving and giving. So God has to rescue us from us. He has to free us from our bondage to ourselves so that we can live for him and for others. And as he does this, God is not taking our humanity from us. He is giving it back to us.
>
> PAUL DAVID TRIPP

DAY 4

READ JAMES 1:12-18

We want to be like God and understand everything. We want our own glory to fill the sky. As Paul Tripp says, "Sin has made us glory robbers." Jesus, on the other hand, didn't need to rob anyone to get glory. He knew who he was and where he was going. He wasn't afraid that people wouldn't appreciate him. And so he was able to say no to all the things we claw and strive for as we seek human approval.

ELYSE FITZPATRICK

Clear conviction of sin is the only true origin of dependence on another's righteousness, and therefore (strange to say!) of the Christian's peace of mind and cheerfulness.

ROBERT MURRAY MCCHEYNE

DAY 5

READ MATTHEW 12:33-37

> The best preparation for the study of this doctrine (that is, of the truth of the gospel) is—neither great intellectual ability nor much scholastic learning—but a conscience impressed with a sense of our actual condition as sinners in the sight of God.
>
> JAMES BUCHANAN

> The solution to the problem of guilt is found in the placement of our hope. If we look to ourselves, we will only find frustration and helplessness. But if we look to Christ and consider his work in our place, we will find hope. The hope we need is found in Christ! His perfect work in our place took us from death to life and changed our eternal destiny, but we cannot forget that he also saved us from the fatigue of trying to meet God's standard every day. He freed us from the danger of trying to be our own functional saviors and of presenting "works of righteousness" that are worthy of God's favor.
>
> BETSY GÓMEZ

> Since the fall, God will not trust us with our own salvation, but it is both purchased and kept by Christ for us, and we for it through faith, wrought by the power of God, which we lay hold of.
>
> RICHARD SIBBES

WEEK 18

OUR SINFUL CONDITION

WESTMINSTER SHORTER CATECHISM QUESTION 18

Q | Wherein consists the sinfulness of that estate into which man fell?

A | The sinfulness of that estate into which man fell, consists in the guilt of Adam's first sin, the want of original righteousness, and the corruption of his whole nature, which is commonly called original sin; together with all actual transgressions which proceed from it.

PRAY *Keep me ever mindful of my natural state, but let me not forget my heavenly title, or the grace that can deal with every sin. Amen.*

WORSHIP GOD BY MEDITATING ON PSALM 77

COMMIT GOD'S WORD TO MEMORY | ROMANS 7:24-25

DAY 1 | Wretched man that I am!
DAY 2 | Who will deliver me from this body of death?
DAY 3 | Thanks be to God through Jesus Christ our Lord!
DAY 4 | So then, I myself serve the law of God with my mind,
DAY 5 | but with my flesh I serve the law of sin.

THE DOOR

One day when I was thirteen years old, I decided to play hooky from school. I wasn't sick or anything else, I just didn't feel like going to school.

That morning I slept in, hung around, and watched some TV, and it wasn't long before boredom took over. So I began to rummage around for something interesting to do. I decided to take the opportunity to clean my shotgun, so I went to my father's closet where the materials were kept and opened the door. While I might not have been feeling sick that morning, I will never forget the sickening feeling that hit me the moment I opened that door. My father's closet was completely empty.

As I looked around at the empty hangers and vacant shoe rack, I realized my father was gone—he had moved out. I was thirteen. Even now as I write these words, my stomach clenches.

I don't think my dad really understood the tsunami effect of his decision to leave us, and the choices that led up to it. I imagine that, to him, it must have seemed simple, even casual and fun. A little flirting here—a short-lived tryst there. My mom was a busy woman and distracted with five children—four of us born within three years of each other. Surely he thought of what might happen if he kept it up.

The day I opened that closet door marked the beginning of a cataclysmic shift in my family's world. Simple choices made by one person over a long period of time formed patterns that added up to devastating results for the rest of us. From that time on, our days never looked as they once had—never mind all the changes that came to Christmas and holidays. As each of my parents moved on, there has never been anything normal about our new normal.

It took me a long time to forgive my dad. And, over time, I came to understand how small choices compound year over year and can lead to devastating outcomes. By God's grace I was finally able to forgive him, and I think it became most clear when I realized how tempted I am to minimize my own sin and my own lust without considering the same ripple effects that wreaked havoc in my own family. One simple sin corrupts an entire human nature before a holy God. Adam's one little sin affects us all. I've lived out the consequences.

....

DAY 1

READ TITUS 1:10-15

<blockquote>

The moral shock suffered by us though our mighty break with the high will of heaven has left us all with a permanent trauma affecting every part of our nature. There is disease both in ourselves and in our environment.

A. W. TOZER

</blockquote>

<blockquote>

But a grave sickness is unlikely to be cured unless the victims face up to the realities of their condition. . . . Like the girl with the kidney disease, we shall have zest and cheerfulness for the daily task only if we have spent our daily three half-hours linked up for the spiritual dialysis which filters out of our system what would otherwise clog its channels of vitality and destroy it.

HARRY BLAMIRES

</blockquote>

DAY 2

READ EPHESIANS 5:1-21

In conclusion, in the course of nineteen years, Jean Valjean, the inoffensive pruner of Faverolles, the miserable convict of Toulon, had become capable—thanks to prison training—of two types of crime: first, a sudden unpremeditated act, rash, instinctive, a sort of reprisal for the wrong he had suffered; second, a serious, premeditated act, debated in his conscience and mulled over with the false ideas such a fate will produce. His premeditations went through the three successive phases to which certain natures are limited—reason, will, and obstinacy. As motives, he had habitual indignation, bitterness, a deep sense of injury, a reaction even against the good, the innocent, and the upright, in the unlikely event he encountered them. The beginning and end of all his thoughts was hatred of human law; that hatred which, if not checked in its growth by some providential event, becomes in time a hatred of society, then hatred of the human race, then hatred of creation, revealing itself by a vague, incessant desire to injure some living being, no matter who. So, the passport was right in describing Jean Valjean as "a very dangerous man."

From year to year this soul had progressively withered, slowly but inevitably. A dry eye goes with a dead soul. When he left prison, he had not shed a tear for nineteen years.

VICTOR HUGO

DAY 3

READ NUMBERS 15:27-31

> Sometimes I lie awake at night, and I ask, "Where have I gone wrong?" Then a voice says to me, "This is going to take more than one night."

CHARLES SCHULTZ

> Take heed of secret sins. They will undo thee if loved and maintained: one moth may spoil the garment; one leak drown the ship; a penknife stab and kill a man as well as a sword; so one sin may damn the soul; nay, there is more danger of a secret sin causing the miscarrying of the soul than open profaneness, because not so obvious to the reproofs of the world; therefore, take heed that secret sinnings eat not out good beginnings.

JEREMIAH BURROUGHS

DAY 4

READ MARK 4:14-23

> Like Israel, we sometimes long for the comfort and security of slavery. They longed for the captivity of Egypt; we long for the captivity of sin. We curse the jails we've built for ourselves, but we also find them strangely comforting. There's a perverse security to our bondage, for like all addicts we begin to believe a lie. We imagine we need our sins to survive. Sometimes we get to the point where we actually feed on alternate fits of rage and remorse. To minds so twisted by sin, forgiveness seems oddly threatening. And so like the Israelites in the wilderness, we sometimes prefer death in slavery to life in freedom. We begin to think that death as slaves to sin is preferable to a life of freedom as the children of God.
>
> HAROLD L. SENKBEIL

> Sin not only leaves us guilty, it leaves us unable. It cripples our ability to be what we are supposed to be and do what we are supposed to do. This is why we need the grace of enablement. Along with forgiveness we need power.
>
> PAUL DAVID TRIPP

DAY 5

READ ROMANS 7:14-25

" Sin is an anomaly, an intruder, a notorious gate-crasher. Sin does not belong in God's world, but somehow has gotten in. In fact, sin has dug in, and, like a tick, burrows deeper when we try to remove it. This stubborn and persistent feature of human sin can make it look as if it has a life of its own, as if it were an independent power or even a kind of person.

CORNELIUS PLANTINGA

" Man is wired so he gets his glory . . . his feelings of rightness with his Maker . . . from God, and this relationship is so strong, and God's love is so pure, that Adam and Eve felt no insecurity at all, so much so that they walked around naked and didn't even realize they were naked. But when that relationship was broken, they knew it instantly. All of their glory, the glory that came from God, was gone.

DONALD MILLER

WEEK 19

THE MISERY OF THE FALL

WESTMINSTER SHORTER CATECHISM QUESTION 19

Q | What is the misery of that estate into which man fell?

A | All mankind by their fall lost communion with God, are under his wrath and curse, and so made liable to all the miseries of this life, to death itself, and to the pains of hell forever.

....

PRAY *When I am afraid of evils to come, comfort me, by showing me that in myself I am a dying, condemned wretch, but that in Christ I am reconciled, made alive, and satisfied. Amen.*

....

WORSHIP GOD BY MEDITATING ON PSALM 81

....

COMMIT GOD'S WORD TO MEMORY | ROMANS 8:18-19

DAY 1 | For I consider that the sufferings
DAY 2 | of this present time are not worth comparing
DAY 3 | with the glory that is to be revealed to us.
DAY 4 | For the creation waits with eager longing
DAY 5 | for the revealing of the sons of God.

GRANDPA

As a World War II veteran, my grandfather was a man of army-style routine. Meal times were at 6 a.m., 11 a.m., and 5 p.m. sharp. These times were to be observed religiously, regardless of outstanding circumstances. I once got stuck in traffic while driving eight hours from Birmingham to Indianapolis to see him, and I had the audacity to arrive at 5:02 p.m. As I pulled into the retirement home parking lot, he was standing there waiting, frantically waving to direct me into a parking space so he could open the car door and usher me into the dinner I was supposed to be enjoying an entire two minutes before. His disciplined life extended beyond meal times: each day at 8 a.m., he took his and my grandmother's blood pressure and logged the results in notebooks and spreadsheets to document their health. He may have been ninety-one years old, but you wouldn't have known it since he was active and mentally sharp. He even kept a Facebook profile.

He spent his last days caring for my grandmother, his wife of sixty-eight years. Every day, he would wake up and help her dress, feed her breakfast and do her hair since a stroke left her unable to do these tasks herself. His devotion and tender care for her and those he came in contact with endeared him to the nurses and staff at their retirement home.

His death was sudden and traumatic. Healthy and active one day, then a hard fall on concrete followed by a quick downward spiral. I've experienced other deaths; they've come in a variety of forms—from friends who died young tragically, to a grandma whose suffering and pain made death a blessing. But his death was different. That fall on pavement wasn't part of his schedule—or mine. The unexpected loss of someone who personified kindness left me heartbroken and reeling with its suddenness and finality. He was the patriarch of our family, whose love and faith over the years provided the soil in which our family grew. He was faithful to pray for me—for all of us—daily. The sense of absence and loss is palpable still.

Walking in this grief, the loss of this dear man, heightens the longing I experience in my everyday life. Pain comes when, as a single woman, I walk through neighborhoods and look into homes full of light and laughter of the family I long for. I feel it when I continually fail or sin and struggle to receive God's grace. I feel it every time I visit the doctor for a health problem that will be with me until I die. This place of brokenness isn't my final destiny, but waiting for Christ's return is heartbreaking. Jesus knew the same grief as he wept for his friend Lazarus. Jesus is a man of sorrows and, as I grieve the loss of my grandfather, I know I am in good company.

DAY 1

> **READ** 2 CORINTHIANS 4:16–5:8

❝ Those who do not weep, do not see.

VICTOR HUGO

❝ We are tempted to say to God, as in the book of Lamentations, "Thou has wrapped thyself with a cloud so that no prayer can pass through." But in fact God is not responsible for the cloud. We are. Our sins blot out God's face from us as effectively as the clouds do the sun.

JOHN STOTT

❝ When God intends to fill a soul, he first makes it empty. When he intends to enrich a soul, he first makes it poor. When he intends to exalt a soul, he first makes it sensible to its own miseries, wants, and nothingness.

JOHN FLAVEL

DAY 2

READ ROMANS 8:18-25

" I happened to see Larry King interview Billy Graham shortly after the shootings at Columbine High School in Littleton, Colorado. I had read an article the previous month about violent video games and their effects on the minds of children, desensitizing them to the act of killing. Larry King asked Billy Graham what was wrong with the world, and how such a thing as Columbine could happen. I knew, because Billy Graham was an educated man, he had read the same article I had read, and I began calculating his answer for him, that violence begets violence, and that we live in a culture desensitized to the beauty of human life and the sanctity of creation. But Billy Graham did not blame video games. Billy Graham looked Larry King in the eye and said, "Thousands of years ago, a young couple lived in a garden called Eden, and God placed a tree in the Garden and told them not to eat from the tree . . ." And I knew in my soul he was right.

DONALD MILLER

DAY 3

READ MATTHEW 25:31–46

> What our flesh wants, maximally, is to be rid of guilt, not sin. But gospel-wakened people want to be free of sin itself, not just the guilt of it.
>
> JARED WILSON

> We cannot begin to understand divine mercy until we first have some understanding of divine justice. When the Bible speaks of God's justice, it usually links it to divine righteousness. God's justice is *according to righteousness*. There is no such thing as justice according to unrighteousness. There is no such thing as evil justice in God. The justice of God is always and ever an expression of his holy character.
>
> R. C. SPROUL

DAY 4

READ PSALM 52

> The gospel can lift this destroying burden [guilty conscience] from the mind, give beauty for ashes, and the garment of praise for the spirit of heaviness. But unless the weight of the burden is felt, the gospel can mean nothing to the man; and until he sees a vision of God high and lifted up, there will be no woe and no burden. Low views of God destroy the gospel for all who hold them.
>
> A. W. TOZER

> We have come to expect God to be merciful. . . . We soon forget that with our first sin we have forfeited all rights to the gift of life. That I am drawing breath this morning is an act of divine mercy. God owes me nothing. I owe him everything.
>
> R. C. SPROUL

DAY 5

READ ECCLESIASTES 12:1-14

> The more we gave 'em away, the more we came to realize the drink would not satisfy, food turned to ash in our mouths, and all the pleasurable company in the world could not slake our lust. We are cursed men, Miss Turner. Compelled by greed we were, but now we are consumed by it.

"BARBOSSA"

> [T]he reason why a natural man is not always perpetually in the pursuit of some one lust, night and day, is because he hath many to serve, every one crying to be satisfied; thence he is carried on with great variety, but still in general he lies towards the satisfaction of self.

JOHN OWEN

WEEK 20

THE COVENANT OF GRACE

WESTMINSTER SHORTER CATECHISM QUESTION 20

Q | Did God leave all mankind to perish in the estate of sin and misery?

A | God, having out of his mere good pleasure, from all eternity, elected some to everlasting life, did enter into a covenant of grace to deliver them out of the estate of sin and misery, and to bring them into an estate of salvation by a Redeemer.

....

PRAY *I bless thee that great sin draws out great grace. Amen.*

....

WORSHIP GOD BY MEDITATING ON PSALM 89

....

COMMIT GOD'S WORD TO MEMORY | 2 THESSALONIANS 2:16–17

DAY 1 | Now may our Lord Jesus Christ himself,
DAY 2 | and God our Father, who loved us
DAY 3 | and gave us eternal comfort and good hope
DAY 4 | through grace, comfort your hearts
DAY 5 | and establish them in every good work and word.

ROLLING

*Fictional names given to protect the innocent.

Last year after a high school dance, a few of my friends and I went to Waffle House. While gathered around the small table, we came up with a plan to TP other students' houses. All smiles and adrenaline, we giggled our way to the house of our first victim: one of our guy friends. Tossing toilet paper over bushes and through tree branches, we quickly went through sixty rolls of toilet paper and worked our way through several more guys' houses before we decided to branch out even more. In the midst of the chaos in the car, someone shouted, "Let's roll Lucy's house!" And I not only joined in shouting her name, but also convinced our driver to take us there. I had a fleeting thought about how Lucy might feel to have some of her close friends roll her house without her. But I shoved the passing thought aside and blurted out the quickest directions.

We spread out and began to conquer her large front lawn, with the final piece bringing us back together to adorn the glorious fountain in the middle. Once finished, we scrambled into our getaway car and drove to safety, ignorant of the weight of pain we'd left behind.

When Monday morning arrived, I walked into school with barely any recollection of Friday's shenanigans dancing in my mind. That is, until I was bombarded by a crowd of friends who were hurt by the mess I'd created. Several girls confronted me angrily with disappointment on their faces. And there, in the back of the group, I saw Lucy, who looked not angry but hurt. After the other girls finished expressing their infuriation and left, she walked up to me, looked me in the eyes, and said, "Just tell me why. That's all I want to know."

I didn't know what to tell her. *Why* would *someone hurt their good friend? Because it was fun?* There was no reasonable answer. My thoughtless indiscretion was evident to everyone, and I was drowning as the realization of my actions caught up to their deep and unwarranted pain. All I could do was shake my head and tell her how sorry I was, and how I obviously didn't think clearly enough to know how she would feel. I told her I knew I had hurt her, and that I wished I could take it back. I continued to talk, pleading my case, fumbling my way through efforts to adequately communicate my misery over my choice, until Lucy interrupted me. She again looked me right in the eyes and said, "Didn't you hear me? I forgive you." And with those three words, I knew it was settled. I knew, because immediately I felt both the weight of her pain and my misery vanish—they dissipated into the kindness of the smile of a friend. A kindness that my actions didn't deserve. The kindness of grace in action.

DAY 1

READ JEREMIAH 31:31-37

" The only perfect Father found occasion to deny the only perfect Son because such denial achieved the only perfect goals: a perfectly qualified high priesthood, reconciliation through the only God-man Mediator, loving atonement for the sins of men, the vindication of the Father's righteousness, and the ever-redounding glory of the Father in the Son and the Son in the Father.

THABITI ANYABWILE

" You can rejoice not only because he is God, but because we are his people, and as such he protects us and provides for us in all ways necessary for us to know him more fully, enjoy him more deeply, and make him known more widely.

JOE THORN

DAY 2

READ GENESIS 17:1-26

> God's covenant is his sovereign, freely bestowed, unconditional promise: "I will be your God," which carries with it a multidimensional implication: therefore "you will be my people." By contrast, a contract would be in the form: "I will be your God if you live as becomes my people." It is the difference between "therefore" and "if." The former introduces the implications of a relationship that has been established; the latter introduces the conditions under which a relationship will be established.
>
> SINCLAIR FERGUSON

> The grace of God means something like: Here is your life. You might never have been, but you are because the party wouldn't have been complete without you.
>
> FREDERICK BUECHNER

DAY 3

READ HEBREWS 8:1-13

> The Snake Crusher is coming back again to wipe away all the bad guys and wipe away every tear. He's coming to make a new beginning and to finish what he started. He's coming to give us the home we once had and might have forgotten that we lost.
>
> So keep waiting for him. Keep believing in him. Keep trusting that the story isn't over yet. God's promises never fail and the Promised One never disappoints.
>
> KEVIN DEYOUNG

> Michael had once read to her how God had cast a man and woman out of paradise. Yet, for all their human faults and failures, God had shown them the way back in.
>
> FRANCINE RIVERS

> Happy the man whose hopes rely
> On Israel's God; he made the sky,
> His truth forever stands secure;
> He saves the oppressed, he feeds the poor
> And none shall find his promise vain.
>
> ISSAC WATTS

DAY 4

> **READ** HEBREWS 9:15-28

" God's jealousy over his people, as we have seen, presupposes his covenant love; and this love is no transitory affection, accidental and aimless, but is the expression of a sovereign purpose. The goal of the covenant love of God is that he should have a people on earth as long as history lasts, and after that should have all his faithful ones of every age with him in glory. Covenant love is the heart of God's plan for his world.

J. I. PACKER

" Grace burst forth spontaneously from the bosom of eternal love and rested not until it had removed every impediment and found its way to the sinner's side, swelling round him in full flow. Grace does away with the distance between the sinner and God, which sin had created. Grace meets the sinner on the spot where he stands; grace approaches him just as he is. Grace does not wait till there is something to attract it nor till a good reason is found in the sinner for its flowing to him. . . . It was free, sovereign grace when it first thought of the sinner; it was free grace when it found and laid hold of him; and it is free grace when it hands him up into glory.

HORATIUS BONAR

DAY 5

READ 2 THESSALONIANS 2:13-17

> The revolutionary thinking that God loves me as I am and not as I should be requires radical rethinking and profound emotional readjustment. Small wonder that the late spiritual giant Basil Hume of London, England, claimed that Christians find it easier to believe that God exists than that God loves them.
>
> BRENNAN MANNING

> The Christian is in a different position from other people who are trying to be good. They hope, by being good, to please God if there is one; or—if they think there is not—at least they hope to deserve approval from good men. But the Christian thinks any good he does comes from the Christ-life inside him. He does not think God will love us because we are good, but that God will make us good because he loves us; just as the roof of a greenhouse does not attract the sun because it is bright, but becomes bright because the sun shines on it.
>
> C. S. LEWIS

WEEK 21

CHRIST, OUR REDEEMER

WESTMINSTER SHORTER CATECHISM QUESTION 21

Q | Who is the Redeemer of God's elect?

A | The only Redeemer of God's elect is the Lord Jesus Christ, who, being the eternal Son of God, became man, and so was, and continues to be, God and man in two distinct natures, and one person, forever.

....

PRAY *Give me unwavering faith that supplications are never in vain, that if I seem not to obtain my petitions I shall have larger, richer answers, surpassing all that I ask or think. Unsought, thou hast given me the greatest gift, the person of thy Son. Amen.*

....

WORSHIP GOD BY MEDITATING ON PSALM 18:1-24

....

COMMIT GOD'S WORD TO MEMORY | JOHN 3:16

DAY 1 | For God so loved the world,
DAY 2 | that he gave his only Son,
DAY 3 | that whoever believes in him
DAY 4 | should not perish
DAY 5 | but have eternal life.

LYING

By the age of eight, I had developed a nasty habit of lying. I wouldn't just lie about things I did wrong for fear of getting in trouble, sometimes I would lie for no good reason. This, of course, disappointed my parents and landed me in the seat of discipline more than a few times.

One day, after hours of bike rides and neighborhood hide-and-seek with some friends and my older brother, we finally went inside for dinner. As we ate, my father asked us about our day, and we told him all about our adventures. In the midst of my brother sharing his view of how the day went, he exposed that I had not stayed with the group like I was supposed to. I quickly opposed the idea and explained that I never left the group. It was a lie, of course, but I stuck to my guns. My father, face downcast as usual when he caught me lying, told me to finish my dinner and that we would discuss it later. For the rest of the meal I was sick to my stomach, scared of what I knew was coming. When dinner was finished, my father told me to meet him in his study so we could talk. I was sure there would be no talking but instead the pain of a well-deserved repercussion.

As my father entered the room, I began to cry. He sat next to me and I blurted out an apology, trying my hardest to reverse my decision to lie and make things better. I would do anything to avoid the pain of the punishment. While I stumbled over my words, my father said, "Stop. It's finished." And I froze. *What does that mean? Why would he say that?* He continued to tell me that he loved me, and all was forgiven. This time, instead of punishing me like I deserved, he showed me mercy. He began to speak straight to my heart, and my heart heard him in a way it never had before. He told me that the punishments for my lie and all the lies I had ever told were paid by Jesus. Christ had died on the cross to pay for all the wrong things I had ever done and would ever do. He finished my punishment; he redeemed it all. In the same way, my father wanted me to know that my lie was paid for. I deserved some not-so-pleasant consequences that day, but my father showed me mercy. And my heart was transformed.

DAY 1

READ JOHN 3:1-21

“ But supposing God became a man—suppose our human nature which can suffer and die was amalgamated with God's nature in one person—then that person could help us. He could surrender his will, and suffer and die, because he was man; and he could do it perfectly because he was God. . . . Our attempts at this dying will succeed only if we men share in God's dying, just as our thinking can succeed only because it is a drop out of the ocean of his intelligence: but we cannot share God's dying unless God dies; and he cannot die except by being a man. That is the sense in which he pays our debt, and suffers for us what he himself need not suffer at all.

C. S. LEWIS

DAY 2

READ ACTS 4:5-12

" Who can understand the riches of the glory of this grace? Here this rich and divine bridegroom Christ marries this poor, wicked harlot, redeems her from all her evil, and adorns her with all his goodness. Her sins cannot now destroy her, since they are laid upon Christ and swallowed up by him. And she has that righteousness in Christ, her husband, of which she may boast as of her own and which she can confidently display alongside her sins in the face of death and hell and say, [as Martin Luther did] "If I have sinned, yet my Christ, in whom I believe, has not sinned, and all his is mine and all mine is his."

GERALD R. MCDERMOTT

" We are not to think of Jesus Christ as a third party wrestling salvation for us from a God unwilling to save. No. The initiative was with God himself. "God was in Christ reconciling the world unto himself." Precisely how he can have been in Christ while he made Christ to be sin for us, I cannot explain, but the same apostle states both truths in the same paragraph.

JOHN STOTT

DAY 3

READ ISAIAH 9:1-7

Through faith in the Messiah, the soul is able to face reality again with cleared vision. As T.S. Eliot said, "Humankind cannot bear very much reality." But through the light shed by the Holy Spirit on the Messiah and his saving work, the soul can take in at a glance the truth about its own standing before God. It can bear the bad news about the justice of God and the depth of its sin, because it can see in the same glance the good news of the grace of Christ available simply through faith.

RICHARD LOVELACE

If you are united to Christ by faith, you should never think that God is punishing you for your sin. How can you be sure? Because someone has already been punished for your sin. The punishment for your bad choices—your utter apathy toward God; your outright rebellion, the ugliest, most shameful things you've ever said or done—has all been laid on Jesus. He was punished for your sin so you don't have to be. Your loving Father will discipline you to make you more holy, but he will not punish you simply to make you pay.

NANCY GUTHRIE

DAY 4

READ 1 TIMOTHY 2:1-7

> We have simply not come to grips with the fact that it isn't hard to live the Christian life. It's impossible! Only Christ can live it. And that's why our only hope is to learn that Jesus Christ did not come just to get men out of hell and into heaven; he came to get himself out of heaven and into men!
>
> BOB GEORGE

> The fact that Jesus came to earth where he suffered and died does not remove pain from our lives. But it does show that God did not sit idly by and watch us suffer in isolation. He became one of us. Thus, in Jesus, God gives us an up-close and personal look at his response to human suffering. All our questions about God and suffering should, in fact, be filtered through what we know about Jesus.
>
> PHILIP YANCEY

DAY 5

READ ISAIAH 55:1-13

> Ah! the bridge of grace will bear your weight, brother. Thousands of big sinners have gone across that bridge, yea, tens of thousands have gone over it. I can hear their trampings now as they traverse the great arches of the bridge of salvation. They come by their thousands, by their myriads; e'er since the day when Christ first entered into his glory, they come, and yet never a stone has sprung in that mighty bridge. Some have been the chief of sinners, and some have come at the very last of their days, but the arch has never yielded beneath their weight. I will go with them trusting to the same support; it will bear me over as it has borne them.

CHARLES SPURGEON

> Knowing God without knowing our wretchedness leads to pride. Knowing our wretchedness without knowing God leads to despair. Knowing Jesus Christ is the middle course, because in him we find both God and our wretchedness.

BLAISE PASCAL

WEEK 22

THE INCARNATION

WESTMINSTER SHORTER CATECHISM QUESTION 22

Q | How did Christ, being the Son of God, become man?

A | Christ, the Son of God, became man, by taking to himself a true body, and a reasonable soul, being conceived by the power of the Holy Spirit, in the womb of the virgin Mary, and born of her, yet without sin.

....

PRAY *I know but little—increase my knowledge of thy love in Jesus, keep me pressing forward for clearer discoveries of it, so that I may find its eternal fullness. Amen.*

....

WORSHIP GOD BY MEDITATING ON PSALM 22:1-31

....

COMMIT GOD'S WORD TO MEMORY | PHILIPPIANS 2:5-7

DAY 1 | Have this mind among yourselves,
which is yours in Christ Jesus,
DAY 2 | who, though he was in the form of God,
DAY 3 | did not count equality with God a thing to be grasped,
DAY 4 | but emptied himself, by taking the form of a servant,
DAY 5 | being born in the likeness of men.

DO YOU SEE ME?

stood in the living room facing my father, sweating . . . and waiting. I carefully studied his face as he looked at my report card. Pleasing him was often a challenge because he demanded a lot from himself and from me, and excellence in education was a requirement. I worked hard to meet his expectations and longed for him to notice my efforts. And even though there was nothing lower than a 95 percent on the report card, I held my breath and searched his face for any flinch of disapproval.

Am I enough? Do you see me? Do I matter?

I've been asking these questions both consciously and subconsciously for as long as I can remember. And I've been a Type A, perfectionist, and people pleaser for as long as I can remember too. Sometimes my father's responses to my hard work were affirming, but on that particular day, he let me know that I hadn't met his expectations: there was room for improvement. I was disappointed but resolute in doubling down on my efforts to please him.

Getting married and having kids has shined a spotlight on this approval mindset that I've internalized over the years. I was a performance addict and a praise junkie . . . and I still am. Having children was part of God's gracious undoing of me. Never in my life had I felt so unproductive. I remember one particular summer afternoon just weeks after having my second child, crying on the bathroom floor while my two-year-old son knocked on the door incessantly because he wanted in. The house wasn't clean, but it was looking good compared to me, and without achievements to translate into tangible accomplishments, I felt like a puddle of failure on that floor. When my husband came home from work later that evening, I found myself standing in the living room of my own house, waiting and sweating once again. He walked in and I studied his face and held my breath.

Am I enough? Do you see me?

I know better; I get frustrated with myself because I often look to the people around me for affirmation instead of running to my Creator who longs to tell me of his goodness and delight in me apart from my performance. When I let him be the One to tenderly answer these questions, his answers deeply satisfy and anchor me in a way that people cannot.

Am I enough, Lord? My grace is sufficient for you (2 Cor. 12:9). *Do you really see me?* I will intercede for you (Rom. 8:26–27). *Do I matter?* You are mine (Isa. 43).

DAY 1

READ LUKE 1:26-38

❝ "The Word became flesh," wrote John, "and dwelt among us, full of grace and truth" (John 1:14). That is what the incarnation means. It is untheological. It is unsophisticated. It is undignified. But according to Christianity, it is the way things are. . . . One of the blunders religious people are particularly fond of making is the attempt to be more spiritual than God.

FREDERICK BUECHNER

❝ The Incarnation shows man the greatness of his misery by the greatness of the remedy which he required.

BLAISE PASCAL

DAY 2

READ MICAH 5:1-5

" The omnipotent, in one instant, made himself breakable. He who had been spirit became piercable. He who was larger than the universe became an embryo. And he who sustains the world with a word chose to be dependent upon the nourishment of a young girl. God as a fetus. Holiness sleeping in a womb. The creator of life being created. God was given eyebrows, elbows, two kidneys, and a spleen. He stretched against the walls and floated in the amniotic fluids of his mother.

MAX LUCADO

" A young wife and mother, overwhelmed by her responsibilities, walked out on her family one day. She just laid down her apron and left. When she called that night, her frantic husband demanded an explanation. But she just hung up. She called every week to check on the children, but she refused to let them know where she was. The husband pleaded with her to return, but she wouldn't listen. Finally, he tracked her down to a dumpy hotel on the other side of the state. When she answered the door, he poured out his love for her and begged her to come home. She fell into his arms and cried for forgiveness. Later, when her husband asked why she hadn't returned before, she replied, "All those claims of love—they were just words before. But then you came."

STEVE BROWN

DAY 3

READ PHILIPPIANS 2:1-11

>> So that is the outline of the official story—the talk of the time when God was the underdog and got beaten, when he submitted to the conditions he had laid down and became a man like the men he had made, and the men he had made broke him and killed him. This is the dogma we find so dull—this terrifying drama of which God is the victim and the hero. If this is dull, then what, in Heaven's name, is worthy to be called exciting?

DOROTHY SAYERS

>> He doth give his joy to all;
He becomes an infant small;
He becomes a man of woe;
He doth feel the sorrow too.
Think not thou canst sigh a sigh
And thy Maker is not by;
Think not thou canst weep a tear
And thy Maker is not near.
O! He gives to us his joy
That our griefs he may destroy;
Till our grief is fled and gone
He doth sit by us and moan.

WILLIAM BLAKE

DAY 4

READ COLOSSIANS 2:8-12

" I stood by the bed where a young woman lies. Her face, post-operative, her mouth, twisted in palsy, clownish. A tiny twig of the facial muscles connecting the face to the mouth has been severed. She will be so from now on. As her surgeon, I have followed with religious fervor the curve of her flesh. Nevertheless, to remove the tumor in her cheek I had to cut that little nerve. And late in the evening I go by to see her. I chance into the room as the shadows are lengthening. Her young husband is in the room. He stands on the opposite side of the bed, and together they seem to dwell in the evening lamplight isolated from me. Who are they? Who are they, I ask myself. He and this woman with a crooked mouth that I have made. They gaze at each other and touch each other so generously. The young woman speaks to me. "Will my mouth always be like this?" "Yes," I say, "it will. It is because the nerve has been cut." She nods, and is silent. Her young husband smiles. "You know," he says, "I like it. It's kind of cute." All at once, I know that I stand on holy ground, so I lower my gaze. Unmindful of me now, he bends to kiss her crooked mouth, and I am so close I see how he twists his own lips to accommodate to hers, to show her that their kiss still works.

RICHARD SELZER

DAY 5

READ 1 TIMOTHY 3:14-17

"For God looked down upon sorrowing, struggling, sinning humanity and was moved with compassion for the contrary, sheep-like creatures he had made. In spite of the tremendous personal cost it would entail to himself to deliver them from their dilemma he chose deliberately to descend and live amongst them that he might deliver them. This meant laying aside his splendor, his position, his prerogatives as the perfect and faultless One. He knew he would be exposed to terrible privation, to ridicule, to false accusations, to rumor, gossip and malicious charges that branded him as a glutton, drunkard, friend of sinners and even an imposter. It entailed losing his reputation. It would involve physical suffering, mental anguish and spiritual agony. In short, his coming to earth as the Christ, as Jesus of Nazareth, was a straightforward case of utter self-sacrifice that culminated in the cross of Calvary. The laid-down life, the poured-out blood were the supreme symbols of total selflessness. This was love. This was God. This was divinity in action, delivering men from their own utter selfishness, their own stupidity, their own suicidal instincts as lost sheep unable to help themselves.

PHILLIP KELLER

WEEK 23

THE OFFICES OF CHRIST

WESTMINSTER SHORTER CATECHISM QUESTION 23

Q | What offices does Christ execute as our Redeemer?

A | Christ, as our Redeemer, executes the offices of a prophet, of a priest, and of a king, both in his estate of humiliation and exaltation.

....

PRAY *May my cry be always, Only Jesus! Only Jesus!*
In him is freedom from condemnation, fullness in
his righteousness, eternal vitality in his given life,
indissoluble union in fellowship with him. Amen.

....

WORSHIP GOD BY MEDITATING ON PSALM 29

....

COMMIT GOD'S WORD TO MEMORY | HEBREWS 4:16

DAY 1 | Let us then with confidence
DAY 2 | draw near to the throne of grace,
DAY 3 | that we may receive mercy
DAY 4 | and find grace to help
DAY 5 | in time of need.

ORDINATION

As far as pastoral ordinations go, the Presbyterian Church in America (PCA) might have one of the most stringent and rigorous of any contemporary denomination, and rightfully so. PCA pastors believe we are called to be "physicians of the soul" and "keepers of the Word." Difficult and demanding training and examination exercises are designed to discern who God is raising up as his chosen leaders.

After months of preparation and study and a lifetime of events leading to this moment, I donned my best suit and walked into the sanctuary to stand before many pastors, elders, friends, and congregants and be confirmed in my calling to be a pastor. The day felt both holy and ordinary. The stress of the past few months had built up a painful dig that lodged in my neck and remained as I took vows to "be zealous and faithful in maintaining the truths of the gospel" and to "be subject to my brothers in the Lord." I had arrived at the final stage of the process, and it had been a long, intense undertaking.

As I listened to my friend, a fellow pastor, speak words of encouragement over me, I felt like a pro-golfer trying to keep his composure through the last putt on the 18th green, finally breaking down when the ball goes in the hole. The enormity of the task behind and before me was as sobering and mysterious as it was celebratory.

My neck began to relax after saying my vows as two dozen men laid hands on me and prayed over me. The elders prayed for strength, wisdom, and compassion for me. They prayed for protection from temptation and evil. They prayed for my family. I teared up from experiencing the Holy Spirit's presence of grace and love in that prayer, knowing they would extend those graces to me in the future as a fellow minister.

So there I was, on my knees, feeling both the weight of those praying hands and the high expectations of my calling. I was humbled. *How did I get here, kneeling on a very public stage with hundreds of witnesses in the congregation?* I wondered. *Surely it wasn't just hard work, and surely it wasn't just because people liked me; sometimes pastors aren't all that popular. Was it because I was so smart? Nah, I'm pretty average.*

The only possible explanation was the divine will of Christ himself. He had placed a vision and a mission on my life to serve him.

Thinking back, I could piece together the events that led up to this pivotal moment. While my childhood could appear to be from the movie, *A Series of Unfortunate Events*, each one of the circumstances molded and shaped me for future use in the lives of others—the painful as well as the beautiful. But here, in the process of my ordination and through the words, prayers, and truths spoken by these men, I experienced the fullness of God and thankfulness for the scars, fears, and pains that led me to accept Christ's calling for my life. And I have never looked back.

DAY 1

READ DEUTERONOMY 18:15-22

  And we have been told also that certain of the prophets themselves became, by the act of anointing, Christs in type, so that all these have reference to the true Christ, the divinely inspired and heavenly Word, who is the only high priest of all, and the only King of every creature, and the Father's only supreme prophet of prophets.

EUSEBIUS

  Christ was anointed, so that he might be our king (*rex*), teacher (*doctor*), and priest (*sacerdos*) for ever. He will govern us, lest we lack any good thing or be oppressed by any ill; he will teach us the whole truth; and he will reconcile us to the Father eternally.

MARTIN BUCER

DAY 2

READ ACTS 3:17-26

“ As powerful as sin is, the blood of Christ is more powerful still. In Christ, the chains of our captivity have been broken, and the light of his grace has shone the way of freedom. But how has he freed us? Christ has secured our freedom because, in the shedding of his blood, he operated in the divinely ordained *munus triplex*, the threefold office of Prophet, Priest, and King. This is why he is called "the faithful witness" (as Prophet); "the firstborn of the dead" (as Priest); and "the ruler of kings on earth" (as King) in Revelation 1:5. In the threefold office of Christ, we are granted our freedom from sin.

ANTHONY CARTER

“ We have a sole prophet, Jesus Christ, who proclaims to us words of life unto our salvation, Christ's word of forgiveness—for us. We have a sole priest who reconciles us by his own body and blood, Christ's shed blood—on our behalf. We have a sole king who exercises complete and just authority over the universe and the church, Christ's authority—over us. We have the quintessential prophet, priest, and king who is for us, acts on our behalf, and is over us.

MATHEW R. RICHARD

DAY 3

READ HEBREWS 4:14–5:6

" Jesus, my Shepherd, Brother, Friend,
My Prophet, Priest and King,
My Lord, my Life, my Way, my End,
Accept the praise I bring.

JOHN NEWTON

" The threefold office of Christ announces three truths. First, it identifies the state of man and how it is remedied in Christ. Man suffers under ignorance, which is resolved by the prophecy of Christ; dwells in alienation from God, which is restored by the priestly work of Christ; and possesses no power to live holily, which is established by the kingship of Christ. Second, Christ's threefold office reveals the way salvation is brought to bear upon man. It is first preached by his prophecy; obtained by his priesthood; and applied by his kingship. Third, the threefold office exposes that salvation is accomplished by Christ. Christ first taught others the will of God; then he offered himself; and afterward he entered to rule in his kingdom.

WILLIAM AMES AND JOHN D. EUSDEN

DAY 4

READ JOHN 18:33-38

> And as little Christs, ordained by the same Father and anointed by the same Spirit, we are to fulfill, in a lesser way, the same offices as our namesake. We confess his name like good prophets, present ourselves as living sacrifices like good priests, and fight our mutual enemies and reign in joint dominion like good kings. Remember this: The work of Christ and the life of a Christian can be summed up in three words: "prophet," "priest," and "king."
>
> KEVIN DEYOUNG

> The nature of our salvation required that it should be revealed by him as a prophet; purchased by him as a priest; and applied by him as a king. His prophetical office, therefore, respects our ignorance; his priestly office our guilt; and his kingly office our pollution, defilement, and thralldom in sin. Accordingly, as a prophet he is made of God unto us wisdom; as a priest, righteousness; as a king, sanctification and complete redemption.
>
> ASHBEL GREEN

DAY 5

READ DANIEL 2:1-45

" This then, is our hope and our comfort—Jesus Christ is the final prophet, the great high priest, and the conquering king. There is a miraculous cure for the disease of ignorance, guilt, and pollution after all. It is what is known by some Reformed theologians as "the triple cure." As Calvin said, in Christ God has fulfilled what he has promised: that the truth of his promises would be realized in the person of the Son. Believers have found to be true Paul's saying that "all the promises of God find their yea and amen in Christ."

KIM RIDDLEBARGER

" The threefold misery of men introduced by sin—ignorance, guilt, and tyranny and bondage by sin—required this conjunction of a threefold office. Ignorance is healed by the prophetic; guilt by the priestly; the tyranny and corruption of sin by the kingly office. Prophetic light scatters the darkness of error; the merit of the Priest takes away guilt and procures a reconciliation for us; the power of the King removes the bondage of sin and death. The Prophet shows God to us; the Priest leads us to God; and the King joins us together and glorifies us with God. The Prophet enlightens the mind by the Spirit of illumination; the Priest by the Spirit of consolation tranquilizes the heart and conscience; the King by the Spirit of sanctification subdues rebellious affections.

FRANCIS TURRETIN

WEEK 24

CHRIST, THE PROPHET

WESTMINSTER SHORTER CATECHISM QUESTION 24

Q | How does Christ execute the office of a prophet?

A | Christ executes the office of a prophet, in revealing to us, by his Word and Spirit, the will of God for our salvation.

PRAY *Help me to place myself always under thy guiding and guardian care. . . . Thou has often wiped away my tears, restored peace to my mourning heart, chastened me for my profit. All thy work for me is perfect, and I praise thee. Amen.*

WORSHIP GOD BY MEDITATING ON PSALM 40

COMMIT GOD'S WORD TO MEMORY | ISAIAH 61:1

DAY 1 | The Spirit of the Lord God is upon me,
DAY 2 | because the Lord has anointed me
to bring good news to the poor;
DAY 3 | he has sent me to bind up the brokenhearted,
DAY 4 | to proclaim liberty to the captives,
DAY 5 | and the opening of the prison to those who are bound.

NUGGETS

When each of our three children turned five, I began taking them on weekly before-school breakfast dates to Chick-fil-A. Initially I simply read to them while they gnawed on chicken nuggets. I read them books such as *Catechism for Young Children*, *The Chronicles of Narnia*, *Pilgrim's Progress*, and other Christian classics. Most of the time I would read a paragraph, stop and explain what it meant in age-appropriate words or illustrations, and then I would attempt to help them think through how what they heard might apply to their lives and often how it applied to my own life.

My desire was to deepen my relationship with them by doing something fun while giving space for Jesus to speak to us through intentional discipleship. At times they would ask me questions related to doctrine, such as creation and dinosaurs . . . or how do we know the Bible is God's Word or that Jesus even lived, or what did obedience look like in their young lives.

As my children grew, our times together became much more interactive. I switched things around and asked them to read aloud and teach me. They began to ask *me* questions! Sometimes we wouldn't even get to the reading because they had something on their hearts that they wanted to share or pray about together.

Those times with my kids at Chick-fil-A were like walking with Jesus and sitting at the foot of the cross together. As we read through the Bible, Jesus would show up during the date and speak tenderly to us about grace, truth, and hope. I had no idea when I started our kindergarten breakfast date tradition that it would last all the way through high school.

When my daughter was in the ninth grade, she went through a season of searching as she struggled with faith, church, and going to a Christian school. For a time, we stopped reading and just talked. Even now my daughter will speak of that pause as a grace period—she felt Jesus and I, by extension, were giving her space to struggle, learn, and process.

Later, my daughter went on to serve as a missionary in Uganda. One of the last things she wanted to do before she left was go on a date to Chick-fil-A. When she returned almost two years later, one of the first things she wanted to do was go on a date . . . back to Chick-fil-A. A couple years ago, during her wedding week, I decided to take her on one last daddy/daughter date. We didn't go to Chick-fil-A—this time it was a much nicer restaurant—but the conversation didn't suffer. It felt as rich and satisfying to us both as it had all through the years gnawing on nuggets.

DAY 1

READ ISAIAH 61:1-11

> A prophet is one who speaks for another. In religious concerns a prophet is one who speaks to men for God. Hence he must be for this purpose a seer, one who sees, and therefore knows, and hence is qualified to speak in God's name. The absolutely necessary qualifications for the office are competent information, adequate powers of expression and unquestionable authority.
>
> A. A. HODGE

> That is, outside Christ there is nothing worth knowing, and all who by faith perceive what he is like have grasped the whole immensity of heavenly benefits . . . and the prophetic dignity in Christ leads us to know that in the sum of doctrine as he has given it to us all parts of perfect wisdom are contained.
>
> JOHN CALVIN

DAY 2

READ LUKE 4:16-30

Often we see that, after a deep humiliation, Christ speaks more peace than before, to witness the truth of this reconciliation, because he knows Satan's enterprises in casting such down lower, because they are most abased in themselves and are ashamed to look Christ in the face, because of their ingratitude.

RICHARD SIBBES

As the prophet of God par excellence, Jesus was both the object and subject of prophecy. His person and his work are the focal point of Old Testament prophecy, yet he himself was a prophet. In Jesus' own prophetic statements, the kingdom of God and his role within the coming kingdom are major themes. A principal activity of a prophet was to declare the Word of God. Jesus not only declared the Word of God, he is himself the Word of God. Jesus was the supreme Prophet of God, being God's Word in the flesh.

R. C. SPROUL

DAY 3

READ ISAIAH 42:1-17

" God is not the sort of person that we are; his wisdom, his aims, his scale of values, his mode of procedure differ so vastly from our own that we cannot possibly guess our way to them by intuition or infer them by analogy from our notion of ideal manhood. We cannot know him unless he speaks and tells us about himself. But in fact he has spoken. He has spoken to and through his prophets and apostles, and he has spoken in the words and deeds of his own Son. Through this revelation, which is made available to us in Holy Scripture, we may form a true notion of God; without it, we never can.

J. I. PACKER

" Jesus was Son of God incarnate, and his teaching, given him by his Father (John 7:16–18; 12:49–50), will stand forever (Mark 13:31) and finally judge its hearers (John 12:48; Matt. 7:24–27). The importance of paying attention to it cannot, therefore, be overstressed. Jesus taught as Jewish rabbis generally did, by bits and pieces rather than in flowing discourses, and many of his most vital utterances are in parables, proverbs, and isolated pronouncements responding to questions and reacting to situations.

J. I. PACKER

DAY 4

READ HEBREWS 2:1–4

> He teaches us to see into our own hearts. Take the most mercurial wits, the greatest politicians, that understand the mysteries of state, they know not the mysteries of their own hearts, they cannot believe the evil that is in them. . . . But when Christ teaches, he [Christ] removes the veil of ignorance, and lights a man into his own heart; and now that he [man] sees swarms of vain thoughts, he blushes to see how sin mingles with his duties, his stars are mixed with clouds; he prays, as Augustine, that God would deliver him from himself.

THOMAS WATSON

> The prophetic office of Christ did not cease when he ascended into heaven, for the role of prophet continues to belong to his essential activities even now. He continues his prophetic work through his church (Mark 16:20). And the Spirit of Jesus continues to work with his messengers.

WALTER A. ELWELL

DAY 5

READ JOHN 15:18-16:4

> Jesus Christ doesn't just give us truths; he is the truth. Jesus Christ is the prophet to end all prophets. He gives us hard-copy words from God, truths on which we can build our lives, truths we have to submit to, truths we have to obey, and truths we have to build our lives on, but he himself is the truth. The core and the center of all the laws and all the regulations and all the words of God we have in the Word is, "... Jesus Christ, and him crucified." Jesus Christ is Lord.

TIM KELLER

> Christ is the Prophet whom we need to instruct us in the things of God so as to heal our blindness and ignorance. The Heidelberg Catechism calls him "our chief Prophet and Teacher, who has fully revealed to us the secret counsel and will of God concerning our redemption." . . . As the Prophet, Jesus is the only one who can reveal what God has been purposing in history "since the world began" and who can teach and make manifest the real meaning of the "scriptures of the prophets." We can expect to make progress in the Christian life only as we heed his instruction and teaching.

JOEL BEEKE

WEEK 25

CHRIST, THE PRIEST

> WESTMINSTER SHORTER CATECHISM QUESTION 25

Q | How does Christ execute the office of a priest?

A | Christ executes the office of a priest, in his once offering up of himself a sacrifice to satisfy divine justice, and reconcile us to God, and in making continual intercession for us.

....

PRAY *Thou hast loved me everlastingly, unchangeably, may I love thee as I am loved. . . . Thou hast died for me, may I live to thee, in every moment of my time, in every movement of my mind, in every pulse of my heart. Amen.*

....

WORSHIP GOD BY MEDITATING ON PSALM 27:1-14

....

COMMIT GOD'S WORD TO MEMORY | ISAIAH 53:6

DAY 1 | All we like sheep have gone astray;
DAY 2 | we have turned—every one—
DAY 3 | to his own way;
DAY 4 | and the Lord has laid on him
DAY 5 | the iniquity of us all.

PEPPER THE SHEEPDOG

Growing up in Choctaw County, Alabama, I was accustomed to dogs off leashes. Every farmhouse had an unfettered hound on the porch operating as security system, doorbell, and table-scrap sweeper. But the farm where I lived had a sheepdog, and his name was Pepper.

To this day, I have never seen a sheep in Choctaw County, so sheep dogs were just as rare. We constantly had to cut cockleburs out of Pepper's long, coarse coat, and summers would have been unbearable for him had we not faithfully sheared his shag in May. But we never cut all his hair away, as dad told us to leave his face and neck untrimmed so Pepper's eyes would be shaded and his neck protected from predators.

Pepper was a local icon. All the other dogs feared him and stood at attention in his presence. I suppose they suspected him to be a fierce and violent beast, the way they barked and became unsettled around him. But their fear, while not warranted, was not lost on Pepper—he learned to enter any environment with regal swagger and soak up every ounce of the attention.

My father marveled at Pepper, probably because he had grown up with hounds as his standard for dog behavior. Pepper loved cows because my dad loved cows, and he was eager to walk among them beside my dad. When we "worked" the cows—meaning doing whatever management or medical actions necessary for the good of the herd—Pepper was always ready to assist. Most of the time, this assistance looked like moving a reluctant animal from one location to another. While this may sound easy and even pastoral, it was actually an innate and focused mixture of strategy and combat bolstered by an unwavering insistence on a fixed end result: the cow was going to go where Pepper desired. Period.

Pepper was as heroic as he was iconic. On one occasion, I saw him protect my dad from an enraged Brahma cow. The speed at which our loveable family sheep dog transitioned to the fierceness of a wolf frightened me. It was the only time Pepper barked, but it was not really a bark as much as a demonic declaration that hell itself had no fury like Pepper. He attacked and dropped the 1600 pound cow the way a linebacker might engage a tackling dummy. And for the remaining years we owned that cow, Pepper would always position himself between him and my dad.

Daddy said that's what sheepdogs do—they fight for what they love, to the death, if necessary.

- -

DAY 1

READ ACTS 8:25-40

“ Whatever the law demanded is perfectly paid. Whatever a sinner needs is perfectly obtained and purchased. Nothing can be added to what Christ hath done. He put the last hand to it when he said, "It is finished."

JOHN FLAVEL

“ You must learn, relearn, and remember your Savior's love and sacrifice for the wicked, the rebellious, the black-hearted—for people like you. And when you see the Holy One's sacrificial love for you, you not only see what love looks like, but also you find strength and power to love like him.

JOE THORN

DAY 2

READ ISAIAH 53:1-12

❝ Shall our sins discourage us, when he appears there only for sinners? Are you bruised? Be of good comfort, he calls you. Conceal not your wounds, open all before him and take not Satan's counsel. Go to Christ, although trembling, as the poor woman who said, "If I may but touch his garment" (Matt. 9:21). We shall be healed and have a gracious answer. Go boldly to God in our flesh; he is flesh of our flesh, and bone of our bone for this reason, that we might go boldly to him. Never fear to go to God, since we have such a Mediator with him, who is not only our friend but our brother and husband.

RICHARD SIBBES

❝ Salvation is only in Jesus Christ because there are two conditions that, no matter how hard we try, we can never meet. Yet, they must be done if we are to be saved. The first is to satisfy the justice of God through obedience to the law. The second is to pay the price of our sins. We cannot do either, but Christ did both perfectly. . . . There is no other way to come into the presence of God than through Christ alone. Jesus' sacrifice took place once only, but he still continues as our great High Priest, the One through whom all acceptable prayer and praise are made to God. In heavenly places, he remains our constant Intercessor and Advocate. . . . We can grow in our enjoyment of access to God only by a deepening reliance on him as our Sacrifice and Intercessor.

JOEL BEEKE

DAY 3

READ HEBREWS 10:1-18

> There is nothing in us or done by us, at any stage of our earthly development, because of which we are acceptable to God. We must always be accepted for Christ's sake, or we cannot ever be accepted at all. This is not true of us only when we believe. It is just as true after we have believed. It will continue to be true as long as we live. Our need of Christ does not cease with our believing, nor does the nature of our relation to him or to God through him ever alter, no matter what our attainments in Christian graces or our achievements in behavior may be. It is always on his "blood and righteousness" alone that we can rest.
>
> BENJAMIN WARFIELD

> Blessed and happy are those who have such a one as Christ to appear for them and intercede for them at the throne of grace.
>
> JONATHAN EDWARDS

> If I could hear Christ praying for me in the next room, I would not fear a million enemies. Yet distance makes no difference. He is praying for me.
>
> ROBERT MURRAY MCCHEYNE

DAY 4

READ HEBREWS 7:11-28

Christ steps into the courtroom, invites the sinner to approach him, lifts him on his shoulders and carries him to his Father who sits in the judge's seat. First, he turns to the sinner. "Be of good cheer! I shall make a plea to our Father as earnestly and dedicatedly as if your case were my own."

Next he turns to God. "Father," he says, "here is a poor sinner who has come to me prayerfully seeking counsel and succor. He has reminded me of the love I have shown the world by dying and rising again in obedience to your command. I beg you now to continue to help him, as you have helped him in the past and, when the time comes, to perfect him with your righteousness."

And to this plea God the Father replies: "My dearest son, I am well pleased with you. You have paid for this sinner with your own obedience to me, having fully satisfied all my demands. I can refuse you nothing. Go, take him with you."

GERALD STRAUSS

DAY 5

READ COLOSSIANS 1:21-23

> Because of the work of our High Priest, we have assurance of faith and can enter into God's presence in confidence, knowing that our sins are forgiven. Though we may fall, we know that we have an advocate with the Father. This is how Jesus continues to perform the role of High Priest in heaven on our behalf. . . . Because of Jesus we have forgiveness for sin and reconciliation [with] God. We can sing with joy, "Because my sinless Savior died, my sinful soul is counted free. For God the just is satisfied, to look on Him and pardon me." We have been pardoned. And since we are fully forgiven through Christ's perfect sacrifice, we need not be ashamed when we fail. When we stumble, we must resist the temptation to hide from God until we can try to make ourselves worthy of his forgiveness. His forgiveness is there; we have only to confess and receive it.

CLAYTON KRABY

> Christ, . . . is no Moses, no lawgiver, no tyrant, but a mediator for sins, a free giver of grace, righteousness and life; who gave himself, not for our merits, holiness, righteousness and godly life, but for our sins.

MARTIN LUTHER

WEEK 26

CHRIST, THE KING

WESTMINSTER SHORTER CATECHISM QUESTION 26

Q | How does Christ execute the office of a king?

A | Christ executes the office of a king, in subduing us to himself, in ruling and defending us, and in restraining and conquering all his and our enemies.

....

PRAY *Let me not be at my own disposal, but rejoice that I am under the care of one who is too wise to err, too kind to injure, too tender to crush. Amen.*

....

WORSHIP GOD BY MEDITATING ON PSALM 2:1-12

....

COMMIT GOD'S WORD TO MEMORY | COLOSSIANS 1:13-14

DAY 1 | He has delivered us from the domain of darkness
DAY 2 | and transferred us to the kingdom
DAY 3 | of his beloved son,
DAY 4 | in whom we have redemption,
DAY 5 | the forgiveness of sins.

STATE OF THE UNION

I still remember the tweed, gray suit because every time I wore it, I felt like a little girl playing dress-up. At age twenty-three and only a few months out of college, I didn't feel grown up enough to work as a congressional staff assistant on Capitol Hill, but I could at least dress the part. About six weeks into the job, my name was randomly selected as the staffer from our office to attend the president's annual State of the Union address. Honestly, I felt awkward that I was chosen; however, my gracious colleagues encouraged me to whole-heartedly take advantage of the opportunity.

With each step my black pumps echoed through the cool, dim underground passageways as I weaved my way to the United States Capitol. Statues and plaques of American greats lined the basement hallways, and the musty air contributed to the reverent ambiance of the capitol complex. Thorough security checkpoints greeted me at the entrance, affirming my decision to bring only my BlackBerry and congressional ID.

Though I gave weekly tours of this chamber, from my bird's eye view in the gallery of the floor below, I felt highly out of place. Representatives mingled, looking happy and important as they shook hands and exchanged pleasantries. In the first lady's box, just thirty feet to my right, the president's honored guests settled into their seats. The Speaker of the House assumed his position at the podium, while the deputy sergeant at arms prepared to announce the arrival of the vice president and senators. As the senators walked the aisle toward their assigned seats, followed by the supreme court justices, the cabinet, and the joint chiefs of staff, I tallied the number of officials who now occupied this space. The estimate: 560.

The boisterous crowd of politicians quieted quickly with the rapping of the gavel, and though I couldn't tell from my seat, it was apparent from their glances toward the door that the sergeant at arms was about to speak. Sure enough, only a moment later came the familiar words, "Ladies and gentlemen, the President of the United States!"

Thunderous applause echoed through the chamber as we instinctively rose to our feet. Members of both parties vied for places along the aisle so they could shake hands or lock eyes, or simply be closer to the leader of the free world. I watched carefully as congressmen who publicly opposed the president, both personally and politically, aggressively moved toward the end of their row for a chance to see and greet the man of the hour.

I had watched the State of the Union on television plenty of times with my dad. I knew the protocol, appreciated the ceremonial aspects of the event, and had even been in that very room on multiple occasions over the past six weeks. So my flushed face and hot tears caught me off guard.

The temperature of the chamber had changed—and the president still hadn't spoken a word.

DAY 1

READ DANIEL 7:9-14

" You and I are kingdom oriented. We are always in pursuit of and in service to some kind of kingdom. We are either living in allegiance to the King of kings, celebrating our welcome into his kingdom of glory and grace, or we are anointing ourselves as kings and working to set up our own little kingdoms of one.

PAUL DAVID TRIPP

" Christianity is the story of how the rightful king has landed, you might say in disguise, and is calling us all to take part in his great campaign of sabotage.

C. S. LEWIS

DAY 2

READ COLOSSIANS 1:9-20

Every child of God is surrounded by a multitude of enemies without and within. . . . What hope or help can we have, but in that all-seeing eye, which sees our condition; that all-sympathizing heart, which feels for us; that all-powerful hand, which delivers the objects of his love from all the snares and traps—and defeats all the plans and projects of these mighty, implacable foes? We daily and hourly feel the workings of our mighty sins, raging lusts, powerful temptations, besetting evils, against the least and feeblest of which, we have no strength!

But as the eye of faith views our enthroned King, we are led by the power of his grace to look unto him, hang upon him, and seek help from him.

J. C. PHILPOT

The guilty soul flies first to Christ crucified, made a curse for us. Thence it is that Christ has right to govern us; thence it is that he gives us his Spirit as our guide to lead us home.

RICHARD SIBBES

DAY 3

READ PSALM 110:1-7

" In the Old Testament, royal succession was a great concern. Many kings tried to establish a dynastic succession in preparation for their own demise. Few of these dynasties endured. The house of David lasted for a season, and the house of Omri for a short period, but Christ's kingship is forever. He is anointed and crowned in heaven itself to become the King of Kings and the Lord of Lords. He is the King in the superlative degree, the ultimate King to whom the Father gives all authority in heaven and on earth.

R. C. SPROUL

" Not all the water in the rough rude sea can wash the balm from an anointed king.

WILLIAM SHAKESPEARE

DAY 4

READ MATTHEW 12:15–32

> Your kingdom come,
> Your will be done,
> On earth as it is in heaven.
>
> On this basis, then the kingdom of God and the kingdom of heaven are the energetic rule of God present in Jesus Christ and directed in power, dominion, and sovereignty against all the evil in the world. God established his kingdom at creation. Satan attacked it in the fall and established his rival reign. In Christ, God's empire has struck back to regain and restore the world and his people.
>
> DAVID NAUGLE

> Let us learn that, as we are all subject to the tyranny of Satan, there is no other way in which he [God] commences his reign within us, than when he rescues us, by the powerful and victorious arm of Christ, from that wretched and accursed bondage.
>
> JOHN CALVIN

DAY 5

READ 1 CORINTHIANS 15:20-28

Don't forget this: Jesus is not just a king; he's a king on a cross. If he were only a king on a throne, you'd submit to him just because you have to. But he's a king who went to the cross for you. Therefore you can submit to him out of love and trust. This means coming to him not negotiating but saying, "Lord, whatever you ask I will do, whatever you send I will accept." When someone gave himself utterly for you, how can you not give yourself utterly to him?

TIM KELLER

All hail the power of Jesus' name! Let angels prostrate fall.
Bring forth the royal diadem,
and crown him Lord of all.
Bring forth the royal diadem, and crown him Lord of all!

EDWARD PERRONET

WEEK 27

THE HUMILIATION OF CHRIST

WESTMINSTER SHORTER CATECHISM QUESTION 27

Q | Wherein did Christ's humiliation consist?

A | Christ's humiliation consisted in his being born, and that in a low condition, made under the law, undergoing the miseries of this life, the wrath of God, and the cursed death of the cross; in being buried, and continuing under the power of death for a time.

PRAY *O my Savior, I thank thee from the depths of my being for thy wondrous grace and love in bearing my sin in thine own body on the tree. Amen.*

WORSHIP GOD BY MEDITATING ON PSALM 17

COMMIT GOD'S WORD TO MEMORY | 2 CORINTHIANS 8:9

DAY 1 | For you know the grace
DAY 2 | of our Lord Jesus Christ,
DAY 3 | that though he was rich,
DAY 4 | yet for your sake he became poor,
DAY 5 | so that you by his poverty might become rich.

THE MANAGER

Years ago, I worked as a technical writer for a software company. About two years into the job, my manager abruptly changed occupations, leaving behind a department that had grown from two to five writers during her tenure. Upper management reviewed their options and named their new manager—someone I wasn't expecting or remotely prepared for: me.

To say I didn't feel I was cut out for this new role is an understatement. I struggled through planning sessions with the department head I now reported to, stumbled through meetings with the writers in my assign (all older than me), and doubted every day my ability to meet their expectations.

I wanted to lead my team to success and be found competent and dependable for the company, but I constantly butted heads with the writers I now managed. One of them, whom I'll call Marsha, would openly challenge departmental decisions and directives. My immaturity and lack of leadership training meant that I didn't know what to do with her disrespect, and over the coming weeks my frustration festered.

One day as I led a team meeting about a fast-approaching deadline we were on track to miss, Marsha challenged me in front of the others: "And just *when* are we supposed to get all this done?" This time, I snapped back, "If you can't get it done during business hours, then you'll have to work this weekend." A long argument ensued. The other writers piled on. It was them versus me, and I knew then that I wasn't up to the task.

Several days later after some management-encouraged time off, I was no longer leading the group. I honestly don't remember whether the demotion was my idea or theirs, but I didn't fight it—I wasn't wired to manage people at this juncture of my life. Humiliated, I limped back to my previous role as a peer and started the search for a new job.

Soon I interviewed with an exciting internet start-up—one of those companies with no dress code and a basketball goal in the office to foster creativity and let off steam. The idea of being part of something new and exciting without the corporate atmosphere was life giving.

After two promising interviews, I told my friends I thought it was my job to lose. Several days later the call finally came in. The start-up had chosen another candidate. I was rejected in what I thought was a done deal. My confidence was gone, my shame restored.

But humiliation wasn't through with me yet. The next morning Marsha arrived with a smile on her face and a resignation letter in her hand. She was leaving the company to go work at an internet start-up. I'll leave it to you to guess which one.

DAY 1

READ LUKE 2:1–21

> The incarnation is a kind of vast joke whereby the Creator of the ends of the earth comes among us in diapers. . . . Until we too have taken the idea of the God-man seriously enough to be scandalized by it, we have not taken it as seriously as it demands to be taken.
>
> FREDERICK BUECHNER

> Maker of the sun, he is made under the sun. In the Father he remains, from his mother he goes forth. Creator of heaven and earth, he was born on earth under heaven. Unspeakably wise, he was wisely speechless. Filling the world, he lies in a manger. Ruler of the stars, he nurses at his mother's bosom. He is both great in the nature of God, and small in the form of a servant.
>
> AUGUSTINE

DAY 2

READ MARK 15:1-39

> There may be no greater inner agony than the loss of relationship we desperately want. If a mild acquaintance turns on you, condemns and criticizes you, and says she never wanted to see you again, it is painful. If someone you're dating does the same thing, it is qualitatively more painful. But if your spouse does this to you, or if one of your parents does this to you when you're still a child, the psychological damage is infinitely worse. We cannot fathom, however, what it would be like to lose not just a spousal love or parental love that has lasted several years, but the infinite love of the Father that Jesus had from all eternity. Jesus' sufferings would have been eternally unbearable.

TIM KELLER

> The whole of Christ's life was a continual passion; others die martyrs, but Christ was born a martyr. He found a Golgotha, where he was crucified, even in Bethlehem, where he was born; for to his tenderness then the straws were almost as sharp as the thorns after, and the manger as uneasy at first as the cross at last. His birth and his death were but one continual act, and his Christmas Day and his Good Friday are but the evening and the morning of one.

NANCY GUTHRIE

DAY 3

READ JOHN 11:30-36

> This, after all, is the master-truth of Scripture, that "Christ died for our sins." To this let us daily return. On this let us daily feed our souls. Some, like the Greeks of old, may sneer at the doctrine, and call it "foolishness." But let us never be ashamed to say with Paul, "Be it far from me to boast, except in the cross of our Lord Jesus Christ" (Gal. 6:14).
>
> J. C. RYLE

> For Christ to be our Saviour there was no other way than the way of the cross. God's righteousness demanded it, our sin required it, and Satan feared it. And for those who would be saved from sin and its consequences, there is no other way than the way of the cross where God's holy conscience has been satisfied, sin has been dealt with and Satan has been routed.
>
> FREDERICK S. LEAHY

DAY 4

READ HEBREWS 5:7-10

> I cannot begin to unfold the meaning of the death of Christ without first confessing that much remains a mystery. Christians believe that the cross is the pivotal event in history. Small wonder that our puny minds cannot fully take it in! One day the veil will be altogether removed. And all riddles will be solved. We shall see Christ as he is and worship him through eternity for what he has done. "Now we see in a mirror dimly, but then face to face. Now I know in part; then I shall understand fully, even as I have been fully understood." So said the great apostle Paul with his massive intellect and his many revelations; and if he said it, how much more should we?"

JOHN STOTT

> "Abba! Father!" is not a calm acknowledgement of a universal truth about God's abstract fatherhood. It is the child's cry in a nightmare. It is the cry of outrage, fear, shrinking away when faced with the horror of the "world"—yet not simply or exclusively protest, but trust as well.

ROWAN WILLIAMS

DAY 5

READ 2 CORINTHIANS 8:1-9

> The Cross is the abyss of wonders, the centre of desires, the school of virtues, the house of wisdom, the throne of love, the theatre of joys, and the place of sorrows. It is the root of happiness, and the gate of Heaven.

THOMAS TRAHERNE AND BERTRAM DOBELL

> It may be profitable to linger yet a little time at the cross, that we may again survey its glory, and feel its soul subduing power. In the cross of Christ, all the divine perfections are gloriously and harmoniously displayed. Infinite love, inviolable truth, and inflexible justice are all seen, in their brightest and most beautifully mingled colors. The heavens declare the glory of God; but the glory of the cross outshines the wonders of the skies. . . . In the presence of the cross, we feel that omnipotent grace has hold of our heart; and we surrender to dying love. The doctrine of the cross needs no other demonstration of its divine origin than its power to sanctify the heart and bring it into willing and joyful subjection to Christ.

JOHN L. DAGG

WEEK 28

THE EXALTATION OF CHRIST

WESTMINSTER SHORTER CATECHISM QUESTION 28

Q | Wherein consists Christ's exaltation?

A | Christ's exaltation consists in his rising again from the dead on the third day, in ascending up into heaven, in sitting at the right hand of God the Father, and in coming to judge the world at the last day.

....

PRAY *Give me the assurance that in Christ I died, in him I rose, in his life I live, in his victory I triumph, in his ascension I shall be glorified. Amen.*

....

WORSHIP GOD BY MEDITATING ON PSALM 68

....

COMMIT GOD'S WORD TO MEMORY | EPHESIANS 4:15

DAY 1 | Rather, speaking the truth in love,
DAY 2 | we are to grow up
DAY 3 | in every way into him
DAY 4 | who is the head,
DAY 5 | into Christ.

CARING FOR MOM

The wheel of life turned, and I began caring for my aging mother. It wasn't something I asked for or ever thought I'd be doing. Mom was a woman of strength in both stature and will. She was an elementary school teacher, passionate about education and its value, and she imparted that message to me from an early age. My mom also placed a high value on music, and as a result my sister and I were in piano lessons every week. She regularly exposed us to a wide variety of places and people, so we would be confident in the world we were preparing to enter.

As I found myself taking care of this woman who taught me so much, I realized one thing she couldn't teach me: how to care for her in her last days. I thought that if I found her the right doctors, tests, and medications she would be back to her strong, independent self. It took ten years before I realized she wasn't going to get better.

The first of those caregiver years began with a stroke while she was living alone in her home. She was in the bathtub and couldn't get out. My heart still aches to think of how I felt when, two days later, I found her and rushed her to the hospital. After that, mom moved in with us. Her age and early dementia kept her from doing many things, but she was still mobile and strong and able to do many of her daily routines—much more slowly, yet still independently.

Two and a half years ago things changed, and mom's functions plummeted. My husband and son had to carry her from one place to another until hospice stepped in to assist with some daily activities. Life carried on until she became more disoriented, contracted pressure wounds, and nearly stopped eating. I sat by her side, her labored breathing a metronome reminding us that her days were getting shorter. Her words were muddled, and she often slept more than she was awake.

The last week of her life, mom slept most of the time, only waking for very short periods. I offered her food and water, but she would cough and choke so violently that the hospice nurses advised we let her rest—her new normal. During our final hours together, I prayed, journaled, and watched this woman who had spent so many days staring into my own eyes as she cared for me. In her final hours, as I tried to get her to swallow droplets of water, I, the daughter, told her, the mother, "It's okay to go be with Jesus." At that moment, I realized she had imparted to me the most important thing: faith in the One seated at the right hand of the Father who promises to wipe away every tear and to do away with death, mourning, crying, and pain.

DAY 1

READ 1 CORINTHIANS 15:1-11

> On the Day of the Lord—the day that God makes everything right, the day that everything sad comes untrue—on that day the same thing will happen to your own hurts and sadness. You will find that the worst things that have ever happened to you will in the end only enhance your eternal delight. On that day, all of it will be turned inside out and you will know joy beyond the walls of the world. The joy of your glory will be that much greater for every scar you bear.
>
> So live in the light of the resurrection and renewal of this world, and of yourself, in a glorious, never-ending, joyful dance of grace.

TIM KELLER

> The resurrection of Jesus offers courage and strength to persevere because his victory over sin and death is ours both in this life and in the one to come. The same spirit that raised Jesus from the dead dwells in us, sanctifies us, and empowers us to follow Christ and serve the mission of the church.

JOE THORN

DAY 2

READ JOHN 20:1-18

> From that moment on, there was no more fear or sadness; no more crying or pain. It never stormed, it never got too cold, and the lights never went out. But most importantly, the family was together—forever and always. And they lived joyfully ever after, because the Star King had made all things new.
>
> ANNE RILEY

> The kingdom is advancing; God's reign is spreading; there will be justice; and when we belong to Christ, it will end with joy.
>
> EDWARD WELCH

DAY 3

READ ACTS 1:1-11

> The truth of the resurrection is of supreme and eternal importance. It is the hinge upon which the story of the world pivots.

TIM KELLER

> But maybe one day when you're alone, unsure, doubting yourself, you'll need these words. Remember this: you are an Annieran. Your father is a king. You are his son. This is your land, and nothing can change that. Nothing.

ANDREW PETERSON

DAY 4

READ EPHESIANS 4:7–16

He will give us to sit upon his throne, for as he has overcome, and is set down with his Father on his throne; he has a crown, and he will not wear his crown, unless he gives us crowns too; he has a throne, but he is not content with having a throne to himself; on his right hand there must be his bride in gold of Ophir. And he cannot be there without his bride; the Saviour cannot be content to be in heaven unless he has his Church with him, which is "the fullness of him that filleth all in all." Beloved, look up to Christ now; let the eye of your faith catch a sight of him; behold him there, with many crowns upon his head. Remember, as ye see him there, ye will one day be like him, and when ye shall see him as he is, ye shall not be as great as he is, ye shall not be as glorious in degree, but still ye shall, in a measure, share the same honors, and enjoy the same happiness and the same dignity which he possesses.

CHARLES SPURGEON

DAY 5

READ HEBREWS 6:13–20

" If you want to be comforted when your conscience plagues you or when you are in dire distress, then you must do nothing but grasp Christ in faith and say, "I believe in Jesus Christ, God's Son, who suffered, was crucified, and died for me. In his wounds and death, I see my sin. In his resurrection, I see the victory over sin, death, and the devil. I see righteousness and eternal life as well. I want to see and hear nothing except him." This is true faith in Christ and the right way to believe.

MARTIN LUTHER

" No coward soul is mine,
No trembler in the world's storm troubled sphere:
I have seen Heaven's glories shine,
And faith shines equal, arming me from fear.

EMILY BRONTË

WEEK 29

PARTICIPATING IN REDEMPTION

WESTMINSTER SHORTER CATECHISM QUESTION 29

Q | How are we made partakers of the redemption purchased by Christ?

A | We are made partakers of the redemption purchased by Christ by the effectual application of it to us by his Holy Spirit.

....

PRAY *Do thou establish me in Christ, settle me, give me a being there, assure me with certainty that all this is mine, for this only will fill my heart with joy and peace. Amen.*

....

WORSHIP GOD BY MEDITATING ON PSALM 107

....

COMMIT GOD'S WORD TO MEMORY | JOHN 6:44

DAY 1 | No one can come to me
DAY 2 | unless the Father
DAY 3 | who sent me draws him.
DAY 4 | And I will raise him up
DAY 5 | on the last day.

THE TREES

Looking through my living room window, I'm drawn to the winter trees on the other side—stark, exposed, gnarled, and immobile—their imperfections, beauty, and emptiness a visual of my own life. The dark branches against the bright morning sky look like arrows pointing to my singleness, my barren womb, my current inability to work, and my health problems. Those unmet longings have been painfully surrendered to the One writing my story. Yet I know that the life held hidden within the seemingly dead branches will soon blossom with dazzling arrays of color, and I find my heart quickening to believe the same could be true of my own desolate places.

A breeze tears the brown, brittle leaves from the trees, and I want to scoop them all up and tell them that I understand the stripping, the pain of ripping pride and self-sufficiency, and what it feels like to fall. When God called me to my last job three years ago, I felt sure and confident, excited to jump into work in a new culture. I never expected to struggle with engaging people, insecurity, health issues, or depression as I left. I was out of my league and needed help, but too proud to ask for assistance, until asking for help was my only option.

The longer I look out the window, the more details I notice—slow and steady movements that catch my eye. The trunks of the giant pine, birch, and oak trees are not stationary, as they first seemed—they are gently swaying in the brisk wind. I imagine the roots gripping deeper into the soil, strengthened and stretched by the assault above, slowly growing and changing them into towers of firm endurance.

I'm reminded that there's more to the trees than meets the eye, more than their discouraging circumstances show—imperceptible growth and strengthening and life are happening beneath the surface, in the dark places. Taking a deep breath, I experience an ache for new life to rise up from within myself, to be able to be at rest despite my situation. I long to trust that the story being written is

God's plan and embrace that he is using me to bring him glory in a way only he can. My head unwaveringly knows this truth while my heart struggles to believe it in full, but I'm sensing a new curiosity and hope—not just in the unseen life, but in the One who gives and takes away.

DAY 1

READ TITUS 3:4-8

> Jesus came to raise the dead. The only qualification for the gift of the gospel is to be dead. You don't have to be smart. You don't have to be good. You don't have to be wise. You don't have to be wonderful. You don't have to be anything . . . you just have to be dead. That's it.
>
> ROBERT FARRAR CAPON

> The more grace, the more spiritual life, and the more spiritual life, the more antipathy to the contrary. Therefore, none are so aware of corruption as those whose souls are most alive.
>
> RICHARD SIBBES

DAY 2

READ 2 TIMOTHY 1:3-10

> The gospel actually redeems our capacity to be a life-giver and to actually do what God has called us to do. . . . It's something that we have to rely on all the time. As we look to Jesus, we are dependent upon him. It's not about us having the capacity to do it. It's his life, through us.

KAREN HODGE

> Behold the Spirit of the Lord, who first of all moved upon chaos and brought forth order, who now visits the chaos of your soul and creates the order of holiness. Behold him as the Lord and Giver of spiritual life, the Illuminator, the Instructor, the Comforter, and the Sanctifier. Behold him as he descends upon the head of Jesus, and then as he rests upon you.
>
> Such an intelligent, scriptural, and experiential belief in the Trinity is yours if you truly know God; and such knowledge brings peace indeed.

CHARLES SPURGEON

DAY 3

READ EZEKIEL 11:14-25

> The Word is the instrumental cause of our conversion, the Spirit is the efficient. The ministers of God are only the pipes and organs; it is the Spirit blowing in them that effectually changes the heart. . . . So it is not the seed of the Word that will effectually convert, unless the Spirit puts forth his sweet influence, and drops as rain upon the heart. Therefore, the aid of God's Spirit is to be implored, that he would put forth his powerful voice, and awaken us out of the grave of unbelief.
>
> THOMAS WATSON

> To what will you look for help if you will not look to that which is stronger than yourself?
>
> C. S. LEWIS

DAY 4

READ 2 CORINTHIANS 3:1-6

> The Spirit operates on the dead soul, communicating the principle of life. The Word holds up to the view of the regenerated soul the evil of sin which leads to repentance, and shows the excellency and suitableness of Christ as a Saviour in all his offices, and reveals the beauty of holiness.

J. W. ALEXANDER

> Clear conviction of sin is the only true origin of dependence on another's righteousness, and therefore (strange to say!) of the Christian's peace of mind and cheerfulness.

ROBERT MURRAY MCCHEYNE

> Often enough, when we think we are protecting ourselves, we are struggling against our rescuer.

MARILYNNE ROBINSON

DAY 5

READ JOHN 6:25-45

> The basis of our knowledge that we are in relationship with God is not our feelings, but the fact that he says we are. The test we are to apply to ourselves is objective rather than subjective. We are not to grub around inside ourselves for evidence of spiritual life, but to look up and out and away to God and his Word.
>
> JOHN STOTT

> Do not be astonished to see simple people believing without argument. God makes them love him and hate themselves. He inclines their hearts to believe. We shall never believe, with an effective belief and faith, unless God inclines our hearts.
>
> BLAISE PASCAL

WEEK 30
REDEMPTION APPLIED

WESTMINSTER SHORTER CATECHISM QUESTION 30

Q | How does the Spirit apply to us the redemption purchased by Christ?

A | The Spirit applies to us the redemption purchased by Christ, by working faith in us, and thereby uniting us to Christ in our effectual calling.

....

PRAY *Grant me never to lose sight of the exceeding sinfulness of sin, the exceeding righteousness of salvation, the exceeding glory of Christ, the exceeding beauty of holiness, the exceeding wonder of grace. Amen.*

....

WORSHIP GOD BY MEDITATING ON PSALM 119:65–96

....

COMMIT GOD'S WORD TO MEMORY | PHILIPPIANS 1:29

DAY 1 | For it has been granted to you
DAY 2 | that for the sake of Christ
DAY 3 | you should not only believe in him
DAY 4 | but also suffer
DAY 5 | for his sake.

THE UGLY TRIPLETS

The ugly triplet chain of fear, anxiety, and worry has circled me again and again since the birth of our profoundly mentally handicapped son twelve years ago. When he was little, we could take him out into the community and manage him (to a degree) and his two siblings. But as he grows bigger and stronger, the reality of leaving the house and taking him out in public is no longer an option much of the time.

My anxiety and fear have grown as my son hit puberty and is now physically stronger, though his mental capacity remains that of a twelve month old. Strangers notice. It seems everywhere I turn I'm being asked, "How are you going to manage him as he gets bigger?" And my answer is always the same: "I don't know . . . yet."

It's not pretty when fear finds an opening in my mind. Without my eyes on the rock of God's promises and his provision, my thoughts wander. I begin to think of the future and the "what ifs" of my circumstances.

What if I am trapped in this house without the ability to go anywhere?

What if he gets so strong I can no longer change his diaper?

What if he wanders off and the tracking device the police have on his ankle doesn't help us find him in time?

The ugly triplets have long ruled over our church attendance. For years I used to go into the sanctuary with our son sitting next to us in his wheelchair aggressively rocking, making high pitched, ear piercing screams, or humming happy sounds. They would create tremendous anxiety for me while sitting through the service. *Are we disrupting everyone around us? Are people annoyed that we are here? Do we make everyone feel awkward? Are we even wanted here?*

Last year a friend told me she happened to overhear a conversation between two of our pastors during worship. One leaned over to the other and whispered, "I hear J.A. worshipping the Lord!"

This pastor still has no idea a comment he likely thought was casual and passing would begin the process of dispelling my angst and insecurity. Those words empowered me to believe and fight against the what-ifs that attempt to shut down my heart. They empowered me to believe that our family is welcome to worship God in our church. And they gave birth to a new set of triplets: faith, hope, and love—words that hold new meaning to me as I offer my apprehensions to the One who perfectly holds my family with the greatest of those virtues.

. . . .

DAY 1

> **READ** 1 CORINTHIANS 2:1-16

> Biblical maturity is never just about what you know; it's always about how grace has employed what you have come to know to transform the way you live.
>
> PAUL DAVID TRIPP

> In the same way a Christian is not a man who never goes wrong, but a man is enabled to repent and pick himself up and begin over again after each stumble—because the Christ-life is inside him, repairing him all the time, enabling him to repeat (in some degree) the kind of voluntary death which Christ himself carried out.
>
> C. S. LEWIS

DAY 2

> **READ** EPHESIANS 3:14-21

❝ The gospel or good news, however, is a doctrine of which even the wisest knew nothing by nature but which is revealed from heaven. In it God does not demand but rather offers and gives us the righteousness that the law requires. This righteousness is the perfect obedience of the suffering and death of Jesus Christ, through which all sin and damnation, made manifest by the law, is pardoned, and washed away (Rom. 5; Gal. 3). Furthermore, God does not give us forgiveness of sins in the gospel on the condition that we keep the law. Rather, even though we never have kept it nor will ever be able to keep it perfectly, he still has forgiven our sins and given us eternal life as an unmerited gift through faith in Jesus Christ.

GEERHARDUS VOS

❝ True redemption involves being struck dumb by the enormity of our failure and then struck even dumber by the enormity of the heart of God that cancels our debt. Redemption brings a level of gratitude that frees the heart to desire the sweet balm of forgiveness for oneself and others. It frees the heart to extend to others what has been so freely given to us.

DAN ALLENDER

DAY 3

READ JOHN 16:1-15

Let us never doubt for a moment that the preaching of Christ cruci-fied—the old story of his blood, righteousness, and substitution—is enough for all the spiritual necessities of all mankind.

It is not worn out. It is not obsolete. It has not lost its power. We need nothing new—nothing more broad and kind—nothing more intellectual—nothing more effectual. We need nothing but the true bread of life, distributed faithfully among starving souls. Let men sneer or ridicule as they will. Nothing else can do good in this sinful world. No other teaching can fill hungry consciences, and give them peace. We are all in a wilderness. We must feed on Christ crucified, and the atonement made by his death, or we shall die in our sins.

J. C. RYLE

Great is his love, and large his grace,
Through the redemption of his Son;
He turns our feet from sinful ways,
And pardons what our hands have done.

ISAAC WATTS

DAY 4

> **READ** PHILIPPIANS 1:2-30

" There is nothing in us or done by us, at any stage of our earthly development, because of which we are acceptable to God. We must always be accepted for Christ's sake, or we cannot ever be accepted at all. This is not true of us only when we believe. It is just as true after we have believed. It will continue to be truest as long as we live. Our need of Christ does not cease with our believing; nor does the nature of our relation to him or to God through him ever alter, no matter what our attainments in Christian graces or our achievements in behavior may be. It is always on his blood and righteousness alone that we can rest.

BENJAMIN WARFIELD

" Our struggle in living the Christian life is not doing, it is believing.

JOHN OWEN

DAY 5

READ EPHESIANS 1:15-23

❝ Grace takes the agency of salvation out of human hands, whereas the heart's desire of every child of Adam and Eve is to keep it there— to strive endlessly to find something we can do to make ourselves legitimate. But grace makes all our efforts to legitimize ourselves irrelevant because it proclaims us already legitimated by the work of Someone Else, without a single effort on our part.

ROBERT FARRAR CAPON

❝ It is a very hard thing to bring a dull and an evasive heart to cry with feeling for mercy. Our hearts, like criminals, until they be beaten from all evasions, never cry for the mercy of the judge. Again, this bruising makes us set a high price upon Christ. Then the gospel becomes the gospel indeed; then the fig leaves of morality will do us no good. And it makes us more thankful, and, from thankfulness, more fruitful in our lives; for what makes many so cold and barren, but that bruising for sin never endeared God's grace to them?

RICHARD SIBBES

WEEK 31

WHAT IS EFFECTUAL CALLING

WESTMINSTER SHORTER CATECHISM QUESTION 31

Q | What is effectual calling?

A | Effectual calling is the work of God's Spirit, whereby, convincing us of our sin and misery, enlightening our minds in the knowledge of Christ, and renewing our wills, he does persuade and enable us to embrace Jesus Christ, freely offered to us in the gospel.

PRAY *My Father, I could never have sought my happiness in thy love unless thou had'st first loved me. Amen.*

WORSHIP GOD BY MEDITATING ON PSALM 42:1–43:5

COMMIT GOD'S WORD TO MEMORY | 2 CORINTHIANS 4:6

DAY 1 | For God, who said,
DAY 2 | "Let light shine out of darkness,"
DAY 3 | has shone in our hearts to give the light
DAY 4 | of the knowledge of the glory of God
DAY 5 | in the face of Jesus Christ.

THE FAIR

We took the long walk from the parking lot to the bustling midway. The sky was electric with lights zooming and flashing and, as we approached, we could hear sounds of carnival games and screams bellowing from the wild rides. The smells of fried food greeted us well before we got to the gate. But even with all the activity and excitement, my husband and I were silent.

This wasn't just another trip to the fair.

We were going to meet for the first time the children we were trying to adopt.

After years of miscarriages and failed infertility treatments, God led us to adoption through the foster care system. We had been waiting about a year when our social worker told us about three siblings, all less than three. I had never considered adopting more than one child at once, but after praying and surrendering to God's profound sense of humor, we agreed to pursue them. Even though we only knew them "on paper" (we hadn't even seen a photograph yet), I felt more drawn to them with every step, as well as more sobered. This was not going to be easy.

We arrived at our designated meeting place and saw them—two blonde girls and a curly-headed boy. For a moment, we drank in the sight, until we realized they wouldn't know who we were until we actually stepped toward them.

And so we did.

That night felt unusually normal. We took them to the petting zoo to feed the goats and observed how each of their reactions revealed their individual personalities, which mimicked ours in many ways—a beautiful surprise. At one point, the curly-headed cutie hopped onto the kiddie coaster. As soon as the ride began, terror set in and he began to cry. I couldn't get to the ride operator fast enough—all I was thinking was, "*Stop this ride!* Can't you see that my son is terrified?" It felt instinctual.

We left the fair exhausted and full of emotion. We shared visions of a curly-headed curious prince and twirling little princesses dancing around stealing our fries.

The weeks that followed weren't easy. We visited them at their foster family's house, and they visited us at ours. The children had to transition from a family they had grown to love into a new home with new parents. Those meetings were both emotional and unpredictable. At times it seemed as though the kids knew we were meant to be, and other times, they did whatever it took to drive us away to stay with what they knew. But that transition time was vital to their emotional health, so we continued the process, even when it hurt.

Despite the many days of being pushed away and rejected, days where we felt little to no relational progress, we kept pursuing them. We loved them, never left them, and in time they were able to move forward into their calling to be our children.

DAY 1

> **READ** MATTHEW 11:25-30

> " Therefore, while it is vital to accept your identity as a sinner, it is not sufficient. You must also live out of a sure grasp of your identity as a child of God's freely given and personally transforming grace. These two identities must be held in a healthy tension and balance. It is only the person who is deeply aware of his sin who gets excited about grace and it is only grace that can give you the courage to humbly face the enormity of your sin.
>
> PAUL DAVID TRIPP

DAY 2

READ ISAIAH 45:1-25

> Indeed, the Word of God is like the sun, shining upon all those to whom it is proclaimed, but with no effect among the blind. Now, all of us are blind in nature in this respect. Accordingly, it cannot penetrate into our minds unless the Spirit, as the inner teacher, through his illumination makes entry for it.

JOHN CALVIN

> Before we can even begin to answer our call to come to him, Jesus comes to us. Because we could never sufficiently humble ourselves, Jesus humbles himself, and by doing so, he became both the model and the means of our own humility.

HANNAH ANDERSON

DAY 3

READ ACTS 16:11–15

" When Christ goes to work, he gets right to the heart of the matter, literally. He tears out my old heart and puts in a new one (Ezek. 36:26). And then, rather than standing outside and telling me what to do with it, he moves inside and directs things from there. He still has laws for me to keep and principles to follow; but now the laws are not merely imposed from without, they arise from within. God's law is now written on our hearts (Jer. 31:33).

Because we embrace the Lawgiver and are embraced by him in a relationship so intimate that we actually "participate in the divine nature" (2 Peter1:4), we want more than ever to keep his laws, but now we see their deeper dimension. We come to realize that biblical principles reflect the heart of someone we love and trust, and we receive his directions, not as required duties (though, of course, they are), but rather as welcomed opportunities to live as he intends, knowing that our good is always on his mind.

LARRY CRABB

DAY 4

READ 2 CORINTHIANS 4:1-6

> He effectually persuades us and, in changing our will, gives us the desire for him that is entirely contrary to our sinful nature.... It has often been called "irresistible grace," but because of the way *irresistible* is used today, I would prefer the term "*intoxicating* grace." For this is what God does by his Spirit: he overwhelms us with his love and grace, liberating us to freely embrace what we had before just as freely rejected.

MICHAEL HORTON

> The immediate and important effect of this inward, purifying change of nature is that the person loves righteousness and trusts in Christ for salvation. Whereas his natural element was sin, it now becomes holiness; sin becomes repulsive to him, and he loves to do good. This effective and irresistible grace converts the will itself and forms a holy character in the person by a creative act.

LORAINE BOETTNER

DAY 5

READ ACTS 26:12-18

> One weekend when I was sitting in the house of God, I was not thinking about the preacher's sermon, for I did not believe it. The thought struck me, "How did you come to be a Christian?" I sought the Lord. "But how did you come to seek the Lord?" The truth flashed across my mind in a moment—I should not have sought him unless there had been some previous influence in my mind to make me seek him. I prayed, I thought, but then I asked myself, "How came I to pray?" I was induced to pray by reading the Scriptures. "How came I to read the Scriptures?" I did read them, but what led me to do so? Then, in a moment, I saw that God was at the bottom of it all, and that he was the Author of my faith, and so the whole doctrine of grace opened up to me, and from that doctrine I have not departed to this day, and I desire to make this my constant confession, "I ascribe my change wholly to God."
>
> CHARLES SPURGEON

> You are a Christian today only because God was the first to seek peace with you. You are now called and equipped to be the first to seek after peace and to attempt to pursue and maintain unity. As you do this you have the high honor of acting as an imitator of God.
>
> THOMAS BROOKS

WEEK 32

THE BENEFITS OF EFFECTUAL CALLING

WESTMINSTER SHORTER CATECHISM QUESTION 32

Q | What benefits do they that are effectually called partake of in this life?

A | They that are effectually called do in this life partake of justification, adoption, and sanctification, and the several benefits which in this life do either accompany or flow from them.

PRAY *Let the Spirit continually reveal to me my interest in Christ, and open to me the riches of thy love in him; may he abide in me that I may know my union with Jesus, and enter into constant fellowship with him. Amen.*

WORSHIP GOD BY MEDITATING ON PSALM 130

COMMIT GOD'S WORD TO MEMORY | ROMANS 8:29-30

DAY 1 | For those whom he foreknew he also predestined
to be conformed to the image of his Son,

DAY 2 | in order that he might be the firstborn among many brothers.

DAY 3 | And those whom he predestined he also called,

DAY 4 | and those whom he called he also justified,

DAY 5 | and those whom he justified he also glorified.

LUCY

We have a very tiny dog and we are her whole world. Lucy doesn't eat, relieve herself, or leave our house without looking to us for permission. She is afraid of just about everything. Her preferred spot is attached to me, preferably in my lap if I'm sitting, or lying flat against my legs if I'm lying down. My standing for any purpose is problematic for Lucy. She often shakes and trembles when her conditions are not perfect.

I'm often annoyed by this quirky, needy, anxiety-ridden little dog. I want to shout at her, "Quit shaking! It's just the mailman bringing the mail!" But, of course, that's ridiculous and impossible. When people walk by or up to our house, Lucy jumps to attention and barks like crazy, sure that the next Amazon or UPS delivery is the sign of our certain doom. Her insecurity seems to be a permanent condition, and we will continue to live with it. After all it was we who decided on a miniature lap dog. But when our doorbell broke and brought a few months peace, I didn't exactly complain.

Yes, in Lucy's world, the sky is always falling except, of course, when conditions are perfect, and she finds herself pressed up against me. I don't necessarily even have to give her any attention—she just wants to be near me, feeling the warmth and presence of me, her person. When that's the case, she relaxes, often sleeps, and stretches out as if she hasn't a care in the world. Codependency, obsessive barking and all, Lucy will always be part of our family, but she only really feels it, or acts like she feels it, when she's near me.

Don't take this metaphor too far, but Lucy is me. Just last week I found myself in the carpool line, rehashing every word of an email conversation, fretting I had overstepped my bounds, been selfish in a request, and showed disrespect for even asking. It was DEFCON 1 and the mental missiles were flying. As I considered *never making another request of another person in my entire life*, a small, reasonable part of me stepped outside of the shaking and agonizing and pressed pause on the whole situation. And I remembered to whom I could surrender my concerns instead of getting swept away by them: the

God who cares for me, the One who sets his affections on me because he loves me. I remembered the fullness of my inheritance as his child, and that I can walk in complete trust and rest and embrace whatever the day holds . . . even when it includes an email delivery.

DAY 1

READ ROMANS 8:26-30

> I must remind myself that the gospel welcomes me out of hiding. It welcomes me to face my darkest parts with hope. It assures me that there is nothing to be known about me that has not already been dealt with in the person and work of the Lord Jesus.

PAUL DAVID TRIPP

> Satan wants to rob us of confidence in our acceptance by God on the basis of Christ's righteousness alone, knowing that the freedom, joy, and courage provided by the unyielding love of God unleashes the Spirit's power in our lives.

BRYAN CHAPELL

DAY 2

READ EZEKIEL 36:22-38

> When I speak of "growth in grace," I do not for a moment mean that a believer's interest (partaking) in Christ can grow. I do not mean that he can grow in safety, acceptance with God, or security. I do not mean that he can ever be more justified, more pardoned, more forgiven, more at peace with God, than he is the first moment he believes. I hold firmly that the justification of a believer is a finished, perfect, and complete work; and that the weakest saint, though he may not know and feel it, is as completely justified as the strongest. I hold firmly that our election, calling, and standing in Christ admit of no degrees, increase, or diminution . . . I would go to the stake, God helping me, for the glorious truth, that in the matter of justification before God every believer is "complete in Christ" (Col 2:10). Nothing can be added to his justification from the moment he believes, and nothing taken away.

J. C. RYLE

> The great objection of a penitent is, I have sinned, and I know not whether God will receive me. Consider, God knows your sin better than you do, yet he kindly calls to you and promises you as good a reception as if you had never sinned.

STEPHEN CHARNOCK

DAY 3

READ 1 PETER 2:21-25

> As Richard Hooker wrote in a sermon which he preached in 1585 when he was master of the Temple, "Let it be accounted folly, or frenzy, or fury, or whatsoever. It is our wisdom and our comfort; we care for no knowledge in the world but this, that man hath sinned and God hath suffered; that God hath made himself the sin of men, and that men are made the righteousness of God." Every Christian can echo these words. There is healing through his wounds, life through his death, pardon through his pain, salvation through his suffering.

JOHN STOTT

> Jesus Christ is the one true Branch, the lost variety. Jesus Christ is the one who alone fears the Lord and who bears good fruit. Jesus Christ is the one who restores both our humility and our humanity. And in his glorious resting place—under the shade of his branches—we find rest.

HANNAH ANDERSON

DAY 4

READ 1 CORINTHIANS 1:26–31

> Let us love, and sing, and wonder,
> Let us praise the Saviour's Name!
> He has hushed the Law's loud thunder.
> He has quenched Mount Sinai's flame:
> He has washed us in his blood.
> He has brought us nigh to God.
> Let us love the Lord who bought us.
> Pitied us when enemies,
> Called us by his grace, and taught us,
> Gave us ears and gave us eyes:
> He has washed us with his blood,
> He presents our souls to God.
> Let us wonder, grace and justice
> Join, and point to mercy's store;
> When through grace in Christ our trust is,
> Justice smiles and asks no more.
> He who washed us with his blood
> Has secured our way to God.

WILLIAM COWPER

DAY 5

READ 2 TIMOTHY 1:8-14

> The treasures of a saint are the presence of God, the favor of God, union and communion with God, the pardon of sin, the joy of the Spirit, the peace of conscience, which are jewels that none can give but Christ, nor none can take away but Christ.

THOMAS BROOKS

> Accordingly the believing soul can boast of and glory in whatever Christ has as though it were its own, and whatever the soul has, Christ claims as his own. Let us compare these and we shall see inestimable benefits. Christ is full of grace, life and salvation. The soul is full of sins, death, and damnation. Now let faith come between them and sins, death and damnation will be Christ's, while grace, life and salvation will be the soul's; for if Christ is a bridegroom, he must take upon himself the things which are his bride's and bestow upon her the things that are his.

MARTIN LUTHER

WEEK 33
WHAT IS JUSTIFICATION

WESTMINSTER SHORTER CATECHISM QUESTION 33

Q | What is justification?

A | Justification is an act of God's free grace, wherein he pardons all our sins, and accepts us as righteous in his sight, only for the righteousness of Christ imputed to us, and received by faith alone.

PRAY *Continue to teach me that Christ's righteousness satisfies justice and evidences thy love. Amen.*

WORSHIP GOD BY MEDITATING ON PSALM 32:1–11

COMMIT GOD'S WORD TO MEMORY | 2 CORINTHIANS 5:21

DAY 1 | For our sake
DAY 2 | he made him to be sin
DAY 3 | who knew no sin,
DAY 4 | so that in him we might become
DAY 5 | the righteousness of God.

THE VICTORY LAP

I t was my senior year of college and I had signed up for as many hours possible so I could finish that year. I didn't want to take a "Victory Lap," or a fifth year of school, which would cost me thousands of dollars. There was one class in particular that caused me more anxiety and stress than any other in all my four years of college: Latin. My friend and I registered for it because unlike every other foreign language class, it didn't have a required speaking lab that was three hours a week on top of the hour-long lecture.

The first test rolled around, and I did worse than I've ever done on any test in my life. I not only failed it, I was nervous I wouldn't even pass the class.

The day after my grade came back, I met with the professor and asked her what I needed to do before the next test. Then I made a plan to study for the hours needed each day for the next month. I needed to make an A to accomplish a passing final average, but it turned out I made an eighty-seven. It wasn't what I wanted, but it was close enough to raise my grade and lower my blood pressure tremendously.

Once my hope of passing was realized, I began to accept the idea of making a C in the class. The final exam was just around the corner and I studied for it, but nowhere near the amount of time I studied for that second test.

The night before the final exam, while texting with my friend in the class, he realized an error in my thinking and typed, "You know a C isn't considered passing, right? You have to have an A or B." I checked the syllabus, and my heart dropped.

Quickly, I did the math—I had to make a ninety-five on the final, cumulative exam. I jumped in my car and drove to the nearby gas station, grabbed some energy drinks and coffee, and prepared for an all-nighter.

The next morning, I walked in the classroom nauseous from the lack of sleep and my Mt. Everest-sized anxiety. Even though I was the last one to leave the testing room, I walked out knowing full well I hadn't made the ninety-five I needed. A few hours later, my professor emailed me my final average for the class: seventy-five.

With hope that seemed smaller than any mustard seed, I emailed her asking if there was anything I could do to raise my final grade. Within minutes, my phone buzzed, alerting me to an email. "Your final average is 82." I could hardly believe it. She had every reason to give me a failing grade, but she didn't. Not only did she give me a passing grade, she awarded me more points than I had even pleaded for. I deserved to have to take that expensive "Victory Lap" and pay for it myself, but by some miracle, instead of counting my failure against me, she went even further and gave credit for what I didn't deserve and never could have earned.

DAY 1

READ ROMANS 3:21-31

“ If I am in Christ, God regards me as guiltless; not only that, God regards me as one who has kept the law fully. Christ has kept it and I am in Christ. I receive all the benefits of his perfect life and atoning death exactly as I am. This is the doctrine: "Just as I am without one plea"—with nothing, nothing at all, indeed to start to do anything is a denial of the doctrine. You can do nothing, Christ has done everything. . . . We must realize that if we lived to be a thousand years old, we would be no more righteous in the sight of God than we are now. You may grow in grace, but on your deathbed your only hope will be the righteousness of Christ.

D. MARTYN LLOYD-JONES

DAY 2

READ ROMANS 4:1–25

> By [Christ's] passion, which he hath suffered, he merited that as many as believe in him shall be as well justified by him, as though they themselves had never done any sin, and as though they themselves had fulfilled the law to the uttermost. For we, without him, are under the curse of the law . . . but Christ with his death hath delivered us from the curse of the law. He hath set us at liberty, and promiseth that when we believe in him, we shall not perish; the law shall not condemn us. Therefore let us study to believe in Christ. Let us put all our hope, trust, and confidence only in him; let us patch him with nothing: for, as I told you before, our merits are not able to deserve everlasting life, it is too precious a thing to be merited by man. It is his doing only. God hath given him unto us to be our deliverer, and to give us everlasting life. O what a joyful thing was this!

HUGH LATIMER

DAY 3

READ GALATIANS 2:15-21

Our need for approval is deeply wired into us. It's not seeking after approval and the personal satisfaction it provides that Jesus condemns; it is seeking approval from the wrong source. If we're always looking for approval from other people, we'll never get enough, and it will never last long enough. In Christ we have already been given all the approval we really need and all the approval that really matters. Jesus was God's beloved Son in whom he was well pleased. Once we are joined to Christ, that approval splashes over onto us. Joined to Christ, we are accepted and approved.

NANCY GUTHRIE

Your justification is not built upon your obedience, but upon Christ's (Rom. 3:24), and how complete and defective soever you be in yourselves, yet at the same instant, "you are complete in him which is the head of all principality and power" (Col. 2:10).

JOHN FLAVEL

DAY 4

READ 2 CORINTHIANS 5:14-21

" How the one love of God, through exceeding regard for men, did not regard us with hatred, nor thrust us away, nor remember our iniquity against us, but showed great long-suffering, and bore with us, he himself took on him the burden of our iniquities, he gave his own Son as a ransom for us, the holy One for transgressors, the blameless One for the wicked, the righteous One for the unrighteous, the incorruptible One for the corruptible, the immortal One for them that are mortal. For what other thing was capable of covering our sins than his righteousness? By what other one was it possible that we, the wicked and ungodly, could be justified, than by the only Son of God? O sweet exchange! . . . That the wickedness of many should be hid in a single righteous One, and that the righteousness of One should justify many transgressors!

MATHETES

DAY 5

READ JEREMIAH 23:1-6

> Your okay-ness rests in the fact that God has forgiven all your sins. You don't have to make up for them or try to justify yourself by blaming others or hope that your good outweighs the bad. You are completely forgiven. If you believe, you are no longer under God's judgment for your sin. You are forgiven.

ELYSE FITZPATRICK

> I must not only wash in Christ's blood, but clothe me in Christ's obedience. For every sin of omission in self, I may find a divinely perfect obedience ready for me in Christ. For every sin of commission in self, I may find not only a stripe or a wound in Christ, but also a perfect rendering of the opposite obedience in my place, so that the law is magnified, its curse more than carried, its demand more than answered.

ROBERT MURRAY MCCHEYNE

WEEK 34

WHAT IS ADOPTION

WESTMINSTER SHORTER CATECHISM QUESTION 34

Q | What is adoption?

A | Adoption is an act of God's free grace, whereby we are received into the number, and have a right to all the privileges of the sons of God.

....

PRAY *Blessed Lord, let me climb up near to thee, and love, and long, and plead, and wrestle with thee. . . . My soul mourns to think it should ever lose sight of its beloved. Amen.*

....

WORSHIP GOD BY MEDITATING ON PSALM 87

....

COMMIT GOD'S WORD TO MEMORY | ROMANS 8:15

DAY 1 | For you did not receive the spirit of slavery
DAY 2 | to fall back into fear,
DAY 3 | but you have received
DAY 4 | the Spirit of adoption as sons,
DAY 5 | by whom we cry, "Abba! Father!"

THE CRIB ROOM

As I walked into the 20' x 20' orphanage crib room, my breath caught as I saw the thirty or more cribs lined up side by side. Each crib held a child who had some sort of special need. My chest tightened. I knew we were on a mission trip—I knew we would see hard things and love on children in difficult circumstances—but I didn't expect this. Having worked in special education for years, I could see that many of these babies and children had severe special needs—cerebral palsy, developmental delays, or needs that even I was unequipped to identify. Several of the children stood in their cribs and reached out for us, and some just stared. Questions came at me like missiles: *What will happen to these children? Will they ever leave this room? Is there any hope? Where are you, God? Don't you care about these babies?* As we walked out of the crib room and into another area, one of my teammates said, "And this is why we do what we do." See, my teammate was an adoption specialist and had worked in-country, building relationships with orphanages for years, helping children with special needs find loving homes all over the world.

Later that day as I was riding the hotel elevator, our non-Christian translator asked, "Do you really believe that those children—the children with special needs—have a purpose?"

My own questions from earlier shot back into my mind, but just as quickly, I heard myself saying to my new friend, "I believe they do, and I can only say this because of Jesus. Only because of what he did can I be okay with my limited understanding."

Where had *that* come from? It seemed moments ago I had hurled the same accusations and questions at the God who had created these children. Only the Holy Spirit could enable me to respond that way.

Over the last ten years, God has allowed me to be involved with a number of families who have adopted children out of similar crib rooms. And watching children reach out to find loving and forever arms to hold them never gets old. Their cries are heard, their needs are met, their wants are seen, and they are fully, rightfully, a part of something bigger than they ever could have imagined.

DAY 1

READ MATTHEW 6:25-34

> Love is holy because it is like grace—the worthiness of its object is never really what matters.
>
> MARILYNNE ROBINSON

> In Uganda I had seen lots of orphans. One had tried to steal my purse as we knelt to pray in the market place. They would kill almost as quickly as steal. Because they had no father to look after them, they made sure they took care of themselves: lying, cheating, stealing, and deceiving to get along. I had been acting like them–as if I had no father, as if I didn't have his authority, his power, his spirit, his heart and his ear.
>
> ROSEMARIE MILLER

DAY 2

> **READ** ROMANS 8:12-25

> I am a child of God. He is my Father. He understands and cares for me. The Christian, of all people, should be increasingly aware of who he really is. That knowledge gives me stability in an unstable world. Knowing the very depths of my being who I am, as I come increasingly to appreciate what it means to be a child of God, has a tremendously powerful effect. It sets me free from the world's anxious quest to "be somebody."

SINCLAIR FERGUSON

> It is important to tell at least from time to time the secret of who we truly and fully are—even if we tell it only to ourselves—because otherwise we run the risk of losing track of who we truly and fully are and little by little come to accept the highly edited version which we put forth in hope that the world will find it more acceptable than the real thing.

FREDERICK BUECHNER

DAY 3

READ NUMBERS 6:22–27

>   As his sons we know we belong to his family. We learn to put out of our lives everything that is not in keeping with the family lifestyle. This is what it means to be "led by the Spirit." We begin to be sensitive to him. . . . We avoid anything that would bring shame on the family name. Our Father's smile has come to mean everything to us; his frown would be our greatest loss.
>
> SINCLAIR FERGUSON

>   Home! All that is wrapped up in that sweet, transcendent word, heightened, sanctified, glorified, and projected everlasting; our Father's house, because Jesus' Father's house, with all it includes, of fellowship with God the Trinity, with holy angels, with glorified saints, with elect relatives, brethren and friends. Ineffable communion! And to this will be added, if to it aught can be added, all outward circumstances of glory which can be collected by an Almighty Father around the brethren of his Son.
>
> J. L. GIRARDEAU

DAY 4

READ GALATIANS 4:1-11

> What is a Christian? The question can be answered in many ways, but the richest answer I know is that a Christian is one who has God as Father. . . .
>
> Some years ago I wrote:
>
> You sum up the whole of New Testament teaching in a single phrase, if you speak of it as a revelation of the Fatherhood of the holy Creator. In the same way, you sum up the whole of New Testament religion if you describe it as the knowledge of God as one's holy Father. If you want to judge how well a person understands Christianity, find out how much he makes of the thought of being God's child, and having God as his Father. If this is not the thought that prompts and controls his worship and prayers and his whole outlook on life, it means that he does not understand Christianity very well at all. For everything that Christ taught, everything that makes the New Testament new, and better than the Old, everything that is distinctively Christian as opposed to merely Jewish, is summed up in the knowledge of the Fatherhood of God. "Father" is the Christian name God.
>
> This still seems to me wholly true, and very important. Our understanding of Christianity cannot be better than our grasp of adoption.

J. I. PACKER

DAY 5

READ HEBREWS 12:1-13

The truly godly have the spirit of adoption, the spirit of a child, and so it is natural to go to God and call upon him, crying to him as to a father.

JONATHAN EDWARDS

While I regarded God as a tyrant, I thought sin a trifle, but when I knew him to be my father then I mourned that I could ever kick against him. When I thought that God was hard, I found it easy to sin, but when I found God so kind, so good, so overflowing with compassion, I smote upon my breast that I could have ever rebelled against one who loved me so and sought my good.

CHARLES SPURGEON

WEEK 35
WHAT IS SANCTIFICATION

WESTMINSTER SHORTER CATECHISM QUESTION 35

Q | What is sanctification?

A | Sanctification is the work of God's free grace, whereby we are renewed in the whole man after the image of God, and are enabled more and more to die unto sin, and live unto righteousness.

....

PRAY *Give me deeper holiness in speech, thought, action, and let me not seek moral virtue apart from thee. Amen.*

....

WORSHIP GOD BY MEDITATING ON PSALM 105

....

COMMIT GOD'S WORD TO MEMORY | GALATIANS 5:22–23

DAY 1 | But the fruit of the Spirit
DAY 2 | is love, joy, peace,
DAY 3 | patience, kindness, goodness,
DAY 4 | faithfulness, gentleness, self-control;
DAY 5 | against such things there is no law.

THE RUNNER

My wife is a runner. High school state champion, Division 1 scholarship athlete, capital "R" Runner. Until I met her, I firmly believed that running any distance over forty yards was a form of cruel and unusual punishment. I am also not a morning person, and certainly not a morning exercise person. In college, I was forced (under threat of punishment by my football coaches) to wake up at 5:00 a.m. and do CrossFit workouts before CrossFit was cool. Although I enjoyed the exercise and team camaraderie, I despised having to be awake before the sun.

Which is why my then-girlfriend of one month was stunned when I informed her in November that I would be joining her in the half marathon she was preparing to run in February.

I quickly discovered my initial desire (wanting to earn her favor) would not work as a long-term motivator for getting myself out of bed at 0-dark-thirty in order to train. This motivation was no match for the temptation to hit snooze and remain in the comfort of my bed, spared from pain and suffering from the freezing weather outside. Moreover, unlike my earlier morning workout experiences, there was now no threat of punishment forcing me to get out of bed. Instead, this time around, the sustaining motivation would have to be love rather than fear.

So, every other morning from December through February, I got out of bed while the rest of my dorm roommates slept, put on my toboggan, and, eyes half-closed, walked slowly to the top of the hill. There, my future wife met me with a smile and a running plan for the morning. During those months, we ran long and far. I felt like a fish out of water—literally, I could not breathe after two miles—but my patient and encouraging soon-to-be wife remained by my side. She prodded me along, despite my grumbling, complaining, and occasional stopping under the guise of needing a water break. She knew just how far to push, setting just the right pace for each day.

As we spent time together crossing the city that winter, my love for her grew and grew. I found myself actually looking forward to the runs because it meant I got to spend time with her. Simultaneously (and miraculously), my lung capacity increased, my leg muscles adapted, and my stamina strengthened with each passing mile. By spending time with my future wife doing what she loved, I was being transformed.

Make no mistake: the transition was not smooth. The running never became easy for me. But by the end of February, it was undeniable that I had been transformed. My relationship with my future wife had deepened. My love for her had increased. And now I had the leg muscles to prove it.

. . . .

DAY 1

READ JOHN 17:13-21

" Sanctification involves not only learning more about God, but loving the God we learn about ever more deeply.

ROB LISTER

" Sanctification, then, is God setting us apart for himself. Thus as saints we have already been sanctified by him. Then he gradually transforms us so that we begin to reflect his attributes and attractiveness. Jesus Christ's life begins to be mirrored in our lives and personalities.

SINCLAIR FERGUSON

DAY 2

READ GALATIANS 5:1-26

> All human nature vigorously resists grace because grace changes us and the change is painful.
>
> FLANNERY O'CONNOR

> Just how do we grow in grace and the power to say no to the world, the flesh, and the Devil? I'm convinced that we have only one of two options. Either we can devote ourselves and our time and our energy to demonstrating the ugliness and futility of sin and the world, hoping that such will embolden our hearts to say no to it as unworthy of our affection, or we can demonstrate the beauty and splendor of all that God is for us in Jesus and become happily and joyfully enticed by a rival affection.
>
> SAM STORMS

DAY 3

READ 1 THESSALONIANS 5:12-24

> The love of God to us, and our love to him, work together for producing holiness. Terror accomplishes no real obedience. Suspense brings forth no fruit unto holiness. No gloomy uncertainty as to God's favor can subdue one lust or correct our crookedness of will. But the free pardon of the cross uproots sin and withers all its branches. Only the certainty of love, forgiving love, can do this.
>
> BRYAN CHAPELL

> It's axiomatic that we begin our Christianity by faith in the righteousness that he [God] supplies through Jesus Christ. What most of us miss is that we progress in our sanctification the same way.
>
> ELYSE FITZPATRICK AND DENNIS JOHNSON

DAY 4

READ ROMANS 6:1-14

> William Romaine (born in 1714) was one of the leaders of the eigh-
> teenth-century revival in England. He wrote, "No sin can be cruci-
> fied either in heart or life, unless it be first pardoned in conscience,
> because there will be want of faith to receive the strength of Jesus,
> by whom alone it can be crucified. If it be not mortified in its guilt,
> it cannot be subdued in its power."
>
> What Romaine was saying is that if you do not believe you are
> dead to sin's guilt, you cannot trust Christ for the strength to subdue
> its power in your life. So the place to begin in dealing with sin in
> your life is to count on the fact that you died to its guilt through
> your union with Christ in his death. This is an important truth you
> need to ponder and pray over until the Holy Spirit convinces you
> of it in both your head and heart.
>
> JERRY BRIDGES

> While sanctification will one day be complete, right now it's an
> ongoing process. It's a journey, not a destination. The real key is
> the direction you're heading, not the distance you've traveled or the
> place you've reached.
>
> DAVID POWLISON

DAY 5

> **READ** 2 CORINTHIANS 6:14–7:1

> *"* While your justification cost you nothing, your sanctification will cost you everything. It will be the laying aside of self at every turn.
>
> JEN WILKIN

> *"* It is no good giving me a play like *Hamlet* or *King Lear*, and telling me to write a play like that. Shakespeare could do it; I can't. And it is no good showing me a life like the life of Jesus and telling me to live a life like that. Jesus could do it; I can't. But if the genius of Shakespeare could come and live in me, then I could write plays like that. And if the Spirit of Jesus could come and live in me, then I could live a life like that.
>
> WILLIAM TEMPLE

WEEK 36

BENEFITS WHILE ALIVE

> WESTMINSTER SHORTER CATECHISM QUESTION 36

Q | What are the benefits which in this life do accompany or flow from justification, adoption, and sanctification?

A | The benefits which in this life do accompany or flow from justification, adoption, and sanctification are assurance of God's love, peace of conscience, joy in the Holy Spirit, increase of grace, and perseverance therein to the end.

....

PRAY *Almighty God, as I cross the threshold of this day, I commit myself, soul, body, affairs, friends, to thy care; watch over, keep, guide, direct, sanctify, bless me. Incline my heart to thy ways. Amen.*

....

WORSHIP GOD BY MEDITATING ON PSALM 147:1-20

....

COMMIT GOD'S WORD TO MEMORY | ROMANS 5:1

DAY 1 | Therefore, since we
DAY 2 | have been justified
DAY 3 | by faith,
DAY 4 | we have peace with God
DAY 5 | through our Lord Jesus Christ.

RAISINETS

A few Christmases ago, my friend Rebecca brought over a gift the size of a child's shoebox. It was wrapped in lime-green paper covered in Santas wearing red and white polka dot mittens, their mouths shaped like o's with little word bubbles saying "JOY." Rebecca's mom Saidie had wrapped the gift over a year ago, when she was still well, still with us. Cancer took her quickly, and we started the new year with bricks in our hearts. But a year later, as Rebecca was cleaning out their basement and going through the small mountain of Christmas items her mom had accumulated and treasured over the years, she found several of these wrapped gifts, bought on a whim, bought because they made Saidie laugh. And one of them was for us, "Merry Christmas" written on the front in her distinct cursive handwriting.

Careful to save the paper because her warm, soft hands had touched it, I opened the gift, curious what it could be. I never could have predicted what was inside: a *pooping reindeer*, including Raisinets to pour inside. Push down on its back and out came a Raisinet. It entertained my two-year-old for an hour with full-on, fall-on-the-floor giggling. And there was Saidie—the life, laughter, and lightheartedness of her right there on my kitchen floor.

I wondered what she imagined our reaction would be when she wrapped that gift. Amusement maybe? A good laugh? My son was barely a year old when she bought and wrapped it, so he wouldn't have enjoyed it as much if she'd given it to us that Christmas she was sick. Instead, the reaction was more than she ever dreamed: a little boy whom she'd loved as dearly as her own grandchild, completely enamored, bubbling over with laughter. And two years later, that same boy sharing the toy with his sister at Christmastime. "Watch this! It poops!" followed by two little souls giggling on the floor and eating more Raisinets than I'd normally let them eat because Saidie would have spoiled them, and this was her gift to my family.

As much as Christmas comes with all the feelings of the Christmas spirit, it also seems to magnify the pain in our lives, and Christmas for me is now bittersweet, in part, because I remember it as the season Saidie was dying. Things aren't as they used to be. It used to be that she'd babysit my son while my husband and I went out for our December anniversary. Or that she'd stop by on New Year's Eve way too late and tell me all the gossip from the party they had just left. That she was *here*. But also, things are not what she expected them to be; they're better than her dreams. I have children she's never met but would've loved. And she has daughters who are women she would be proud of and who laugh her same laugh. And in there somewhere is a truth for us all: things aren't the way they used to be, but they're going to be better than we imagine, because out of death comes life bubbling over.

DAY 1

READ ZEPHANIAH 3:8–20

> You are God's poem, his work of art. There's no one else he made quite like you. So when he becomes one with you, he still preserves and delights in your unique particularity. As he restores his image in you, as you become more like his Son, you are becoming more and more yourself—more and more the you God dreamed up when he first dreamed you up.
>
> RANKIN WILBOURNE

> Let God have you, and let God love you—and don't be surprised if your heart begins to hear music you've never heard and your feet learn to dance as never before.
>
> MAX LUCADO

DAY 2

READ ROMANS 5:1-11

> God made us alive and secured us in Christ so that he could make us the beneficiaries of everlasting kindness from infinite riches of grace. This is not because we are worthy. Quite the contrary, it is to show the infinite measure of his worth.

JOHN PIPER

> "Salvation" is a wonderfully comprehensive term. It is a great mistake to suppose that it is merely a synonym for forgiveness. God is as much concerned with our present and future as with our past. His plan is first to reconcile us to himself, and then progressively to liberate us from our self-centeredness and bring us into harmony with our fellow men. We owe our forgiveness and reconciliation chiefly to the death of Christ, but it is by his Spirit that we can be set free from ourselves and in his church that we can be united in a fellowship of love.

JOHN STOTT

DAY 3

READ JEREMIAH 31:1-14

> Shattered dreams are the prelude to joy. Always. In the middle of our pain, God is working for our joy. At some point, he works in ways we can see.
>
> LARRY CRABB

> If we let him . . . he will make the feeblest and filthiest of us into a god or goddess, a dazzling, radiant, immortal creature, pulsating all through with such energy and joy and wisdom and love as we cannot now imagine, a bright stainless mirror which reflects back to God perfectly (though, of course, on a smaller scale) his own boundless power and delight and goodness. The process will be long and in parts very painful; but that is what we are in for. Nothing less.
>
> C. S. LEWIS

DAY 4

> **READ** HABAKKUK 3:16-19

" You aren't the mistakes you've made. You aren't the labels that have been put on you. And you aren't the lies the Enemy has tried to sell you.

You are who God says you are.

You are a child of God.

You are the apple of God's eye.

You are sought after.

You are more than a conqueror.

You are a new creation in Christ.

You are the righteousness of Christ.

One more thing. You can do all things through Christ who strengthens you.

All our identity issues are fundamental misunderstandings of who God is.

Guilt issues are a misunderstanding of God's grace.

Control issues are a misunderstanding of God's sovereignty.

Anger issues are a misunderstanding of God's mercy.

Pride issues are a misunderstanding of God's greatness.

Trust issues are a misunderstanding of God's goodness.

If you struggle with any of those issues, it's time to let God be the loudest voice in your life!

MARK BATTERSON

DAY 5

READ 1 JOHN 4:7-21

> Therefore the godly heart feels in itself a division because it is partly imbued with sweetness from its recognition of the divine goodness, partly grieves in bitterness from the awareness of its calamity; partly rests upon the promises of the gospel, partly trembles at the evidence of its own iniquity; partly rejoices at the expectation of life, partly shudders at death. This variation arises from imperfection of faith, since in the course of the present life it never goes so well with us that we are wholly cured of the disease of unbelief and entirely filled and possessed by faith.

JOHN CALVIN

> The heart overflows with gladness, and leaps and dances for the joy it has found in God. In this experience the Holy Spirit is active, and has taught us in the flash of a moment the deep secret of joy. You will have as much joy and laughter in life as you have faith in God.

MARTIN LUTHER

WEEK 37

BENEFITS AT DEATH

WESTMINSTER SHORTER CATECHISM QUESTION 37

Q | What benefits do believers receive from Christ at death?

A | The souls of believers are at their death made perfect in holiness, and do immediately pass into glory; and their bodies, being still united in Christ, do rest in their graves, till the resurrection.

....

PRAY *May I arrive where means of grace cease and I need no more to fast, pray, weep, watch, be tempted . . . where nothing defiles, where is no grief, sorrow, sin, death, separation, tears, pale face, languid body, aching joints, feeble infancy . . . griping fears, consuming cares. . . . Where is full knowledge of thee. Amen.*

....

WORSHIP GOD BY MEDITATING ON PSALM 16

....

COMMIT GOD'S WORD TO MEMORY | PHILIPPIANS 1:21

DAY 1 | For to me
DAY 2 | to live
DAY 3 | is Christ,
DAY 4 | and to die
DAY 5 | is gain.

THE CT SCAN

t was early December when I felt a strange pain that wouldn't go away. I assumed it was some kind of infection and that a round of antibiotics would take care of it.

I went to see my doctor and he casually asked if I had time to do an ultrasound that day. I did. The following morning, the office called to ask if I had time to do a CT scan in the next hour or so. They could "work me in" and I would have the results immediately afterwards. I thought to myself, *They're really on top of this.* So within a few hours I was lying on a cold CT scan table with the Tim McGraw song "Live Like You Were Dying" playing and replaying in my head.

It's probably safe to say that most of us wonder if we'll get cancer. That strange lump, that unusual pain, the spot that wasn't there before. It's human nature to jump to the worst possible conclusion and think cancer. It was certainly hard not to let my mind go there after having an ultrasound, then a CT scan the very next day. I felt it was grounds for legitimate worry.

And it turns out it was. The results showed a mass and the doctor wanted to remove it right away and have it biopsied. I wrote in my journal a few days after the surgery:

As I write this, I am waiting on the pathology report from the mass my doctor removed. The blood work showed no tumor markers and the CT scan came back clear. Though not likely, there is still a chance that it's an early stage of cancer. I've been very sick from the antibiotics and anesthesia, or maybe I have a bug, but I really haven't had the mental capacity to truly grasp the possibilities.

It was nearly a week later before I got the report—a week of waiting and wondering, trying to think of something else—anything else—as I went about my routines at work and home.

Ironically, the week before the results came in, I'd taught a Sunday school class on what happens to believers when they die. The focus was on God's promises for new bodies, transformation, and being together forever with the fullness of the Trinity. I told the class that, one day, there would be a test of faith for each of us—we will all come face to face with the holy God, and our record of righteousness will not stand without an intermediary. What I really meant was, there would be a test for them . . . not for me.

It was Stage 2 cancer, but the doctor caught it early, and I went through radiation for the next month. I prayed that God would impact me through my journey—that I wouldn't just make it through, but that my faith would grow even deeper as a result of this trial.

Looking back, almost a year later, my belief is stronger than ever that the sacrifice Jesus made allows me to be with him forever. And one day there'll be no more sickness, no more sorrow, no more pain— only real and abundant life.

Come, Lord Jesus, come.

DAY 1

READ JOB 19:23-27

When John Owen, the great Puritan, lay on his deathbed his secretary wrote (in his name) to a friend, "I am still in the land of the living." "Stop," cried Owen. "Change that and say, I am yet in the land of the dying, but I hope soon to be in the land of the living."

JOHN M. DRESCHER

Death used to be an executioner, but the gospel has made him just a gardener.

GEORGE HERBERT

DAY 2

READ 1 THESSALONIANS 4:13-18

> My comfort and my confidence is: even if I outlive my love for Jesus, I will never outlive his love for me. . . . So how does it feel to be an old lady? It feels like a tired, very dependent, very happy little girl, being carried in the arms of her Father, and she's calling to her friends, "Look how good and strong my Daddy is!" And she knows that when she falls asleep in his arms, she'll wake up at home.

SUSAN HUNT

> For subjects of King Jesus, death and tragedy are never the last word. The goodness of our God is certain. He has given up his very Son for our redemption. There is no reason to doubt him. The resurrection punctuates how the last word is one of blessing and joy.

EDWARD T. WELCH

DAY 3

READ PHILIPPIANS 1:21-26

> The Bible teaches that we do not lose consciousness when we die. We will be in heaven, aware of Christ, aware of God, and aware of the other saints who are there. We will not be clothed with our resurrected bodies at that point, but we will be in an intermediate state, in which the soul exists without the body. . . . Life in the intermediate state is far better than it is now, Paul said, because we are then in the immediate presence of Jesus. However, it is still not the best. The best will come at the final resurrection, when our souls will be united with our glorified bodies. We will live forever in that glorified state.
>
> R. C. SPROUL

> Do you know that if at birth I had been able to make one petition, it would have been that I was born blind? Because when I get to heaven, the first face that shall ever gladden my sight will be that of my Savior.
>
> FANNY CROSBY

DAY 4

READ ISAIAH 57:1-2

> As he drove his children to his wife's funeral, Donald Barnhouse stopped at a traffic crossing. Ahead of them was a huge truck. The sun was at such an angle that it cast the truck's shadow across the snow-covered field beside it. Dr. Barnhouse pointed to the shadow and spoke to his children. "Look at the shadow of that truck on the field, children. If you had to be run over, would you rather be run over by the truck or by its shadow?"
>
> The youngest child responded first, "The shadow. It couldn't hurt anybody."
>
> "That's right," said Barnhouse, "And remember children, Jesus let the truck of death strike him, so that it could never destroy us. Mother lives with Jesus now—only the shadow of death passed over her."
>
> BRYAN CHAPELL

> O what a blessed day that will be when I shall . . . stand on the shore and look back on the raging seas I have safely passed; when I shall review my pains and sorrows, my fears and tears, and possess the glory which was the end of all!
>
> RICHARD BAXTER

DAY 5

> **READ** 2 CORINTHIANS 5:1-10

"" As a result of Christ's righteous life, his atoning death, his bodily resurrection and his ascension to the Father's throne in glory, those who are united to Christ through faith alone are no longer condemned. They no longer face God's wrath and eternal ruin, but are already able to stand upright in God's presence, unashamed, clothed in the righteousness of Christ and washed in his precious blood. If they were to die at that very moment, like the repentant thief on the cross, they would be presented "holy in his sight, without blemish and free from accusation."

PHILIP EVESON

"" For a close, remember this, that your life is short, your duties many, your assistance great, and your reward sure; therefore faint not, hold on and hold up, in ways of well-doing, and heaven shall make amends for all.

THOMAS BROOKS

WEEK 38

BENEFITS AT RESURRECTION

> WESTMINSTER SHORTER CATECHISM QUESTION 38

Q | What benefits do believers receive from Christ at the resurrection?

A | At the resurrection, believers, being raised up in glory, shall be openly acknowledged and acquitted in the day of judgment, and made perfectly blessed in the full enjoying of God to all eternity.

....

PRAY *May I never think I prosper unless my soul prospers, or that I am rich unless rich toward thee, or that I am wise unless wise unto salvation. Amen.*

....

WORSHIP GOD BY MEDITATING ON PSALM 84:1–12

....

COMMIT GOD'S WORD TO MEMORY | 1 JOHN 3:2

DAY 1 | Beloved, we are God's children now,
DAY 2 | and what we will be has not yet appeared;
DAY 3 | but we know that when he appears
DAY 4 | we shall be like him,
DAY 5 | because we shall see him as he is.

HANDS

M y eight-year-old son sat next to me in church and leaned into my left side throughout the service, bored stiff. Actually, if he had been stiff, it would have been a rare blessing, indeed. The book he begged to bring along held no interest. All the puzzles and activities in the children's bulletin were finished long before the sermon started. Instead, he twisted and turned and spun and made faces at me. He asked if church was almost over about three minutes after the sermon started. He played with the zipper on my jacket. He put his hand in my pocket. And he grabbed my hand.

My hand was now a toy, which of course was fashioned into a gun to shoot imaginary bullets into the air, and then balled up into a fist, followed by trying to see how far back he could pull my fingers. But what really got me was when he placed his hand on top of mine and his small, soft hand sat light and warm on top of my forty-six-year-old hand. His goal was to show me how much my fingers had grown compared to the size of his. But I noticed something different.

I'd never noticed the wrinkles and age of my own hands before. Seeing the difference between our two hands put my own middle-aged life in sharp contrast. *I am growing old.* I am growing old, and for the first time in my life I had to reckon with this fact that stands completely outside of the most earnest opinion. No protest of "forty-six years old is not old" would change this reality. Being old was always someone else's experience. It was a condition beyond my reality. Age had never looked at me from my own hands.

Before he could pull his hand away, I saw an image of my father's hands. My wife says our eight-year-old has my hands, so it makes sense. There in my lap, I saw my own hand against the hand of the aged hand I had known best. And I took a deep breath because my father has now been gone for four and a half years. One day I, too, will be gone from this earth into the glorious wonders of the resurrection.

And then a bittersweet thought dawned on me like the first light of a day when the sun stays hidden behind a gathering storm: One day my son will be sitting in a church or a theater or lying on a blanket under a star-pocked sky and his own child will play with his newly wrinkled hands.

And I will be the one no longer around. I will have gone on to trace for eternity the immeasurable fingers of God on all things.

DAY 1

READ PHILIPPIANS 3:12–4:1

> Heaven is not here, it's there. If we were given all we wanted here, our hearts would settle for this world rather than the next. God is forever luring us up and away from this one, wooing us to himself and his still invisible kingdom, where we will certainly find what we so keenly long for.

ELISABETH ELLIOT

> The gauge of health in the Christian is the degree of his gravitation to the future, eternal world.

GERHARDUS VOS

DAY 2

READ 1 JOHN 2:28-3:3

MEMORIES OF THE FUTURE PAST

Remember those summer nights
   when you were young
   and dusk hung in the air
   like that kiss
   from the girl around the corner?
And the fireflies
   lit the yard of freshly cut grass?
And your dreams were bigger
   and brighter than the
   mirror-ball moon
   hanging among stars
   you pretended to throw
   into the night sky?
One day.
One day, my friend.
It will come with no end.
And our parents in all their
   forgotten strength
   will lay down their newspapers
   and their dish rags
   and join you in the joy

as the screen door slams
   shut behind them.
The ice cream churn will hum
   and the smell of the
   community pool
   will lie thick upon
   your sunned skin
   and you will crave the
   breeze traveling
   fast like the trains
   you hear down in the valley.
It will come with no end.
And the tears of cancer
   and the tears of Alzheimer's
   and divorce
   and all the broken-
   hearted times will end
   and give way to a taut
   thread of moments
   that taste like the honied
   memory of dusk unending.

MATT REDMOND

DAY 3

READ MALACHI 3:13-4:3

"I didn't think it would end this way."

Gandalf looked at him curiously, "End? No, the journey doesn't end here. Death is just another path, one that we all must take. The grey rain-curtain of this world rolls back, and all turns to silver glass, and then you see it."

"What? Gandalf? See what?"

"White shores, and beyond, a far green country under a swift sunrise."

"Well, that isn't so bad."

"No. No, it isn't."

J. R. R. TOLKIEN

The Biblical view of things is resurrection—not a future that is just a consolation for the life we never had but a restoration of the life you always wanted. This means that every horrible thing that ever happened will not only be undone and repaired but will in some way make the eventual glory and joy even greater.

TIM KELLER

DAY 4

READ 1 CORINTHIANS 15:35-58

> One day all of us in Christ will sit around an enormous table exquisitely set with a feast of rich foods, prepared in divine kitchens. No one will be left out. No one will be alone. No one will be nameless. No one unknown. No one with nowhere to go. We will finally be Home.

BETH MOORE

> Boughton says he has more ideas about heaven every day. He said, "Mainly I just think about the splendors of the world and multiply by two. I'd multiply by ten or twelve if I had the energy."

MARILYNNE ROBINSON

DAY 5

READ DANIEL 12:1-3

> Daniel sees an *ultimate* and *eternal* victory of Christ over all the powers and dominions of this world. Christ's final work is not completed. Jesus is coming back to reign. All will be subject to his authority. Awaiting you is his kingdom, where there shall be no more tears or trials. . . . Our trials will not last forever; his rule will be eternal. Unfairness, injustice, pain, and difficulty will end. All will be put right.

BRYAN CHAPELL

> Christian, believe this, and think about it—you will be eternally embraced in the arms of the love which was from everlasting, and will extend to everlasting—of the love which brought the Son of God's love from heaven to earth, from earth to the cross, from the cross to the grave, from the grave to glory—that love which was weary, hungry, tempted, scorned, scourged, buffeted, spat upon, crucified, pierced—which fasted, prayed, taught, healed, wept, sweated, bled, died. That love will eternally embrace you.

RICHARD BAXTER

WEEK 39

THE DUTY OF MAN

WESTMINSTER SHORTER CATECHISM QUESTION 39

Q | What is the duty which God requires of man?

A | The duty which God requires of man, is obedience to his revealed will.

PRAY *May I view and long after holiness as the beauty and dignity of the soul. Amen.*

WORSHIP GOD BY MEDITATING ON PSALM 78:1–39

COMMIT GOD'S WORD TO MEMORY | 1 JOHN 5:3

DAY 1 | For this is the love of God,
DAY 2 | that we keep his commandments.
DAY 3 | And his commandments
DAY 4 | are not burdensome.

THE FUNDRAISER

The day started with promise. I was still buzzing from the success of our adoption fundraiser the night before, so I had extra pep in my step as I climbed the hill toward the school entrance. I spotted two moms of children in my son's class and stopped to say hello.

It quickly became obvious that one of the moms was not happy with me. She began firing questions at me about our adoption process and then got irate about our fundraiser. Come to find out, she was an adoptive parent herself, and the fundraiser I was approved to have was much more difficult for her to get consent for, and she didn't understand why. Her perception of my much simpler experience had deeply offended this woman.

She was furious. Through anger, she told me how she had contacted other parents. The school principal too. While I had been celebrating a successful event that encouraged our community and brought us one step closer to bringing our daughter home, I was the subject of a behind-the-scenes firestorm and countless less-than-favorable conversations. And I had no idea.

I hurried down the hill, no longer pulled by the buzz of a fun night, but by shame and embarrassment. The pain of being misunderstood and slandered cut to the core. Cheeks burning, my tears morphed into full-blown heaving sobs by the time I reached my car. When I got home, I threw myself onto my bed and cried some more.

"Why, Lord? I thought I was doing the right thing. All I wanted to do was invite others into our adoption story and help bring our little girl home. And *this* is what I get?! Gossip? Rejection? Humiliation?"

Then a scripture came to mind: "So far as it depends on you, live peaceably with all" (Romans 12:18).

Me *live at peace?* Me?! *But I didn't do anything wrong! My intentions were good!*

"So far as it depends on you . . ."

My armor cracked. Truth was, my intentions didn't matter. I had hurt someone whether I meant to or not. Sure, she could have handled things differently. She could have come straight to me with her concerns instead of firing up the phone lines. But that wasn't my responsibility. My responsibility—what God was calling me to do—was to make things right from my end.

Oh, man. Obedience did not feel easy, especially when it was the opposite of what I wanted to do.

Hands trembling, I picked up the phone and dialed her number. When she answered, I almost hung up. My voice shook as I apologized for hurting her. "Could you meet me for coffee today?" I asked. "I'd really like to hear more of your story."

And so we met. I apologized again for the pain I caused her, and then I listened. And she listened to me. We didn't walk away best friends, but I know I left changed.

DAY 1

READ PSALM 119:17–24

" Do you know that the word disciple means "learner"? As a disciple of Christ, you and I are called to learn, and learning requires effort. It also requires good study methods. We know this to be true in our schooling, but do we know it to be true of following Christ?

JEN WILKIN

" Grace is not opposed to effort, it is opposed to earning. Earning is an attitude. Effort is an action. Grace, you know, does not just have to do with forgiveness of sins alone.

DALLAS WILLARD

DAY 2

READ 1 JOHN 5:1-5

> For he willeth that we be occupied in knowing and loving till the time that we shall be fulfilled in heaven. . . . For of all things the beholding and the loving of the Maker maketh the soul to seem less in his own sight, and most filleth him with reverent dread and true meekness, with plenty of charity for his fellow Christians.

JULIAN OF NORWICH

> When love and duty are one, then grace is in you.

W. SOMERSET MAUGHAM

DAY 3

READ 1 SAMUEL 15:1-26

❝ The law of God is relentlessly rigid. It never gives anyone a break because no one, regardless of what he or she has suffered, deserves a break. Total other-centeredness is required of us at every moment, whether in the presence of a caring friend or an unfaithful spouse. The slightest compromise with purity ends any hope of acceptance by God. People who present the quality of their lives to God as grounds for relationship with him will instead be removed from his presence.

LARRY CRABB

❝ Only he who believes is obedient, and only he who is obedient believes.

DIETRICH BONHOEFFER

DAY 4

READ MATTHEW 5:17–48

> In fact the church is both the celebrator of grace and the poet of holiness. It is not an error for Christians to live righteous lives or to strive to live out the fruit of the Holy Spirit in their private lives as well as in the broader culture. But we fail when certain standards of behavior, rather than grace and forgiveness, are assumed to be the core of Christianity. The heart of our faith is not a set of rules, but the Cross. The result of a standards-oriented religion is the rise, if not the dominance, of a self-righteousness for those who appear to be doing what is expected. For those who aren't as adept at deceiving others, the outcome of a standards-driven Christianity will be shame.
>
> DAN ALLENDER

> We must first be made good before we can do good; we must first be made just before our works can please God, for when we are justified by faith in Christ, then come good works.
>
> HUGH LATIMER

DAY 5

> **READ** DEUTERONOMY 29:29–30:14

So great is the goodness of God towards men, that he will have those good things to be our good duties which are his own gifts.

COELESTIUS

Someone near you right now has lost his way. Someone near you is feeling alone. Someone near you is overwhelmed. Someone near you is being tempted to step off God's pathway. Someone near you is doubting God's presence and love. The God who is love now lives inside of you, enabling you to love as you have been loved. He has chosen you to be one of his ambassadors, incarnating his love in the lives of those he has placed you near. Open your eyes and your heart and offer to others what you have been given. There is no better way to live in this fallen world.

PAUL DAVID TRIPP

WEEK 40

THE MORAL LAW

WESTMINSTER SHORTER CATECHISM QUESTION 40

Q | What did God at first reveal to man for the rule of his obedience?

A | The rule which God at first revealed to man for his obedience was the moral law.

....

PRAY *Help me when I helpless lie, when my conscience accuses me of sin, when my mind is harassed by foreboding thoughts, when my eyes are held awake by personal anxieties. . . . Permit me to commit myself to thee awake or asleep. Amen.*

....

WORSHIP GOD BY MEDITATING ON PSALM 100

....

COMMIT GOD'S WORD TO MEMORY | MICAH 6:8

DAY 1 | He has told you, O man, what is good;
DAY 2 | and what does the Lord require of you
DAY 3 | but to do justice,
DAY 4 | and to love kindness,
DAY 5 | and to walk humbly with your God.

CARROT CAKE

t's not easy being two years old. My daughter's days are filled gathering data about the world she lives in and reacting to it with laughter, hitting, licking, crying, or dancing. And while she's driven by her wants and felt needs, I've noticed that what motivates her most is pleasing me. She's intuitive, so when my tone of voice is frustrated, her little eyes lock in on mine. With a tilt of her head, she leans in with a smile. "Hey . . . mama." Her voice inflection high, she's wanting to make me smile. A fast learner, she repeats the phrase until I soften.

The apple didn't fall far because pleasing others is in my blood. It comes straight down the shoot from my dad and grandmother who both thrived on serving others, even at great cost to themselves. Yet their gifts of service had a blind spot.

As the story goes, Dad always liked my grandmother's carrot cake. When he was a teenager, she made carrot cake for his birthday, and apparently, he expressed how much he enjoyed it. So for the next forty years, he found himself eating carrot cake on his birthday. As an adult, I remember my grandmother telling me how she always had to make him that cake because it was his favorite. The pleaser in Dad never had the heart to tell her the carrot cake actually wasn't his favorite; the diligent servant in my grandmother never paused and asked Dad what cake he would like. They both wanted the same thing—to love each other well. But because Dad wasn't honest and my grandmother wasn't curious, neither got to experience their relationship to its fullest. The two components of intimacy—honesty and curiosity—were woefully never present at the same time, and they wound up "serving each other" forty years of carrot cake.

So, when I see those little eyes and hear "Hey . . . mama," I have to fight my desire to please her back, to bake my own carrot cakes of sorts and make her feel as though I like everything she does. To know me, she'll have to see the honest me that sometimes likes order where she would prefer chaos, or solitude when she would prefer extroversion. And I hope she will learn to express curiosity about me, not just trying to be cute and making me smile, but to ask questions in order to understand me.

It's hard to say whether or not she'll like my grandmother's carrot cake or continue to work for a smile, but I want to foster the sort of environment where intimacy grows through honesty and curiosity. If I, as my daughter's authority, am honest about who I am and what I expect, and she, in turn, is curious to know me and my ways, we will have intimacy. By grace, we're baking a different kind of cake—one that helps us to truly know each other as mother and daughter.

DAY 1

READ ROMANS 2:11-16

" Each commandment represents some aspect of the likeness of God, and, therefore, obedience to God's law gives expression to what we really are, beings in God's likeness, and results in our true freedom.

J. A. MOTYER

" The knowledge of God and the knowledge of self always go hand in hand. In fact, there can be no true knowledge of self apart from the knowledge of God. He is the only reference point that is reliable.

JEN WILKIN

DAY 2

READ JOB 1:1–2:3

> To observe the law is not evil, but to be in slavery to it is. A person is in slavery to the law if he obeys it out of fear, as if he had to do so in order to become righteous. . . . The prophets observed the law not in order to be made righteous but in order to show their love to God.
>
> MARTIN LUTHER

> After God delivered his people from Egypt, he gave them a lot of commandments. This wasn't to punish them but to help and protect them. They were good commandments. And if they obeyed the commandments, God's people would be blessed. There would be food and children and long life and protection and a new home. It would be just like they were in Paradise again. That's where God wanted to lead them all along, back to the garden.
>
> KEVIN DEYOUNG

DAY 3

READ MICAH 6:6-8

" The law of God is holy, just, and good; and we should make the proper use of it. But we cannot derive from it pardon, righteousness, or strength. It teaches us to adorn the doctrine of God our Savior, but it cannot supply the place of that doctrine. As no mercy comes from God to sinners but through Jesus Christ, no man can come to the Father but by him; no man can know God, except as he is made known in the only begotten and beloved Son.

MATTHEW HENRY

" In vain we ask God's righteous law
To justify us now,
Since to convince and to condemn
Is all the law can do.
Jesus, how glorious is Thy grace!
When in Thy name we trust,
Our faith receives a righteousness
That makes the sinner just.

ISAAC WATTS

DAY 4

READ GENESIS 9:1-7

> The Old Testament saint knew that while condemned by the law he had breached, its ceremonial provisions pointed him to the way of forgiveness. He saw Christ as really (if opaquely) in the ceremonies as he did in the prophecies. He also knew as he watched the sacrifices being offered day after day and year after year that this repetition meant these sacrifices could not fully and finally take away sin—otherwise he would not need to return to the temple precincts. He was able to love the law as his rule of life because he knew that God made provision for its breach, pointed to the redemption in its ceremonies, and gave him direction through its commandments. It should not, therefore, surprise us or grieve us to think that the Christian sees Christ in the law.

SINCLAIR FERGUSON

> The law sends us to the gospel for our justification; the gospel sends us to the law to frame our way of life.

SAMUEL BOLTON

DAY 5

READ ROMANS 13:1–5

66 The law wasn't simply a legal code, but a heart-piercing call to a higher way of living. It was a call to sacrifice. It is the gospel in the Old Testament.

CAROLYN CUSTIS JAMES

66 It is after you have realized that there is a real Moral Law, and a Power behind the law, and that you have broken that law and put yourself wrong with that Power—it is after all this, and not a moment sooner, that Christianity begins to talk. When you know you are sick, you will listen to the doctor. When you have realized that our position is nearly desperate you will begin to understand what Christians are talking about.

C. S. LEWIS

WEEK 41

TEN COMMANDMENTS SUMMARIZED

WESTMINSTER SHORTER CATECHISM QUESTION 42

Q | What is the sum of the ten commandments?

A | The sum of the ten commandments is to love the Lord our God with all our heart, with all our soul, with all our strength, and with all our mind; and our neighbor as ourselves.

....

PRAY *Let me see thy love everywhere, not only in the cross, but in the fellowship of believers and in the world around me. Amen.*

....

WORSHIP GOD BY MEDITATING ON PSALM 112

....

COMMIT GOD'S WORD TO MEMORY | MATTHEW 22:37

DAY 1 | You shall love

DAY 2 | the Lord your God

DAY 3 | with all your heart

DAY 4 | and with all your soul

DAY 5 | and with all your mind.

COMMUNICANTS' CLASS

'm no gardener, but I do know that when you plant a seed in fertile soil and give it plenty of water and sunshine, it grows into something of beauty or sustenance, or both. But while that seed is deep in the dark dirt, it's easy to wonder if anything is happening, even if you're watering and protecting it as you should.

After twenty years of teaching children, I'm still learning to be patient, still learning that the growth of a heart isn't my job, but that the watering of it is.

Most of my teaching includes the hope that growth is happening under the surface of those kids' squirmy bodies and darting eyes, and occasionally God flashes small shoots flicking up out of the soil, revealing life. On one such occasion, I'd been teaching the Communicants' class at church, which prepares children who have come to faith in Jesus for their first communion—a role I genuinely enjoy. Weeks after the class ended, I received a note from one of the children explaining how she came to know Jesus in that very class. Even though attendance in the Communicants' class is intended to demonstrate that a child has put their faith in Jesus, the Holy Spirit was at work during our class in such a way that this child felt the full assurance of her salvation. Tears welled as I considered what God had done to draw her heart to him.

And God hasn't just grown hearts while I was teaching well; he's grown them when my teaching was at its worst. It's hard to forget royal failures, and one Sunday night lesson on Jonah was no exception. I felt underprepared, distracted, and uninspiring.

Early the next Sunday morning as I walked down the preschool hall, a mother spotted me and picked up her pace. "Wait!" she called out. "I need to talk to you!" I swallowed hard. "What did you say during your lesson last Sunday night? My daughter has talked about it all week and I have to know what you said." Quickly, my mind pulled up everything I could remember from the lesson, searching for something I might need to explain or even apologize for, when she interrupted my mental spin. "You don't understand. My daughter has been talking about being a missionary and taking God's Word to those who don't have it." I looked into her eyes, finding assurance where I thought I would see frustration. I hadn't spoken well or clearly that night. How did her daughter get that message from anything I'd said?

Simply put, it wasn't me—*God* delivers his message to his people. Just as he grows trees in the middle of concrete in Brooklyn, he does so on rolling hills by a stream. He used Moses with all his objections, didn't he? Regardless of his people's inability, shortcomings, or waning confidence, God makes a way. I'm no Moses, but the way God has worked through me gives me hope that in some way, I'm a little like him. And since he was a lot like Jesus, that's fine by me.

DAY 1

READ GALATIANS 6:1-18

> None of us keeps the Great Commandment for five minutes. We may think that we do in a surface way, but upon a moment's reflection it is clear that none of us loves God with our whole heart or our whole mind or our whole strength. No one loves his neighbor as he loves himself. We may do everything in our power to avoid thinking about this at a deep level, but there is always that nagging certain knowledge that in fact we violate the Great Commandment every day.
>
> R. C. SPROUL

> The law was there to emphasize human sinfulness and to direct people to put their trust in the promise contained in the law.
>
> PHILIP EVESON

DAY 2

READ ROMANS 13:8-14

> The law could promise life to me
> If my obedience perfect be;
> But grace does promise life upon
> My Lord's Obedience alone. . . .
> An angry God the law reveal'd;
> The gospel shows him reconcil'd:
> By that I know he was displeas'd;
> By this I see his wrath appeas'd. . . .
> Lo! in the law Jehovah dwells
> But Jesus is concealed
> Whereas the gospel's nothing else
> But Jesus Christ reveal'd.

RALPH ERSKINE

> The Ten Commandments is the Bible's fundamental statement of "the law of liberty." The fact that it is in the main a series of prohibitions has led to the unthinking charge that it is negative in tone and purpose. This is to forget that a negative command is far more liberating than a positive one, for a positive command restricts life to that one course of action, whereas a negative command leaves life open to every course of action except one!

J. A. MOTYER

DAY 3

READ EXODUS 20:1-17

> They say that it came as a legal code, those Ten Commandments—
> but it is more. . . .
>
> The Ten Commandments are more than God saying, "Here is
> my law for you"—they are God saying, "Here is my love for you."
>
> *Here, I take you to be mine, to be my treasured possession—have
> no other gods, no other lovers that woo you, that take your attention
> or affection, but me.*
>
> *Here, I give you my name, my very name to make you mine—do
> not use it in vain.*
>
> *Here, I long to spend time with you, holy time for you and me—set
> apart the Sabbath day as holy time for you and me.*
>
> *Here, I love you, bride—be united, not coveting or lying or stealing
> or murdering or cheating one another, but honoring and loving and
> living out of our love.*
>
> And three times the Israelites say yes, this we will do—we do, we
> do, we do.
>
> God gives his people this gift, these two tablets of stone with his
> handwritten commitment to love, and he aches.
>
> "Oh, that their hearts would be inclined to fear me and keep all
> my commands."
>
> ANN VOSKAMP

> The gospel never overthrows God's law for the simple reason
> that both the law and the gospel are expressions of God's grace.
> Therefore the reverse is true: grace confirms the law and its true
> character.
>
> SINCLAIR FERGUSON

DAY 4

READ MATTHEW 22:23-40

>> In response to his grace his people desire to please him, obey him, and never grieve him. The law, therefore, and obedience to it must never be abstracted from the character of the Person who gave it. What was true in the old covenant of Sinai is just as true in the new covenant in Christ. For at Calvary God's covenant commitment and its implications are spelled out in large letters: "I have loved you like this; trust and love me in return, for this is my commandment, that you love one another as I have loved you." Thus love for the brethren in the New Testament, while motivated by the love of Christ for us, remains simultaneously obedience to the commandment. For love does not ignore the law; rather, it fulfills it.

SINCLAIR FERGUSON

>> God gives the commandments to us—and God gives God to keep the commandments for us. God gives us the commitment of love at the top of Mount Sinai, and he staggeringly keeps our commitment to love at the top of Calvary.

ANN VOSKAMP

DAY 5

READ JAMES 1:19-2:13

> O direct my life towards thy commandments, hallow my soul, purify my body, correct my thoughts, cleanse my desires, soul, and body, mind and spirit, heart and reins. Renew me thoroughly, O God, for, if Thou wilt, Thou canst.

LANCELOT ANDREWES

> All of the wonderful obligations of the law will then help us on our way toward godly living and sanctification. Since we cannot be made any more perfect in God's eyes than we already are, we are now free to make the law serve us. It will serve us by making us more thankful for Christ when we see how we fail to obey it, and it will serve us by showing us how to love God and our neighbor as we long to.

ELYSE FITZPATRICK AND DENNIS JOHNSON

WEEK 42

OUR INABILITY

WESTMINSTER SHORTER CATECHISM QUESTION 82

Q | Is any man able perfectly to keep the commandments of God?

A | No mere man, since the fall, is able in this life perfectly to keep the commandments of God, but does daily break them in thought, word, and deed.

....

PRAY *Teach me that I cannot satisfy thy law, that this effort is a resting in my righteousness, that only Christ's righteousness, ready-made, already finished, is fit for that purpose. Amen.*

....

WORSHIP GOD BY MEDITATING ON PSALM 39

....

COMMIT GOD'S WORD TO MEMORY | 1 JOHN 1:9

DAY 1 | If we confess our sins,
DAY 2 | he is faithful and just
DAY 3 | to forgive us our sins
DAY 4 | and to cleanse us
DAY 5 | from all unrighteousness.

PHONE MESSAGE

I don't remember my brother being born, but apparently it rocked my only-child world. Researchers have shown that when a firstborn experiences the addition of another child into the family, he or she often becomes more of a people-pleaser and perfectionist in order to regain the apparent lost affection of his or her parents. Thus, my journey to Perfection Summit began. I was two.

I developed certain skills in my quest to maintain perfection status: rationalizing, blame shifting, and, if all else failed, flat out lying—anything to convince my parents that I was worthy of their love and devotion. When there were slip-ups, I kept them hidden, explained them away, or blamed someone else.

As I grew into adulthood, another aspect of my perfectionism grew as well: the expectation that everyone else should be perfect too. And that is how I approached the imperfect world of parenting imperfect children.

One day, as I was sitting in my white minivan on a hot Alabama day waiting on my son to finish swim team practice, I looked up to see practice had finished, but my son was nowhere to be seen. When I spotted him, I saw him sauntering to the van where his personal chauffeur waited while he extended his final high fives. My frustration mounted. By the time he climbed into the seat next to me, the tirade was underway as I listed his imperfections with furrowed brows and flailing arms. "Why are you so late? Your practice ended fifteen minutes ago! Why didn't you come straight to the car? Where are your goggles? Don't tell me you broke another pair!"

As I settled back into my seat, I noticed that my emphatic arm motions had bumped my cell phone, which had apparently dialed a number. I ended the call and thought nothing more of it.

Eventually I cooled off and later that day checked in with my mom. As we chatted, she mentioned that she had received an unusual phone message. My face reddened, my stomach knotted, and my mind raced to find ways to hide my imperfection, my hateful heart.

I could tell her it was a wrong number. Or that she didn't know the whole story. Or how he deserved what he got. But before any words could come out of my mouth, my mother spoke four words that I did not deserve to hear: "I erased your message." Instead of what I deserved to hear, she ended our conversation with what I longed to hear: "I love you."

· ·

DAY 1

READ JAMES 3:1-12

❝ The concept of self-help is like putting your broken hand in a garbage disposal, flipping the switch, and expecting it to be healed. We know that help comes from outside of ourselves, from our loving God via the alien righteousness of Jesus Christ dispensed by the Spirit who is not our own.

JARED C. WILSON

❝ When something happens that punctures our sense of self—when we see someone with more than we have or who is more successful than we are—our ego begins to deflate. We feel smaller, not because we are smaller than other people, but because we had been thinking of ourselves "more highly than [we] ought." We have lifted ourselves up; and as the most basic laws of physics demand, what goes up must come down.

HANNAH ANDERSON

DAY 2

READ ROMANS 7:1-25

> If you aren't daily admitting to yourself that you are a mess and in daily and rather desperate need for forgiving and transforming grace, and if the evidence around has not caused you to abandon your confidence in your own righteousness, then you are going to give yourself to the work of convincing yourself that you are okay.

PAUL DAVID TRIPP

> God is inviting you every day to wake up and say, "I can't do this."

GLORIA FURMAN

DAY 3

READ GENESIS 8:20-22

" When we believe that God expects us to try hard to become who Jesus wants us to be, we will live in that blurry, frustrating land of Should Be rather than trust in The One Who Is. We will do whatever it takes to please God rather than receive the acceptance that has already been given. We will perform to live up to what we believe his expectation is of us rather than expectantly wait on him.

EMILY P. FREEMAN

" I can hide my heart, and my past, and my future plans, from those around me, but I cannot hide anything from God. I can talk in a way that deceives my fellow creatures as to what I really am, but nothing I say or do can deceive God. He sees through all my reserve and pretense; he knows me as I really am, better indeed than I know myself. A God whose presence and scrutiny I could evade would be a small and trivial deity.

J. I. PACKER

DAY 4

READ ECCLESIASTES 7:19-29

" God gave them other rules, like don't make yourselves pretend gods; don't kill people; or steal; or lie. The rules showed God's people how to live, and how to be close to him, and how to be happy. They showed how life worked best.

"God promises to always look after you," Moses said. "Will you love him and keep these rules?"

"We can do it! Yes! We promise!"

But they were wrong. They couldn't do it. No matter how hard they tried, they could never keep God's rules all the time.

God knew they couldn't. And he wanted them to know it, too.

Only one Person could keep all the rules. And many years later God would send him—to stand in their place and be perfect for them.

Because rules couldn't save them.

Only God could save them.

SALLY LLOYD-JONES

DAY 5

READ 1 JOHN 1:5-2:6

❝ We aren't what we do but what God has done to and for us.

MICHAEL HORTON

❝ Sinners that we are, we shall either reduce the law's demands to something which we can live with, as the Pharisees did, or we shall relapse into a sense of hopelessness when we realize that such an undertaking is beyond our powers. The freedom of the gospel which Paul proclaimed was a freedom from hypocrisy and despair—the twin agents of the power of sin within us.

GERALD L. BRAY

WEEK 43
SIN'S PENALTY

WESTMINSTER SHORTER CATECHISM QUESTION 84

Q | What does every sin deserve?

A | Every sin deserves God's wrath and curse, both in this life, and that which is to come.

....

PRAY *I am pardoned through the blood of Jesus—give me a new sense of it. Amen.*

....

WORSHIP GOD BY MEDITATING ON PSALM 34

....

COMMIT GOD'S WORD TO MEMORY | ROMANS 6:23

DAY 1 | For the wages
DAY 2 | of sin is death,
DAY 3 | but the free gift of God
DAY 4 | is eternal life
DAY 5 | in Christ Jesus our Lord.

THE QUESTION

The diagnosis hadn't come lightly, nor had the reality. The appointments came and went, week after week, month after month, then year after year. It's a strange thing to feel both immense gratitude for modern medicine and skilled doctors and, at the same time, feel anything but grateful to be there. As I sat in the sterile room, boring and drab and too quiet for my comfort, I realized the appointments had begun feeling like an obligation—something cancer required of me that I had to accommodate. By now I knew the answers to all the doctor's questions: *Yes, this prescription seems to be working fine. No, there aren't any new lumps that I'm aware of.*

The knock on the door pulled me from my thoughts. *Here we go. Same questions, same drill.* But the question the doctor asked this time wasn't related to the cancer at all. It was one I didn't see coming and didn't know how to answer: "How's the writing?" His three small words jarred me, revealing his sincere care for me as a person and my own false assumptions about his intentions.

Since I was too stunned to speak, the doctor continued, "Please, tell me the latest piece you've finished." And so I began to talk, still processing how I could have misjudged (even judged) him. My tower of self-centeredness and unfair conclusions toppled as I realized and repented of my belief that I knew more and better than the God of the universe. I begged forgiveness from God for far more than ungratefulness.

With new eyes and a humbled spirit, I stopped noticing the sterile room and paper gown and instead refocused my attention to find the words I actually wanted to speak. "You see patients like me all day long, walking in and out of cancer-laden doors, and you've got a wife and two small children? How do you do it? It must be so discouraging." Because he took time to really see me, and because I was no longer standing in judgment over him, we were both able to share vulnerably, straying a bit from the trivia of cancer.

All this time in and out of that patient room, week after week, year after year, and I thought cancer was my greatest problem. Turns out it's my sin and the consequences it brings—separation from God and others. I had forgotten the depth of my sin nature in lieu of the in-your-face issues of cancer. But God, in his infinite kindness, made a way of redemption and called him Jesus. And he unveils my sin in the most tender and kind ways, inviting my repentance and reconciliation. In light of my heart that's bent toward thinking I know best, his kindness leaves me speechless . . . again.

DAY 1

> **READ** REVELATION 6:1–17

" So when the devil throws your sins in your face and declares that you deserve death and hell, tell him this: "I admit that I deserve death and hell, what of it? For I know One who suffered and made satisfaction on my behalf. His name is Jesus Christ, Son of God, and where he is there I shall be also!"

MARTIN LUTHER

" If men will not understand the meaning of judgment, they will never come to understand the meaning of grace.

DOROTHY SAYERS

DAY 2

READ ROMANS 6:15-23

    At the Cross, God's unbending demand for truth came face-to-face with his mercy; his unchanging demand for perfect righteousness came together with peace made possible by Christ's atoning sacrifice.

NANCY GUTHRIE

    If we can see the true seriousness of our sin, we will no longer object to God's supposed severity, but marvel at his mercy.

VERN S. POYTHRESS

DAY 3

READ 1 THESSALONIANS 2:9-16

<blockquote>
The gospel is the gospel of salvation, and salvation is, first of all, salvation from sin in its guilt, defilement, and power. If our emphasis on the judgment of God upon sin is minimal, correspondingly minimal will be our esteem of salvation and of the savior.

JOHN MURRAY
</blockquote>

<blockquote>
On the day of judgment God's wrath will silence all who have rejected his grace, for they are without excuse. And on that day, we, the redeemed of the Lord, will be spellbound as we enter into our eternal inheritance.

SCOTTY SMITH AND MICHAEL CARD
</blockquote>

DAY 4

READ MATTHEW 23:1-39

Oh! my soul, if you would view sin in darkest colors and most terrible effects. . . . Go to Bethlehem, and ask, "Why did the King of heaven become infant of days? Why was he who fills all space, wrapped in swaddling clothes and laid in a manger?" Go to Gethsemane and ask, "Why did the incarnate God agonize and sweat great drops of blood?" Go to Calvary and ask, "Why did the innocent suffer such indignities? Why was the guiltless condemned to die? Why did the Lord of glory hang on the accursed tree? Why did the Lord of life condescend to pour out his soul unto death?" Let this view of sin, and of a sin bearing Savior, humble you in his presence and empty you of pride and vain glory. Let it, at the same time, fill you with gratitude to God for having provided such a remedy against the evils of the fall.

THOMAS READE

Unless you believe in Hell, you will never know how much Jesus loves you.

TIM KELLER

DAY 5

READ ISAIAH 33:1-24

> The reason Mount Zion—the place where God's people dwell—cannot be shaken is because of what happened on the hill of Golgotha. . . . The only reason the Lord "surrounds his people, both now and forever" is because of that Friday when the Father did not surround his Son.

NANCY GUTHRIE

> Our story is a story of God doing what we can't, in order to make up for us doing what we shouldn't. The Christ suffers for our sin, that we might share in his sinlessness.
>
> And so deliverers are born to die. Things fall apart so they can come together. God kicks his own people out of Paradise and then does whatever it takes to bring them back again.

KEVIN DEYOUNG

WEEK 44

WHAT GOD REQUIRES

WESTMINSTER SHORTER CATECHISM QUESTION 85

Q | What does God require of us, that we may escape his wrath and curse, due to us for sin?

A | To escape the wrath and curse of God, due to us for sin, God requires of us faith in Jesus Christ, repentance unto life, with the diligent use of all the outward means whereby Christ communicates to us the benefits of redemption.

....

PRAY *I forget to submit to thy will, and fail to be quiet there. But Scripture teaches me that thy active will reveals a steadfast purpose on my behalf, and this quietens my soul, and makes me love thee. Amen.*

....

WORSHIP GOD BY MEDITATING ON PSALM 4

....

COMMIT GOD'S WORD TO MEMORY | MARK 1:15

DAY 1 | The time is fulfilled,
DAY 2 | and the kingdom of God
DAY 3 | is at hand;
DAY 4 | repent and believe
DAY 5 | in the gospel.

THE FRONT DOOR

For close to sixty years, I've been afraid of being alone at night. So it was ironic when my husband and I moved to a house that sits off the road in the middle of some woods, and at night it is very, very dark. We talked and prayed about my fear prior to deciding to move there, so I viewed it as an opportunity to grow in my trust in God's protection. But I also knew I would have a security system in place and get familiar with the sounds the house made before I would have to be alone overnight for the first time. You can probably guess where this is going . . .

A couple of weeks after we moved in, my husband was called away on an unexpected two-week ministry trip. That meant thirteen nights alone by myself in the house in the middle of the big, dark, scary woods. That first night I crawled into bed and knew I had a decision to make. I could continue on fearful and fretting and imagining all sorts of horrible things, or I could choose to really believe what I say I believe: God is my refuge, he will never leave me, and he holds my soul, which cannot be touched by evil, ever. God has transformed me to be a very different woman than the one I was sixty or thirty or even five years ago. His power has shown up time and again in circumstances where my actions proved I either trusted him or I didn't, and by his grace I am now living more on the "trust him" side of that fence.

Well, in his kindness, that first night in the bed alone, God invited me—unexpectedly—to repent. He revealed to me my nighttime atheism—how I trusted him in the daylight but not when I'm blinded by the dark. How I put my faith in what I could see rather than the unseen. So I confessed the ways that walking in fear had blocked my intimacy with him, and I began to mourn over grieving his heart. In my repentance I experienced a new freedom from this long-lived fear, and within minutes I was fast asleep. To some that may seem like a small thing, but to me, it wasn't. I am still blown away by the outcome—I slept! In true freedom and trust and rest, I slept.

The following morning, I got up and happened to walk by the front door—the *unlocked* front door. In all my fretting, I had forgotten to lock the door! And that discovery quickly confirmed the truth I have come to know: it is God who protects me, not chariots or horses, a security system, or any locked door (Psalm 20:7). I stood there and laughed out loud at my misplaced thinking and vain, flawed attempts at trying to feel safe. While I still lock the front door at night, I can now say with full confidence that he is my real protector—my job is merely to rest securely in my place as his child.

DAY 1

READ MARK 1:1-15

❝ When my conscience under the Holy Spirit makes me aware of a specific sin I should at once call that sin sin and bring it consciously under the blood of Christ. Now it is covered and it is not honoring to the finished work of Jesus Christ to worry about it, as far as my relationship to God is concerned. Indeed, to worry about it is to do spite to the infinite value of the death of the Son of God. My fellowship with God is restored.

FRANCIS SCHAEFFER

❝ After we are in a state of grace, if we are overtaken with any sin, we must remember to have recourse first to Christ's mercy to pardon us, and then to the promise of his Spirit to govern us.

RICHARD SIBBES

DAY 2

READ 1 KINGS 8:46-53

> Christ has done everything necessary for salvation. Nothing now stands between the sinner and God but the sinner's good works. Nothing can keep him from Christ but his delusion that he doesn't need him and that his good works can actually satisfy God. All he needs is need, all he must have is nothing, all that is required is acknowledging the guilt, but alas he cannot part with his virtues. He has none that are anything but imaginary, but they are real to him and therefore grace becomes real. The real grace of God he spurns to hold onto the illusory virtues of his own. His eyes are fixed on a mirage. He will not drink of the real water of grace and so dies of thirst in the midst of an ocean of grace.

JOHN GERSTNER

> The whole gospel is contained in Christ. . . . To move even a step from Christ means to withdraw oneself from the gospel.

JOHN CALVIN

DAY 3

READ LUKE 13:1-9

> Repentance out of mere fear is really sorrow for the consequences of sin, sorrow over the danger of sin—it bends the will away from sin, but the heart still clings. But repentance out of conviction over mercy is really sorrow over sin, sorrow over the grievousness of sin—it melts the heart away from sin. It makes the sin itself disgusting to us, so it loses its attractive power over us. We say, "This disgusting thing is an affront to the one who died for me. I'm continuing to stab him with it!"
>
> TIM KELLER

> Since our direction, ever since the fall, is to be "curved in on ourselves," as Augustine put it, our natural tendency is to trust our own inner righteousness (legalism) and our own inner light (antinomianism). However, the gospel is the answer to both: it calls us out of ourselves, to look to someone else both to save and rule over us.
>
> MICHAEL HORTON

DAY 4

READ ACTS 16:22-34

In Luke 18, a rich young man comes asking Jesus what he must *do* to inherit eternal life. He wants to be in the spotlight. It is no coincidence that Luke juxtaposes the passage of Jesus and the children immediately preceding the verses on the young aristocrat. Children contrast with the rich man simply because there is no question of their having yet been able to merit anything. Jesus' point is: there is nothing any of us can do to inherit the Kingdom. We must receive it like little children. And little children haven't done anything. The New Testament world wasn't sentimental about children and had no illusion about any pretended innate goodness in them. . . . Children are our model because they have no claim on heaven. If they are close to God, it is because they are incompetent, not because they are innocent. If they receive anything, it can only be as a gift.

BRENNAN MANNING

When you remember your sins, you learn humility, love Jesus, and make much of the gospel.

JOE THORN

DAY 5

READ NUMBERS 21:4-9

The life of faith is a constant coming to Jesus for daily, hourly, and fresh supplies. Let every circumstance and event, every trial, sorrow, and need, be an echo of the gracious life inspiring words: "Go to Jesus!" Go to Jesus, confessing sin. Go to Jesus, unveiling grief. Go to Jesus, telling need. Go to Jesus, breathing love, desire, and hope. You are still in the land of famine and of need. But your heavenly Father would remind you that he has anticipated and provided . . . for all your requirements, for all your history, for your daily demands, in him whom whose fullness fills all in all. Take the hard heart, or the broken heart; take the cold heart, or the glowing heart; take your barrenness, or your fruitfulness; take the sunbeam of prosperity, or the cloud of adversity; take the joy, take the sorrow; take all to Jesus! Let him participate in all, keep you in all, sympathize with all; for Jesus is your Brother, raised up to befriend, relieve, and preserve you in your time of need.

OCTAVIUS WINSLOW

WEEK 45

WHAT IS FAITH

WESTMINSTER SHORTER CATECHISM QUESTION 86

Q | What is faith in Jesus Christ?

A | Faith in Jesus Christ is a saving grace, whereby we receive and rest upon him alone for salvation, as he is offered to us in the gospel.

....

PRAY *Give me a deeper trust, that I may lose myself to find myself in thee, the ground of my rest, the spring of my being. Amen.*

....

WORSHIP GOD BY MEDITATING ON PSALM 37

....

COMMIT GOD'S WORD TO MEMORY | EPHESIANS 2:8–9

DAY 1 | For by grace you have been saved through faith.
DAY 2 | And this is not your own doing;
DAY 3 | it is the gift of God,
DAY 4 | not a result of works,
DAY 5 | so that no one may boast.

MOTHERING

"If ever a monk could go to heaven by his monkery, it was I."
-MARTIN LUTHER

"If ever a mother could get her kids to heaven by her mothering, it is I."

onkery" didn't work for Martin Luther and "mothering" isn't working for me. My adulting kids aren't following my highway to heaven. They've no plans to get married, especially to my hand-picked list of godly possibilities. They're not going to church or connecting in Christian community. And they are unapologetic about it.

What's a mother to do?

First, I swirl in self-punishment: *Why didn't I homeschool? Why didn't I send them to "that" summer camp where those other kids' lives changed and they embraced a deep faith? Where did I go wrong?*

Then, I get busy interceding and weeping. After all, it worked for Monica who pursued her son, Augustine of Hippo, around the known world for fifteen years and pleaded with the early church leaders to convert her adult son. Bishop Ambrose finally, in mercy, told her, "Surely the son of so many tears will not perish." See how Augustine turned out with a mother like that?

Maybe I haven't prayed hard enough. Maybe there's another book I can read or anonymous support group of failed moms I can join. So I focus on "mother martyrdom" because, surely, if I sacrifice enough, God will see my efforts and reawaken my children's faith.

I'm sure it's hard having a martyr for a mother. My children endure my subtle mentions of local churches and inspirational books they should read. And to their credit, they politely acknowledge all the relevant messages by cool millennial pastors I forward them on Facebook.

Monica's my patron saint, but my role model should be the prodigal's father, who waited in faith for his son to return. The father who got on with his life and loved and enjoyed his children when he was with them. Jesus didn't mention the prodigal's mother for a reason. How could a mother just wait and believe without nagging her husband to go out and look for their son?

In my head I hear, "I gave you one job to do and look how that turned out." But it isn't God's voice. He's smiling and saying, "That's not your responsibility. Your only work is to believe" (John 6:28–29). And even that belief is a gift (Eph. 2:8).

So, I'm trying to stop negotiating and start enjoying them. But along with the waiting, I'm still talking to God about what I think he should do and when. Because, well, I'm a still a mother.

DAY 1

READ PHILIPPIANS 3:1-11

" For what befits faith more than to recognize that we are bare of all virtue, in order to be clothed by God? That we are empty of all good, in order to be filled by him? That we are slaves of sins, to be rescued by him? Blind, to be illumined by him? Lame, to be set on our feet by him? Frail, to be sustained by him? And to cast aside every motive for vainglory, so that he alone might be glorified, and we in him?

JOHN CALVIN

" The resurrection turns us from law-keeping to gospel-believing and from self-righteousness to an alien righteousness in Jesus Christ. It turns us from trying to earn God's love by our good deeds to freely accepting God's love as a gift through faith in his Son.

THABITI ANYABWILE

" Faith is the force of life.

LEO TOLSTOY

DAY 2

READ 1 PETER 1:1-12

> Jesus having taken the place of the believer—having rendered a full equivalent to divine wrath for all that his people ought to have suffered as the result of sin, the believer can shout with glorious triumph, "Who shall lay anything to the charge of God's elect?" Not God, for he hath justified; not Christ, for he hath died, "yea rather hath risen again." My hope lives not because I am not a sinner, but because I am a sinner for whom Christ died; my trust is not that I am holy, but that being unholy, *he* is my righteousness. *My faith rests not upon what I am, or shall be, or feel, or know, but in what Christ is, in what he has done, and in what he is now doing for me.*

CHARLES SPURGEON

> We both believe, and disbelieve a hundred times an hour, which keeps believing nimble.

EMILY DICKINSON

DAY 3

> **READ** EPHESIANS 2:1-21

> The gospel of the grace of God awakens an intense longing in human souls and an equally intense resentment, because the revelation which it brings is not palatable. There is a certain pride in man that will give and give, but to come and accept is another thing. I will give my life to martyrdom, I will give myself in consecration, I will do anything, but do not humiliate me to the level of the most hell-deserving sinner and tell me that all I have to do is to accept the gift of salvation through Jesus Christ. We have to realize that we cannot earn or win anything from God; we must either receive it as a gift or do without it. The greatest blessing spiritually is the knowledge that we are destitute . . . we have to enter into his Kingdom through the door of destitution.

> OSWALD CHAMBERS

> Earnest prayers, long fasting, and burning tears may seem befitting, but cannot move the heart of infinite love to a greater willingness to save. God's time is now. The question is not, What have I been? Or What do I expect to be? But, Am I now trusting in Jesus to save to the uttermost? If so, I am now saved from all sin.

> PHOEBE PALMER

DAY 4

READ HEBREWS 11:1-40

If a random sample of one thousand American Christians were taken today, the majority would define faith as a belief in the existence of God. In earlier times it did not take faith to believe that God existed—almost everyone took that for granted. Rather, faith had to do with one's relationship to God—whether one trusted in God. The difference in faith as "belief that something may or may not exist" and faith as "trusting in God" is enormous. The first is a matter of the head and the second a matter of the heart. The first can leave us unchanged, the second intrinsically brings change.

BRENNAN MANNING

This freedom from sin is the miraculous healing that is beyond our understanding, and the too-good-to-be promise of the gospel—that when we come to him in repentance and faith, Jesus gives us his righteousness and takes our sin upon himself in a miraculous and mysterious exchange. It is not merely having faith that saves us. Our faith is a conduit by which this miraculous healing exchange takes place. When we come to Christ in faith, we are essentially saying, "I'm sick and I can't get well on my own. Jesus, I trust you and depend on you to make me acceptable to God."

NANCY GUTHRIE

DAY 5

READ JOHN 4:1-42

> Jesus came to us to help us overcome our fear of God. As long as we are afraid of God, we cannot love God. Love means intimacy, closeness, mutual vulnerability, and a deep sense of safety. But all of those are impossible as long as there is fear. Fear creates suspicion, distance, defensiveness, and insecurity.
>
> The greatest block in the spiritual life is fear. Prayer, meditation, and education cannot come forth out of fear. God is perfect love, and as John the Evangelist writes, "Perfect love drives out fear" (1 John 4:18). Jesus' central message is that God loves us with an unconditional love and desires our love, free from all fear, in return.

HENRI NOUWEN

> Faith means receiving something, not doing something or even being something. To say, therefore, that our faith saves us means that we do not save ourselves even in the slightest measure, but that God saves us.

J. GRESHAM MACHEN

WEEK 46

WHAT IS REPENTANCE

WESTMINSTER SHORTER CATECHISM QUESTION 87

Q | What is repentance unto life?

A | Repentance unto life is a saving grace, whereby a sinner, out of a true sense of his sin, and apprehension of the mercy of God in Christ, does, with grief and hatred of his sin, turn from it unto God, with full purpose of, and endeavor after, new obedience.

....

PRAY *Take away my roving eye, curious ear, greedy appetite, lustful heart; show me that none of these things can heal a wounded conscience. . . . Then take me to the cross and leave me there. Amen.*

....

WORSHIP GOD BY MEDITATING ON PSALM 38

....

COMMIT GOD'S WORD TO MEMORY | 2 CORINTHIANS 7:10

DAY 1 | For godly grief
DAY 2 | produces a repentance
DAY 3 | that leads to salvation without regret,
DAY 4 | whereas worldly grief
DAY 5 | produces death.

THE PARKING METER

I was dressed for a job interview that day, so I decided to park in the metered spaces right next to the law school. I would have to go straight from the interview to my international law class. The timing was tight, but if I loaded up the parking meter, it would be just enough to cover both, after which I would move my car to the distant student lot for the remainder of the day.

My interview went well, and the professor who taught my class was interesting and entertaining as always. On this particular day, however, he ran over and I didn't have a single minute to spare. Afterward, I power-walked to the metered space where I had parked my car. As soon as I turned the corner, I saw him.

The meter man stood there in a dull brown uniform, scrutinizing my parking meter, and my heart began to pound. He took out a pen and scribbled on his ticket pad. Hot anger tingled my cheekbones. "Please don't give me a ticket!" I called out, running toward him as fast as I could, a knot forming in my throat. "My class ran over!" He kept writing, unfazed by my plea, and then glanced over at his subsequent target—the meter beside me belonging to his next victim. I glanced too: three minutes left. I grabbed some quarters, and quickly fed them into the neighboring meter. *Take that!* I thought, taking delight in thwarting his effort to penalize my fellow student.

Despite my frenzied act of altruism, he seemed unmoved and calmly handed me my parking ticket. I no longer swallowed the lump in my throat and gave him a piece of my mind. I argued my case, looked him in the eyes and said, "Don't you have anything better to do with your time?"

I found my fists clenching when I recounted the incident to my husband later that night. Then I waited for him to take my side and compliment my advocacy skills. Instead, there was a long pause before he gently said, "That doesn't sound like you."

It took a while for those words to soak in. But when they did, I felt ashamed of how I had treated the officer, an image-bearer doing his job. I looked for him when I went to the Parking and Transportation

Office to pay my ticket, but he wasn't there, so I stopped and asked God for an opportunity to apologize.

To my surprise, the opportunity came a few weeks later at a football game. As I left the stadium, there he was, working as event staff. God had answered my prayer, but could I follow through? Could I live with myself if I didn't?

I walked over, reminded him how I had treated him, and apologized. I couldn't retract my previous words, but I could acknowledge my arrogance in speaking them. I couldn't change what I had done, but God had changed me. Then he graciously gave me the opportunity to pursue reconciliation with my fellow image-bearer.

DAY 1

READ JOEL 2:12-29

> Repentance is not about earning grace but entering it; not about quenching his wrath but quieting the accusations of our hearts; not about unlocking his mercy but releasing our sin-sick sorrow to the Savior, who already rejoices to receive it.
>
> BRYAN CHAPELL

> No sooner is the proud heart humbled, and the hard heart broken into contrition, than Jehovah is near with his healing balm. To heal the broken in heart and to revive the spirit of the contrite ones is the delight of Immanuel.
>
> ARCHIBALD ALEXANDER

DAY 2

READ 2 TIMOTHY 2:22-26

> One can no more keep the mind from returning to an idea than the sea from returning to a shore. For the sailor, this is called the tide; in the case of the guilty, it is called remorse. God stirs up the soul as well as the ocean.

VICTOR HUGO

> Repentance does not mean changing, or becoming a super-Christian, or engaging in self-flagellation. Repentance is simply agreeing with God about who you are, what you have done, and what you need to change. I used to think that repentance couldn't be repentance unless there was true change. If that is true, most of us have never repented. In the case of the son in Jesus' story, repentance involved going to the Father. That is what repentance is. It is going to the Father.

STEVE BROWN

DAY 3

READ AMOS 5:12-15

> The conscience is never touched by vague generalities; we must come to particulars. Thus and thus hast thou done.
>
> JAMES HENLEY THORNWELL

> The call to repent assaults the Old Adam in us: the life of the flesh, our involvement in the sinful structures of this world, our stubborn refusal to yield to God's will. We cherish our sin, we clutch it, it kills us but we love it. The gospel demands that we choose life, rejecting sin and its ungodly demands. So the love of God in the gospel works like a surgeon. Cutting out sin's cancer, with pain like death, the gospel heals.
>
> DAVID HANSEN

DAY 4

READ PSALM 119:57-64

> True apologies never explain, they only admit, acknowledging that the error was without justifiable cause. Repentant people realize that inexcusable wrong can either be judged or forgiven, never understood and overlooked, and so they beg for forgiveness with no thought of deserving it. Truly repentant people are the ones who begin to grasp God's amazing grace, the ones who know that they need only confess to experience the forgiveness that is always there in infinite supply.

LARRY CRABB

> I must never think a sin too small to need immediate application to the blood of Christ. If I put away a good conscience, concerning faith I make shipwreck. I must never think my sins too great, too aggravated, too presumptuous—as when done on my knees, or in preaching, or by a dying bed, or during dangerous illness—to hinder me from fleeing to Christ. The weight of my sins should act like the weight of a clock; the heavier it is, it makes it go faster.

ROBERT MURRAY MCCHEYNE

DAY 5

READ 2 CORINTHIANS 7:2-13

> False repentance is less concerned with the spiritual contamination of sin than it is with the personal consequences of sin. True repentance is chiefly concerned with the wrong we have done to our Savior and to others. Repentance of the first kind is self-preoccupied; true repentance is a selfless seeking of spiritual fellowship and renewal. False repentance flees correction; true repentance seeks it. True repentance is evident when we are as much concerned about deep and hidden sins as we are about the faults that others can observe. The repentant heart desires full confession. It is more concerned about relationship with God than about relationship among men (Ps. 51:4–6).

BRYAN CHAPELL

> The repentance we are called to is about choosing one audience over another.

DONALD MILLER

WEEK 47

THE MEANS OF GRACE

WESTMINSTER SHORTER CATECHISM QUESTION 88

Q | What are the outward and ordinary means whereby Christ communicates to us the benefits of redemption?

A | The outward and ordinary means whereby Christ communicates to us the benefits of redemption are, his ordinances, especially the Word, sacraments, and prayer; all which are made effectual to the elect for salvation.

....

PRAY *May his shed blood make me more thankful for thy mercies, more humble under thy correction, more zealous in thy service, more watchful against temptation, more contented in my circumstances, more useful to others. Amen.*

....

WORSHIP GOD BY MEDITATING ON PSALM 73

....

COMMIT GOD'S WORD TO MEMORY | ACTS 2:42

DAY 1 | And they devoted themselves
DAY 2 | to the apostles' teaching
DAY 3 | and the fellowship,
DAY 4 | to the breaking of bread
DAY 5 | and the prayers.

THE SOLDIER

t seems to me a good picture will evoke powerful memories of people, times, and places like nothing else. I'm thinking specifically of a fifty-year-old photo I have, taken of a young soldier who's unaware of the photographer. He's not soldiering at the moment, but resting and intently reading a letter, blessedly forgetful of his circumstances—if only for a moment. The soldier has been away from home now four months, with eight months to go on his tour of duty. His army unit would spend days in the fields and jungles of Vietnam, punctuated by brief breaks for the combatants to rest bodies and nerves. It's during one of these times that the photographer captured the soldier reading that very special letter. Letters from family members and friends were nice, but the ones from his new bride were life giving to his soul.

The newlyweds only had a few days before the war separated them, so their love for each other would have to be sustained by these letters. She was his rock, possessing an inner peace and confidence that she claimed came from a personal, unconditional relationship with God.

Her correspondence spoke constantly of her love for him, her new husband. She regularly encouraged him, reminding him not to be overwhelmed by what he was experiencing, no matter how terrible. *God is in control*, she claimed with an admirable assurance. He drank in every line and especially loved when she told him about herself. Always wanting to know more, he asked her to write even the mundane details of what was happening in her life, and together from afar, they dreamed of what their future could look like. There were many plans: experiences to share, college to finish, babies and careers to nurture. But her primary message was to trust God. *He is protecting you, he loves you, and I am asking him to bring you home to me.*

After their year apart, God did bring the soldier home to be with the love of his life, and joined him to Christ seven years after that.

I know this story so well because the man in the photo is me. I often go back to it because it reminds me of the unseen hand of God in my life, even before I knew him in the personal way my wife did. Through her prayers and the words of scripture she wrote to me through the war and decades since, I began to think of the Word of God as his love letter, given so I would know him more intimately and be encouraged in my daily spiritual battles—battles just as fierce as those fought fifty years ago in a strange country. Today I still need the promise of a future hope—a homecoming to the One who loves me dearly.

Of all the interesting details this particular photo communicates—the heat of the country, the cramped quarters, and the quiet contentment on my face—what's most unusual is how unaware I was that the photo was being taken. The photographer's lens may have been focused on me in that moment, but it was the eye of God that never left me—and never leaves me—even when I'm unaware of his presence.

DAY 1

> **READ** ACTS 2:42-47

❝ The "means of grace" are such as Bible reading, private prayer, and regularly worshipping God in Church, wherein one hears the Word taught and participates in the Lord's Supper. I lay it down as a simple matter of fact that no one who is careless about such things must ever expect to make much progress in sanctification.

J. C. RYLE

❝ True spiritual development is something which God himself gives. . . . Our greatest need is to recognize, and to put our lives under, the influences which God uses to produce growth in Christian character.

SINCLAIR FERGUSON

DAY 2

READ MATTHEW 28:16-20

> No man is so regenerate, but that continually he has need of the means which Christ Jesus has appointed to be used in his church.

RICHARD G. KYLE

> Akin to the preaching of the gospel, we have another help to our faith in the sacraments in regard to which, it greatly concerns us that some sure doctrine should be delivered, informing us both of the end for which they were instituted, and of their present use. First, we must attend to what a sacrament is. It seems to me, then, a simple and appropriate definition to say, that it is an external sign, by which the Lord seals on our consciences his promises of good-will toward us, in order to sustain the weakness of our faith, and we in our turn testify our piety towards him, both before himself and before angels as well as men. We may also define more briefly by calling it a testimony of the divine favour toward us, confirmed by an external sign, with a corresponding attestation of our faith towards him.

JOHN CALVIN

DAY 3

READ 1 PETER 1:13-25

❝ Worship is the strategy by which we interrupt our preoccupation with ourselves and attend to the presence of God.

EUGENE PETERSON

❝ Let us remember that grace is increased, in the exercise of it, not by virtue of the exercise itself, but as Christ by his Spirit flows into the soul and brings us nearer to himself, the fountain, so instilling such comfort that the heart is further enlarged. The heart of a Christian is Christ's garden, and his graces are as so many sweet spices and flowers which, when his Spirit blows upon them, send forth a sweet savor. Therefore keep the soul open to entertain the Holy Ghost, for he will bring in continually fresh forces to subdue corruption.

RICHARD SIBBES

DAY 4

READ EPHESIANS 6:10-20

“ God has given us the Disciplines of the spiritual life as a means of receiving his grace. The Disciplines allow us to place ourselves before God so that he can transform us. . . . This is the way it is with the Spiritual Disciplines—they are a way of sowing to the Spirit. The Disciplines are God's way of getting us into the ground; they put us where he can work within us and transform us. By themselves the Spiritual Disciplines can do nothing; they can only get us to the place where something can be done. They are God's means of grace. The inner righteousness we seek is not something that is poured on our heads. God has ordained the Disciplines of the spiritual life as the means by which we place ourselves where he can bless us.

In this regard it would be proper to speak of "the path of disciplined grace." It is "grace" because it is free; it is "disciplined" because there is something for us to do. In *The Cost of Discipleship* Dietrich Bonhoeffer makes it clear that grace is free, but it is not cheap. The grace of God is unearned and unearnable, but if we ever expect to grow in grace, we must pay the price of a consciously chosen course of action which involves both individual and group life. Spiritual growth is the purpose of the Disciplines.

RICHARD J. FOSTER

DAY 5

READ NEHEMIAH 9:1-38

> I can flip a switch, but I don't provide the electricity. I can turn on a faucet, but I don't make the water flow. There will be no light and no liquid refreshment without someone else providing it. And so it is for the Christian with the ongoing grace of God. His grace is essential for our spiritual lives, but we don't control the supply. We can't make the favor of God flow, but he has given us circuits to connect and pipes to open expectantly. There are paths along which he has promised his favor. . . . Our God is lavish in his grace; he is free to liberally dispense his goodness without even the least bit of cooperation and preparation on our part, and often he does. But he also has regular channels. And we can routinely avail ourselves of these revealed paths of blessing—or neglect them to our detriment.
>
> DAVID MATHIS

> I must take care above all that I cultivate communion with Christ, for though that can never be the basis of my peace—mark that—yet it will be the channel of it.
>
> CHARLES SPURGEON

WEEK 48

HOW THE WORD WORKS

WESTMINSTER SHORTER CATECHISM QUESTION 89

Q | How is the Word made effectual to salvation?

A | The Spirit of God makes the reading, but especially the preaching, of the Word, an effectual means of convincing and converting sinners, and of building them up in holiness and comfort, through faith, unto salvation.

....

PRAY *Order all my ways by thy holy Word and make thy commandments the joy of my heart, that by them I may have happy converse with thee. May I grow in thy love and manifest it to mankind. Amen.*

....

WORSHIP GOD BY MEDITATING ON PSALM 119:25–48

....

COMMIT GOD'S WORD TO MEMORY | ROMANS 10:17

DAY 1 | So faith
DAY 2 | comes from hearing,
DAY 3 | and hearing
DAY 4 | through the word
DAY 5 | of Christ.

A NEW CHURCH

Sweaty palms and hearts beating, we entered the school cafeteria, which was to be our new church home. We sat at laminate lunch tables that were flipped over to act as benches. After the service, people began talking to one other, and my family and I stood off to the side. I whispered encouragement to my darling daughter, my fragile introvert. "I know it's awkward and hard not knowing anyone, but I promise it will get easier." I had already given myself the same pep talk at home—I had butterflies in my stomach too. I knew that the first day at a new church with new people was the hardest.

We stood alone, we four. We braced ourselves for the variety of handshakes—some too firm, some limp, some so quick there was no time to squeeze back. And the barrage of new names came and went. We shook and smiled back, doing our best to make a connection and begin establishing ourselves in a new community of believers.

Growing up the daughter of a U. S. Marine Corps dad, I attended many different churches of a variety of denominations. As a military spouse, I relived all those firsts again with every move. Only now, my feelings were multiplied by three as I felt the awkwardness for myself plus my two children.

Despite how uncomfortable we felt, and despite all the hands shaken, names forgotten, and the blur of being "new," we knew we needed to be in church before we unpacked all the boxes, learned our way around town, or met our neighbors. Church would always be our hub.

Each time our family visited a new church, the sense of community was never a guarantee. Some congregations were warm and welcoming, but some were not. For us, the driving force was wanting to hear God's Word preached. We needed to commune with him that way, and we knew if we went to church, his Word would be living and active there in a unique way.

Over the years, we've been pastored by military chaplains, new seminary graduates, and venerable old fellows. Some pastors were wonderful orators and storytellers, some taught like professors, some fumbled the phrases, and some meandered. Still, in one way or another, all of them served us well. All of them read God's Word and did their best to honor it, unpack it, and plant it in our hearts.

Though I have not sat under one pastor my whole life, I have sat under one Spirit. And the Lord has woven his Word into the fabric of my heart in many different ways. But no matter where I lived, it wasn't meeting the neighbors or unpacking the boxes or finding my way around town that made me feel at home—it was the Word of God shared with brothers and sisters in his Spirit, even when I didn't know their names.

DAY 1

READ ROMANS 10:5-17

❝ The personality of Jesus emerged from the Gospels with astonishing consistency. Whenever they were written, they were written in the shadow of a personality so tremendous that Christians who may never have seen him knew him utterly: that strange mixture of unbearable sternness and heartbreaking tenderness.

SHELDON VANAUKEN

❝ You cannot have spiritual life when this book [the Bible] is closed . . . you can't.

CONRAD MBEWE

DAY 2

READ ACTS 20:17-32

> I think the greatest weakness in the church today is that almost no one believes that God invests his power in the Bible. Everyone is looking for power in a program, in a methodology, in a technique, in anything and everything but that in which God has placed it—his Word. He alone has the power to change lives for eternity, and that power is focused on the Scriptures.
>
> R. C. SPROUL

> Christians don't simply learn or study or use Scripture; we assimilate it, take it into our lives in such a way that it gets metabolized into acts of love, cups of cold water, missions into all the world, healing and evangelism and justice in Jesus' name, hands raised in adoration of the Father, feet washed in company with the Son.
>
> EUGENE PETERSON

DAY 3

READ 1 THESSALONIANS 1:1-10

> His commands expose our guilt, making us flee to Jesus the Curse-bearer. His promises turn our trust to Jesus the Law-keeper, who gives us his perfect record by grace alone, through faith alone. Viewed through the lens of Jesus' redeeming work, the law unveils the Spirit's design for renewing us into God's image.
>
> DENNIS JOHNSON

> All of the wonderful obligations of the law will then help us on our way toward godly living and sanctification. Since we cannot be made any more perfect in God's eyes than we already are, we are now free to make the law serve us. It will serve us by making us more thankful for Christ when we see how we fail to obey it, and it will serve us by showing us how to love God and our neighbor as we long to.
>
> ELYSE FITZPATRICK AND DENNIS JOHNSON

DAY 4

> **READ** EZEKIEL 37:1-14

" When the Holy Spirit works in your heart so that the gospel suddenly makes sense, you repent and believe. You become a new person with a new way of looking at life and a new motivation. Now, with the help of the Holy Spirit, you may begin to develop a new understanding of yourself and the world based on the explanation God provides in the Bible.

LUDER G. WHITLOCK

" Though the Bible never uses the word *guidance,* it does talk about a Guide. You may seek guidance, but God desires to give something better: himself. The point I'm making is a profound one. It is more than a play on words. And deep in your heart it is a guide, even more than guidance, that you want. Which would you prefer to have while driving in heavy traffic through a strange city, a complicated set of instructions from someone on the sidewalk or a kindly stranger who says, "Look, I'm on my way there right now. If you'll let me hop in, I'll show you the way."

JOHN WHITE

DAY 5

READ ROMANS 16:25-27

> When you read the word of God, you will also become aware that in your heart you really hate the commands of God. You will see that you are under God's wrath for breaking his commands, and that it is impossible for you to be saved by your own works. Once you realize all these things, you will run to Christ for safety, and trust only in the free grace of God for your justification. Once you are a Christian, you will continue to run to Christ for the strength to keep the law in your daily Christian life.

WALTER MARSHALL

> Mind renewal is a slow, active work. In it, we let God's Word tell us how to think and see and feel. Then life begins to change as the mind changes.

JACKIE HILL PERRY

WEEK 49

READING AND HEARING THE WORD

WESTMINSTER SHORTER CATECHISM QUESTION 90

Q | How is the Word to be read and heard, that it may become effectual to salvation?

A | That the Word may become effectual to salvation, we must attend thereunto with diligence, preparation, and prayer; receive it with faith and love, lay it up in our hearts, and practice it in our lives.

. . . .

PRAY *Keep me feeding in the pastures of thy strengthening Word, searching Scripture to find thee there. Amen.*

. . . .

WORSHIP GOD BY MEDITATING ON PSALM 1

. . . .

COMMIT GOD'S WORD TO MEMORY | PSALM 1:1–2

DAY 1 | Blessed is the man who walks not in the counsel of the wicked,
DAY 2 | nor stands in the way of sinners,
DAY 3 | nor sits in the seat of scoffers;
DAY 4 | but his delight is in the law of the LORD,
DAY 5 | and on his law he meditates day and night.

A MERRY JIG

I awakened to the songs of clamoring birds and the gentle melody of the Gulf waves. The music was an invitation I couldn't refuse. Leaving my husband in the bed, his chest rising and falling in the tell-tale rhythm of deep sleep, I quietly put on a jacket, made some hot tea, and stepped out of our camper with my Bible, journal, and pen. I settled into a folding chair left near the fire pit from the previous night to watch dawn break at the campground. The sun began to shed its early light. Only the animals stirred.

To my left, a fat, fuzzy rodent rustled out of the underbrush—scurrying around, nose to the ground, in search of food. He found a pinecone, slightly taller than he was and much wider in circumference. He grabbed it like I would seize a massive redwood that was too large for me to wrap my arms around. Amused, I wondered what he planned to do with his colossal discovery.

He grasped its mammoth girth and began to bounce it up and down, slamming it to the ground with all his strength. Next, he jumped up off the ground and twisted about, forcing his few ounces of unreliable weight onto the top of the giant. It landed with him on top. He rolled with it, resituated himself, and then leapt up and down again and again, first twirling one way, then the next. Without meaning to, I smiled.

What was he up to? Was this some sort of game he enjoyed playing with large pinecones? I chuckled more than once as he twirled with it in the dust, walloping and working it over tirelessly. This was a well-rehearsed dance. He had done it before. Then it dawned on me: he was trying to get to the pine nuts that were clinging to the center.

He was persistent, furiously single-minded, and patiently optimistic. He knew nourishment was there and that his life depended on that food. I watched as he went from cone to cone, searching for seeds on the ground after he'd led each giant in a merry jig. Sometimes he paused to munch, but often he stored the tiny nuts in his little jowls, saving them for later. I observed for a good fifteen minutes—until he saw me. Then off he went with God's provision in his belly and pouch.

Grateful for the lesson on how to find nourishment in the center of something much larger than myself, I grinned as I watched my dance teacher scamper into the brush.

Then, I opened my Bible and journal and began to waltz.

DAY 1

READ 1 SAMUEL 3:1-10

> Entering the day without a serious meeting with God, over his Word and in prayer, is like entering the battle without tending to your weapons. It's like taking a trip without filling the tires with air or the tank with gas. . . . We replenish our hearts not with sleep, but with the Word of God and prayer. Thousands of saints have discovered throughout the centuries that starting the day by filling the mind with the Word of God will bring more joy and more love and more power than traveling on yesterday's gas.
>
> JOHN PIPER

DAY 2

READ 2 CHRONICLES 34:14-34

> Remember that it is not hasty reading, but serious meditation on holy and heavenly truths, that makes them prove sweet and profitable to the soul. It is not the mere touching of the flower by the bee that gathers honey, but her abiding for a time on the flower that draws out the sweet. It is not he that reads most, but he that meditates most, that will prove to be the choicest, sweetest, wisest, and strongest Christian.

THOMAS BROOKS

> Be very careful that you do not fall into the trap that some people fall into. Do not think that you will love God or live a holy life merely by reading about God in his Word. You can read the Word of God and learn much about God.... However, just learning about these things will not automatically mean you live a godly life. There is a deeper dynamic you must understand. When you meditate upon all God's truth, and upon his character, your conscience will understand how high God's standards of holiness really are. As you see this, you will go in faith to Christ for life and strength to live in holiness.

WALTER MARSHALL AND BRUCE MCRAE

DAY 3

READ EXODUS 24:1-8

> I know not a better rule of reading the Scripture, than to read it through from beginning to end and when we have finished it once, to begin it again. We shall meet with many passages which we can make little improvement of, but not so many in the second reading as in the first, and fewer in the third than in the second: provided we pray to him who has the keys to open our understandings, and to anoint our eyes with his spiritual ointment.
>
> JOHN NEWTON

> It's important to realize that the Bible not only tells a true story; it also demands a response. The authors of Scripture write with intention—their words are meant to provoke a response from the reader. In other words, the Bible is a story that provokes action! It not only informs; it also transforms our life. It's a message that invites us to turn from unbelief and participate in the life of the One who . . . forgives our sin and gives us new life through the Spirit.
>
> MICHAEL EMLET

DAY 4

READ ACTS 17:10-15

> I was sitting in church in the West Indies, tired, distracted and not paying attention to what was going on. I was vaguely aware that the minister was reading scripture, and it was a long passage from the Old Testament, and he was going on and on and I was really not listening. But I heard a woman sitting near me saying something. Not very loudly, but enough for me to hear. As the minister read the scripture I heard her say out loud, "Yes, that is true, yes, that's true." Throughout that chapter she was punctuating the Word of God with those kinds of statements. It startled me awake, and I said, "David, listen! This is God's Word." This brought me back to consciousness that this was God's Word and it was precious and holy.

DAVID CALHOUN

> The reason we come away so cold from reading the Word is, because we do not warm ourselves at the fire of meditation.

THOMAS WATSON

DAY 5

READ ISAIAH 66:1-6

> Meditation is the activity of calling to mind, and thinking over, and dwelling on, and applying to oneself, the various things that one knows about the works and ways and purposes and promises of God. It is an activity of holy thought, consciously performed in the presence of God, under the eye of God, by the help of God, as a means of communion with God. Its purpose is to clear one's mental and spiritual vision of God, and to let his truth make its full and proper impact on one's mind and heart. It is a matter of talking to oneself about God and oneself; it is, indeed, often a matter of arguing with oneself, reasoning oneself out of moods of doubt and unbelief into a clear apprehension of God's power and grace.
>
> J. I. PACKER

> The transforming vision of the glory of Jesus is found in the anointed portrayal of him in the Holy Scripture. When we humbly kneel before the inspired authority of the written Word and diligently seek out the rich treasures buried within it, the Spirit of God shines a light in our hearts awakening us to the person of Jesus. . . . When we eat and drink from the fountain of Scripture, Jesus comes alive in our souls.
>
> SAM STORMS

WEEK 50

WHAT IS BAPTISM

> WESTMINSTER SHORTER CATECHISM QUESTION 94

Q | What is baptism?

A | Baptism is a sacrament, wherein the washing with water in the name of the Father, and of the Son, and of the Holy Spirit, does signify and seal our ingrafting into Christ, and partaking of the benefits of the covenant of grace, and our engagement to be the Lord's.

....

PRAY *May I remember the dignity of my spiritual release, never be too busy to attend to my soul, never be so engrossed with time that I neglect the things of eternity; thus may I not only live, but grow towards thee. Amen.*

....

WORSHIP GOD BY MEDITATING ON PSALM 51

....

COMMIT GOD'S WORD TO MEMORY | PSALM 51:1-2

DAY 1 | Have mercy on me, O God,
DAY 2 | according to your steadfast love;
DAY 3 | according to your abundant mercy blot out my transgressions.
DAY 4 | Wash me thoroughly from my iniquity,
DAY 5 | and cleanse me from my sin.

GETTING ENGAGED

At coffee a few months ago, I asked a friend how she and her husband met. Before she opened her mouth, I'd practically written her response in my mind, complete with a dreamy sunset-at-the-beach proposal. But her version was a little different. "I was so furious with him when he asked me to marry him! We were in the middle of a fight, so the last thing I expected was a tender, romantic proposal."

As I listened to her story, relief washed over me because I had also been fighting with my soon-to-be husband when he asked me to marry him, and that wasn't something I eagerly shared with anyone. We had talked about marriage for over a year, but our timetables for becoming Mr. and Mrs. didn't exactly line up. When he finally did propose, I had graduated from college, moved back to my hometown and into an apartment, and taken a stressful job while he was still in college, hanging out with friends and having a great time. I knew I wanted to marry him—that he was the one for me—but a part of me also thought that a ring on my finger would have saved me from the stress of a new job and starting over in a city that was supposed to feel like home but felt anything but. Life was moving forward, and I felt the pressure to hurry up and get married, but he just didn't—hence, the fight on the day he proposed. He did everything right. He set a romantic mood by reminiscing about times we had come to that particular spot and recalled some great conversations. And while he talked about our dating history together with sentimentality that would make my friends swoon, all I was thinking about was how hungry and cold and mad at him I was. Blinded by my self-absorption, I didn't even realize what was going on: he was asking me to marry him!

The examples of other friends' engagements weren't easy to live up to, either. One friend got engaged in Europe, in a gorgeous seaside town in Italy. Another got engaged on the Fourth of July, with patriotic music playing as fireworks lit the sky. And I carry the shame of feeling as though I ruined my husband's proposal with my bad attitude and selfishness. Hearing my coffee-date friend's story gave me the freedom to share mine with her without fear of being judged. And through our sharing, the truth was realized that, despite our rocky beginnings, God has ordained and redeemed both of our marriages.

While it's not my proudest moment, I've come to love my engagement story because my husband chose me when I was at my worst—ungrateful, thinking of myself, and trying to live and seek fulfillment in the wrong things. It was *then* that he declared his love; *then* that he called me his. Not because I was loveable, but because he loved me even when I wasn't.

DAY 1

READ COLOSSIANS 2:11–15

" We don't think of our baptism enough. Whether you were baptized as an adult or a child or even as an infant, you should think of your baptism often. This may mean remembering the actual event of your baptism or simply remembering that you are baptized and have been sealed with the promise of God's forgiveness. When you trip up and overeat to the point of gluttony, when you lose it with your kids, when you lament that you have such a critical spirit, you should remember your baptism. By faith you are forgiven and have been washed clean. Baptism is that reminder, a symbol of forgiveness we have received.

KEVIN DEYOUNG

DAY 2

READ GENESIS 17:1-21

❝ Sheep carry a mark on their wool to show to whom they belong—a sign of their shepherd. . . . Our baptism is the mark of our Shepherd, Jesus. . . . Remember the promises you were given at your baptism: Jesus knows you and he loves you. Let those promises wash over you like the water off the pastor's hands! And then run with the song to those who haven't heard about our Shepherd. Sing the songs of the good pasture and of the Good Shepherd who knows and loves his sheep.

ELIZABETH HARWELL

❝ Baptism is not only a sacrament of our union with Christ; it is also a sacrament of our communion as the body of Christ.

MICHAEL HORTON

DAY 3

READ GALATIANS 3:23-29

> If you want God's grace, all you need is need, all you need is nothing. But that kind of spiritual humility is hard to muster. We come to God saying, "Look at all I've done," or maybe "Look at all I've suffered." God, however, wants us to look to him.
>
> TIM KELLER

> There is an authentic identification of God's people with Christ's humiliation and his exaltation, and that identification with Christ is signified by baptism. An individual's baptism says to the world, "I belong to Christ and he belongs to me." For this reason, the New Testament speaks of our being buried with Christ in baptism. Our baptism signifies our identity with him in his humiliation and in his exaltation—in his suffering and in his resurrection.
>
> R. C. SPROUL

DAY 4

READ EPHESIANS 5:25–27

“ The sun had come up brilliantly after a heavy rain, and the trees were glistening and very wet. On some impulse, plain exuberance, I suppose, the fellow jumped up and caught hold of a branch, and a storm of luminous water came pouring down on the two of them, and they laughed and took off running, the girl sweeping water off her hair and her dress as if she were a little bit disgusted, but she wasn't. It was a beautiful thing to see, like something from a myth. I don't know why I thought of that now, except perhaps because it is easy to believe in such moments that water was made primarily for blessing, and only secondarily for growing vegetables or doing the wash. I wish I had paid more attention to it. My list of regrets may seem unusual, but who can know that they are, really. This is an interesting planet. It deserves all the attention you can give it.

MARILYNNE ROBINSON

DAY 5

READ HEBREWS 10:19-25

> Christian baptism is a naming ceremony. The baptized person is given a name, not the name on a baptismal certificate, but the name of the Triune God. A flustered pastor performing an infant baptism may address little Martha as Margaret, but he is not giving her that name. The name that he gives her is the name of the Triune God. Baptism gives Christians their family name, the name they bear as those called the children of God. . . . If we understand the giving of God's name, we will recognize how fully baptism centers on Jesus Christ, the son of God. To bear his name is to be united to him, who gives us his righteousness and bears our sins; it is to share his glory.
>
> EDMUND P. CLOWNEY

WEEK 51
WHAT IS THE LORD'S SUPPER

WESTMINSTER SHORTER CATECHISM QUESTION 96

Q | What is the Lord's Supper?

A | The Lord's Supper is a sacrament, in which, by giving and receiving bread and wine, according to Christ's appointment, his death is showed forth; and the worthy receivers are, not after a corporal and carnal manner, but by faith, made partakers of his body and blood, with all his benefits, to their spiritual nourishment, and growth in grace.

PRAY *As the outward elements nourish my body, so may thy indwelling Spirit invigorate my soul, until that day when I hunger and thirst no more, and sit with Jesus at his heavenly feast. Amen.*

WORSHIP GOD BY MEDITATING ON PSALM 23

COMMIT GOD'S WORD TO MEMORY | JOHN 6:35

DAY 1 | Jesus said to them,
DAY 2 | "I am the bread of life;
DAY 3 | whoever comes to me shall not hunger,
DAY 4 | and whoever believes in me
DAY 5 | shall never thirst."

RIBS

'll have the ribs."

"Sorry, sir. We just ran out of ribs."

You've got to be kidding. This, after waiting in line for twenty minutes, subjecting my senses to smells so spicy and sweet I'd already begun mentally licking my fingers. I sighed (dramatically, I'll admit) and ordered something else.

A few weeks later as I recalled the disappointing ribs experience, I found myself insatiably hungry once again, but this time in an entirely different arena. While at our denomination's annual meeting, I arrived a few minutes late to the opening worship service. It was standing room only, without even a place to stand. So I found a seat in the overflow section in front of a monitor where I could watch and listen. As I did, my heart stirred in response to the liturgy, songs, prayers, and sermon. When the pastor stood before the communion table at the end of the service with the bread and cup in front of him, describing how Jesus comes to meet us, give us grace, and to nourish and strengthen our souls, I realized my own soul was famished. Jesus was being offered inside the sanctuary, and I had to get in.

I had to have Jesus.

Opening the doors, I squeezed inside among the crowd, eagerly watching as the trays were passed. My hunger grew. The trays came nearer and became emptier, and I became desperate as I realized my spiritual starvation. Maneuvering my way forward, I came to the loaf, pulled off a piece, and placed it in my mouth. As I tasted the bread, I sensed fresh hope, courage, and joy. Jesus didn't leave me disappointed. I was instantly filled and refreshed by the One who came to die so I might really live.

But the experience highlighted some lingering questions: *Why is my soul not that hungry every time I take the Lord's Supper? Why am I not that desperate on a daily basis? Why do I sometimes feel more urgency when waiting for ribs than I do when waiting for Jesus?* I know Scripture—I know the One who promises not to leave me hungry and disappointed. But the serpent's lie that God is withholding good from me screams so loudly that I, like so many Christ-followers before me, listen to the lie. Perhaps that's why Jesus' reason for eating the bread and drinking the cup is to *remember*. To remember *him*, the Bread of Life (John 6:35), the Lamb of God (John 1:29), who takes away the sins of the world and satisfies us in parched places (Isaiah 58:11).

DAY 1

READ 1 CORINTHIANS 11:17-34

> This is the greatest mystery of all the practicals of our Christian religion, a way of receiving Christ by eating and drinking, something peculiar, that is not in the hearing of the Word nor in any other part of divine worship whatsoever; a peculiar participation of Christ, a peculiar acting of faith towards Christ.
>
> JOHN OWEN

> We are weak. God knows that. . . . He indulges our weakness and doubt, offering us physical, tangible tokens of inward grace. Instead of condemning us for doubt, fear, anxiety and faithlessness, Christ offered himself as food for the journey in the desert—the Bread of heaven.
>
> MICHAEL HORTON

DAY 2

READ LUKE 22:14-23

“ To aid our encounter with the "immense invisibles," God acti-
vates all five senses. We see the elements; we hear the word of the
cross; we hold the loaf and the cup; we smell and taste them both.
The gospel, as proclaimed both verbally and visibly, is "the power
of God for salvation," for wholeness in every sense of the word.
The heart in all its dimensions is nourished. . . . Appropriating its
saving benefits liberates us from paralyzing guilt; feeding upon
Christ provides healing for deep emotional wounds. Our wills are
activated. Contemplation of Christ's sacrifice moves us to a sacrifice of our own.

J. KNOX CHAMBERLIN

“ In the word preached, we hear Christ's voice; in the sacrament, we
feed on him. . . . The word preached begets grace, the Lord's Supper
nourishes it.

THOMAS WATSON

DAY 3

READ JOHN 6:35-58

You called and cried out loud and shattered my deafness. You were radiant and resplendent, you put to flight my blindness. You were fragrant, and I drew in my breath and now pant after you. I tasted you, and I feel but hunger and thirst for you. You touched me, and I am set on fire to attain the peace which is yours.

AUGUSTINE

Jesus Christ still stands in the midst of Christian congregations to teach them with his Holy Word. And he still sits at table to dine with lowly sinners in his Holy Supper. As it was in Jerusalem in the breaking of bread, as it was in Jericho at the table of Zacchaeus, so it is each time we eat the bread and drink the cup of the Lord. Salvation comes to call. The bread of heaven comes down to feed us with his body once broken and to give us to drink of his blood once shed for the forgiveness of sins. And there is life in that blood; for it is the blood of God.

HAROLD L. SENKBEIL

DAY 4

READ EXODUS 12:1-32

" We bring ourselves to the eucharistic table and enter into that grand four-fold shape of the liturgy that shapes us: taking, blessing, breaking, giving—the life of Jesus taken and blessed, broken and distributed. That eucharistic life now shapes our lives as we give ourselves, Christ in us, to be taken, blessed, broken, and distributed in lives of witness and service, justice and healing.

But that is not the American way. The great American innovation in congregation is to turn it into a consumer enterprise. We Americans have developed a culture of acquisition, an economy that is dependent on wanting more, *requiring* more. We have a huge advertising industry designed to stir up appetites we didn't even know we had. We are insatiable.

EUGENE PETERSON

" The Lord's Supper is a sign-action that displays the gospel and, together with the preached Word, draws us into the drama of God's work. Through the Word preached and received in the Lord's Supper, we encounter and receive Jesus Christ by the Spirit. In him, we find forgiveness and new life, justification and sanctification. In him, we receive nourishment and enter into loving fellowship.

J. TODD BILLINGS

DAY 5

READ REVELATION 19:1-9

" We don't come to the table to fight or to defend. We don't come to prove or to conquer, to draw lines in the sand or to stir up trouble. We come to the table because our hunger brings us there. We come with a need, with fragility, with an admission of our humanity. The table is the great equalizer, the level playing field many of us have been looking everywhere for. The table is the place where the doing stops, the trying stops, the masks are removed, and we allow ourselves to be nourished, like children. We allow someone else to meet our need. In a world that prides people on not having needs, on going longer and faster, on going without, on powering through, the table is a place of safety and rest and humanity, where we are allowed to be as fragile as we feel.

SHAUNA NIEQUIST

WEEK 52

WHAT IS PRAYER

WESTMINSTER SHORTER CATECHISM QUESTION 98

Q | What is prayer?

A | Prayer is an offering up of our desires unto God, for things agreeable to his will, in the name of Christ, with confession of our sins, and thankful acknowledgment of his mercies.

. . . .

PRAY *Teach me to live by prayer as well as by providence, for myself, soul, body, children, family, church; give me a heart frameable to thy will so might I live in prayer and honor thee. Amen.*

. . . .

WORSHIP GOD BY MEDITATING ON PSALM 62

. . . .

COMMIT GOD'S WORD TO MEMORY | PHILIPPIANS 4:6-7

DAY 1 | Do not be anxious about anything,
DAY 2 | but in everything by prayer and supplication with thanksgiving
DAY 3 | let your requests be made known to God.
DAY 4 | And the peace of God, which surpasses all understanding,
DAY 5 | will guard your hearts and your minds in Christ Jesus.

PRAYERS OF THE PEOPLE

For most of my life, I've believed that the Lord is faithful and hears the prayers of his people, but that promise took on new depth in the hours, days, and weeks after my husband unexpectedly passed away. In an instant, my life changed. I was faced with a barrage of decisions—notifying friends, making funeral arrangements, telling my children that their daddy was gone. It was all so overwhelming and seemed impossible.

But I found solace in the Lord and the ways he worked through his Spirit, knowing none of what I was able to do in those dark days (nor anything since) was ever possible in my own strength. I have sought the Lord since I was a child, for as long as I can remember, but have never experienced the power of prayer like I did in those difficult days.

My desire was that the Lord would be glorified in my husband's death. I uttered this prayer many times as I began to make arrangements for the funeral. The day before the service, as I was asking the Lord for guidance, almost immediately the order, song choices, and message became clear. The next day, even though I knew what the day held, I was able to get up out of bed, get dressed, and care for my young sons. I look back in awe because there is no doubt that God gave me the strength I needed through his Spirit, and continuing prayers of other believers.

When I arrived at my home to begin the visitation, I was exhausted. It had been an unbearable day at the funeral home, being asked to make decisions that no thirty-six-year-old should have to make. I dreaded facing friends and family for the first time since his death. I begged the Lord for strength and prayed Psalm 61:2, "Lead me to the rock that is higher than I." The Lord fulfilled his promise. For two hours, I stood, grieved, and received comfort from dear friends. One friend even handed me a tube of waterproof mascara—a small and seemingly meaningless gesture that meant everything to me in the moment. The Lord continued to encourage and strengthen me as friend after friend, face after face, filed by me at our front door and told me time and time again, "I am praying for you." Those words may not seem like much—they express such a simple sentiment—but their words were raw and sheer power for my soul. I knew the prayers of the Lord's saints were sustaining me.

Even now, months later, the Lord continues to sustain us as we connect with him in prayer. Every night my boys and I make two specific requests of God: we ask for his mercy and provision. And in his goodness, he does not fail to answer. Through prayer, he imparts to us the strength, guidance, and wisdom we need.

DAY 1

> **READ** MATTHEW 6:5-15

> Is your own personal prayer life characterized by the simplicity, childlike candor, boundless trust, and easy familiarity of a little one crawling up in Daddy's lap? An assured knowing that the daddy doesn't care if the child falls asleep, starts playing with toys, or even starts chatting with little friends, because the daddy knows the child has essentially chosen to be with him for that moment? Is that the spirit of your interior prayer life?
>
> BRENNAN MANNING

> True prayer is bound up with a persuasion of our inability and complete dependence on God.
>
> IAIN MURRAY

DAY 2

READ 1 SAMUEL 1:1-20

❝ Prayer is a refusal to live as an outsider to my God and my own soul.

EUGENE PETERSON

❝ We will be tempted to give up on prayer. It takes so long, the world moves so slowly, justice seems so far away. He [Jesus] is calling us to faithfulness in unfailing prayer for the manifestation of righteousness. The temptation in petitionary prayer is always to submit, to acquiesce to what is, to come to terms with the unjust and unsaved world around us. We lose our anger at the wrongness of what is and lose with it our desire to persevere. We succumb to Doris Day theology: *que será, será,* the situation is unchangeable, what is will always be. No, says God, do not faint. And what is the mark of that confidence that God does build his kingdom of grace and justice? Shamelessness in prayer to the Father.

HARVIE M. CONN

DAY 3

READ PHILIPPIANS 1:3-11

❝ God not only has spoken clearly and powerfully to us through Christ and the Scriptures, He also has a Very Large Ear continuously open to us. He will hear every prayer of his children, even when our prayers are weaker than a snowflake.

DONALD S. WHITNEY

❝ Prayer in the time of trouble brings comfort, help, hope, and blessings, which, while not removing the trouble, enable the saint the better to bear it and to submit to the will of God. Prayer opens the eyes to see God's hand in trouble. Prayer does not interpret God's providences, but it does justify them and recognize God in them. Prayer enables us to see wised ends in trouble. Prayer in trouble drives us away from unbelief, saves us from doubt, and delivers from all vain and foolish questionings because of our painful experiences.

E. M. BOUNDS

DAY 4

READ LUKE 18:1-17

“ When a man is speaking to God he is at his very acme. It is the highest activity of the human soul, and therefore it is at the same time the ultimate test of a man's true spiritual condition. There is nothing that tells the truth about us as Christian people so much as our prayer life. Everything we do in the Christian life is easier than prayer. . . . Ultimately, therefore, a man discovers the real condition of his spiritual life when he examines himself in private, when he is alone with God.

D. MARTYN LLOYD-JONES

“ Deep in our psyches we want an experience with God or an experience in prayer. Once we make that our quest, we lose God. *You don't experience God; you get to know him.* You submit to him. You enjoy him. He is, after all, a person.

Consequently, a praying life isn't something you accomplish in a year. It is a journey of a lifetime. The same is true of learning how to love your spouse or a good friend. You never stop learning this side of heaven.

PAUL E. MILLER

DAY 5

READ PHILIPPIANS 4:4-9

❝ Prayer is the open admission that without Christ we can do nothing. And prayer is the turning away from ourselves to God in the confidence that he will provide the help we need. Prayer humbles us as needy and exalts God as wealthy.

JOHN PIPER

❝ God will answer your prayers better than you think. Of course, one will not always get exactly what he has asked for. . . . We all have sorrows and disappointments, but one must never forget that, if commended to God, they will issue in good. . . . His own solution is far better than any we could conceive.

FANNY CROSBY

POSTFACE

For holidays and special events, our music ministry often has a full choir. On those days it's not unusual for me to be moved to tears—though not for the reasons you might expect. While every element of their performances lean toward extraordinary, it's not typically the excellence of the music, song selection, or instrumentation responsible for the heightened emotion. No, what happens has more to do with the opportunity to look on the faces of those who make up the full choir. From the vantage point of my congregant seat, I recognize friends and acquaintances and I know so many of their stories. I see the hurt of miscarriage and infertility. I know the struggle of caring for aging parents. I see the couple who knows the heartbreak of the wayward and unrepentant child. There is the pain of singleness one woman doesn't feel called to. These are not mere faces in a crowd but rather fellow members of the church body I love and long to serve.

And they are worshiping.

Their very act of worship moves me and softens my often cold, self-righteous, and severe heart. It's a heart that longs to embrace the truth that it is kept and held by the Father who made it, but in reality struggles to live out that beautiful truth on a daily basis. I see the stories on the faces of those I know in the choir and I remember God's faithfulness to me in my own story, and together *we glorify God* and lean into *enjoying him forever.*

When I lift my eyes and see the chorus singing his renown, my life is no longer about me, but rather the chorus of we—then, with grace upon grace, it's not about us either. For I remember what we are doing—how we are all singing the glories of the One who saw fit to relentlessly chase after and save us. We are all bringing an offering of praise to the One who envelops us into his triune self, and then urges us into life-giving community with one another.

Believer in Jesus, we never sing for ourselves and we never sing solo. We sing for the glory of God alongside the body—the invisible church of God's elect throughout the entirety of history. The heavenly communion of saints, full in their glory, now seated with Christ in the heavenly places, are belting out the praise of reckless abandon and perfect pitch alongside us. Even now, this side of heaven, may we remember how they join us.

As I've had the pleasure to help curate this devotional, God has grown in me a deep appreciation for believers who have already gone on—even centuries before—and I'm struck by our *sameness*. While these pages hold the stories of Oak Mountain Presbyterian Church, we are not unique. In each gospel-preaching church around the world, you could find similar stories of God's faithfulness in trial, kindness in joy, and presence in suffering. You would see the trace of the God of the ages working faith into the hearts of his believers.

It won't be long now before we will find ourselves part of church history as well. May we join the chorus of all the saints—past, present, and future—who testify: he never left our side. And may we testify alongside those who have gone before, alongside those of the Westminster Assembly, and beside believers in Jesus who haven't yet been born: he is worthy of all worship and delight.

Soli Deo Gloria.
Holly Mackle
with Cara Johnson, Greg Poole, Matt Redmond,
and Elisabeth Welty

ACKNOWLEDGMENTS

The contributors would like to thank Dr. Stephen Estock, Marlys Roos, and the Committee on Discipleship Ministries (CDM) for their enthusiasm and support of this project. We are grateful for your faithful ministry to the PCA and beyond. Thank you to Lisa Stilwell, whose thoughtful editorial eye melded the stories and voices found in these pages, and to Greg Jackson of Thinkpen Design for bringing our vision to life. Our heartfelt thanks to Banner of Truth Trust, who graciously allowed us to include portions of prayers from their book, *Valley of Vision*, as well as Andrew Peterson, who allowed his song "The Good Confession (I Believe)" to inspire our title. This song, plus Andrew's responsive song "Is He Worthy" set the tone for the heart behind this project: reaching up in worship of the One True God, and reaching out to do so together, in community. Additional thanks go to Val Peterson and Kayla Neely for their input and direction. List of Contributors:

Keri Adams
Braxton Baker
Linda Barrett
Joie Black
Katy Blackburn
Mary Branch
Nancy Carroll
Emily Dagostin
Jim Doggett
Lisa Donohue
Bob Flayhart
Meg Flowers
Drew Goneke
Robyn Granberry
Melany Guzzo
Justin Hale
Jessica Hale
Sandra Hardy

Sue Harris
Varina Hart
Ann Maura Hinton
Billy Ivey
Cara Johnson
Ken Jones
Stu Jones
Kara Jones
Lauren Kirkland
Britta Lafont
Barbara Lindsey
Mark Long
David Mackle
Holly Mackle
Tim McCracken
Kristy McKinney
Jim Murdock
Tom Patton

Val Peterson
Jennifer Phillips
Greg Poole
Gary Purdy
Matt Redmond
Anne Riley
Jason Sears
Dana Smith
Tyler Tilford
Chad Walker
John Welch
Elisabeth Welty
Sarah Wentworth
Chase Williams
Brooke Wingard
Tirzah Zaccagni

NOTES

WEEK ONE:

J. I. Packer, *Knowing God* (Downers Grove: InterVarsity Press, 1993).

Edward T. Welch, *Running Scared: Fear, Worry, and the God of Rest* (Greensboro: New Growth Press, 2007).

Ron Livingston, *Office Space*. Directed by Mike Judge. (Los Angeles: Twentieth Century Fox. 1999), DVD.

D. Martyn Lloyd-Jones, *God's Ultimate Purpose* (Grand Rapids, Baker House, 1978).

Augustine, *The Works of Saint Augustine: A Translation for the 21st Century*. Translated by Edmund Hill and John E. Rotelle (Brooklyn: New City Press, 1990).

C. S. Lewis, *Reflections on the Psalms* (New York: Harcourt, 1958).

A. W. Tozer, *Pursuit of God* (Abbotsford: Aneko Press, 2015).

Thomas Watson, *A Body of Divinity: Contained in Sermons Upon the Westminster Assembly's Catechism* (London: Banner of Truth Trust, 1965).

Joe Loconte, *A Hobbit, A Wardrobe, and a Great War: How J.R.R. Tolkien and C. S. Lewis Rediscovered Faith, Friendship, and Heroism in the Cataclysm of 1914-1918* (Nashville: Nelson Books, 2017).

Jared C. Wilson, *Gospel Wakefulness* (Wheaton: Crossway, 2011).

WEEK TWO:

J.K. Rowling and Mary GrandPré, *Harry Potter and the Prisoner of Azkaban* (New York: Arthur A. Levine Books, 1999).

Thomas Merton, *The Sign of Jonas* (New York: Harcourt, Brace, 1953).

J. I. Packer, *Knowing God* (Downers Grove: InterVarsity Press, 1993).

Louisa May Alcott, *Little Women* (New York: Scholastic, 1954).

James C. Wilhoit and Evan B. Howard, *Discovering Lectio Divina: Bringing Scripture into Ordinary Life* (Downers Grove: Formatio/IVP Books, 2012).

Gabriela Mistral, *Desolation: A Bilingual Edition*, translated by Michael P. Predmore and Liliana Baltra (Ithaca, NY: Latin American Literary Review Press, 2013).

Rosaria Butterfield, *The Secret Thoughts of an Unlikely Convert: An English Professor's Journey into Christian Faith* (Pittsburgh: Crown & Covenant, 2012).

Samuel Taylor Coleridge, *Confessions of an Inquiring Spirit.* (London: Cassell & Company, 1892).

C. S. Lewis, *Mere Christianity* (New York: Harper Collins, 2001).

John R. W. Stott, *Culture and the Bible* (Westmont, IL: InterVarsity Press, 1979).

WEEK THREE:

J. C. Ryle, *Expository Thoughts on the Gospels, John, Volume III* (Cambridge and London: James Clarke & Co. Ltd, 1969).

Stephen Smallman, *The Walk: Steps for New and Renewed Followers of Jesus* (Phillipsburg: P&R, 2009).

Leif Enger, *Peace Like a River* (New York: Atlantic Monthly Press, 2002).

Jen Wilkin, *Women of the Word: How to Study the Bible with Both Our Hearts and Our Minds* (Wheaton: Crossway, 2014).

David Powlison, "If you look at God through the lens of your human experience, you do so at your peril," Facebook, January 26, 2018 https://www.facebook.com/ccef.org/?hc_ref=ART140EDDXHyXC8-dxVf2y4YD1bkwsE4Wx3qK9tB95cyV4oVQkV8iSVAV6uQwp6C1ac&fref=nf

Elisabeth Elliot, *Discipline: The Glad Surrender* (Grand Rapids: Revell, 1982).

Michael R. Emlet, *CrossTalk: Where Life & Scripture Meet* (Greensboro: New Growth Press, 2009).

J. A. Motyer, *Look to the Rock: An Old Testament Background to Our Understanding of Christ* (Leicester: Inter-Varsity Press, 1996).

William Cowper, "Tirocinium: or, A Review of Schools," in *Cowper: Poetical Works,* H. S. Milford, 4th ed., corrections and additions Norma Russell (London: Oxford University Press, 1967).

Paul D. Tripp, *Broken-Down House: Living Productively in a World Gone Bad* (Wapwallopen, PA: Shepherd Press, 2009).

WEEK FOUR:

Thomas Watson, *A Body of Divinity: Contained in Sermons Upon the Westminster Assembly's Catechism* (London: Banner of Truth Trust, 1965).

Flannery O'Connor and Sally Fitzgerald, *The Habit of Being: Letters* (New York: Farrar, Straus, Giroux, 1979).

Annie Dillard, *Teaching a Stone to Talk: Expeditions and Encounters* (New York: Harper & Row, 1982).

Roland H. Bainton, *Here I Stand: A Life of Martin Luther* (New York: Abingdon-Cokesbury, 1950).

Jen Wilkin, *None Like Him: 10 Ways God is Different From Us (And Why That's a Good Thing)* (Wheaton, Illinois: Crossway, 2016).

A. W. Tozer, *The Knowledge of the Holy: The Attributes of God, Their Meaning in the Christian Life* (San Francisco: Harper & Row, 1978).

Joe Thorn, *Note to Self: The Discipline of Preaching to Yourself* (Wheaton: Crossway, 2011).

A. W. Tozer, *The Knowledge of the Holy: The Attributes of God, Their Meaning in the Christian Life* (San Francisco: Harper & Row, 1978).

Joni Eareckson Tada, *A Place of Healing: Wrestling with the Mysteries of Suffering, Pain, and God's Sovereignty.* (Colorado Springs: David C. Cook, 2015).

R. C. Sproul, *The Holiness of God* (Wheaton: Tyndale House, 1985).

Hilary of Poitiers, *De Trinitate* (Scotts Valley, CA: Create Space, 2012).

WEEK FIVE:

Attributed to Martin Luther

D. Martyn Lloyd-Jones quoted in Steven J. Lawson, and Max E. Anders, *Psalms 76-150.* (Nashville: Holman Reference, 2006).

A. W. Tozer, *The Knowledge of the Holy: The Attributes of God, Their Meaning in the Christian Life* (San Francisco: Harper & Row, 1978).

Augustine, *The Confessions of Augustine in Modern English*, ed. Sherwood E. Wirt (Grand Rapids: Zondervan, 1977).

J. I. Packer, *Knowing God* (Downers Grove: InterVarsity Press, 1973).

Peter Jeffery, *Bitesize Theology* (Darlington: Evangelical Press, 2000).

James M. Boice, *The Sovereign God* (Downers Grove: InterVarsity Press, 1978).

Victor Hugo, *Les Misérables* (London: Penguin Classics, 2012).

William B. Ullathorne, *Patience and Humility: A Handbook for Christians* (Manchester: Sophia Institute Press, 1998).

WEEK SIX:

Charles R. Swindoll, *Wisdom for the Way: Wise Words for Busy People* (Nashville: J. Countryman, 2001).

Michael Green, *Illustrations for Biblical Preaching* (Grand Rapids: Baker Book House, 1993).

Charles Spurgeon, *Morning and Evening* (Fearn: Christian Focus, 1994).

David Kinnaman, *Good Faith: Being a Christian When Society Thinks You're Irrelevant and Extreme* (Grand Rapids: Baker Books, 2016).

C. S. Lewis, *Mere Christianity* (New York: Harper Collins, 2001).

Max Lucado, *Traveling Light* (Nashville: Thomas Nelson, 2010).

C. S. Lewis, *Mere Christianity* (New York: Harper Collins, 2001).

Eugene Peterson, *Christ Plays in Ten Thousand Places* (Grand Rapids: Eerdmans, 2005).

Sinclair B. Ferguson, *Devoted to God: Blueprint for Sanctification* (Edinburgh: Banner of Truth Trust, 2016).

WEEK SEVEN:

Jonathan Edwards. "Christians a Chosen Generation, A Royal Priesthood, A Holy Nation, A Peculiar People," https://www.monergism.com/thethreshold/articles/onsite/chosengeneration.html, accessed September 6, 2018.

A. W. Tozer, *The Knowledge of the Holy: The Attributes of God, Their Meaning in the Christian Life* (San Francisco: Harper & Row, 1978).

Elton Trueblood as quoted, https://www.allchristianquotes.org/quotes/D_Elton_Trueblood/1051/, accessed September 6, 2018.

Beryl Markham, *West with the Night*. (New York: Open Road Media, 2012).

Joni Eareckson Tada, *The God I Love: A Lifetime of Walking with Jesus*. (Grand Rapids: Zondervan, 2003).

John R. Stott, *Basic Christianity* (Grand Rapids: Eerdmans, 1971).

Attributed to Archbishop William Temple

John Calvin, *Institutes of the Christian Religion* (Peabody: Hendrickson Publishers, 2008).

R. C. Sproul, *Truths We Confess: A Layman's Guide to the Westminster Confession of Faith*, (Phillipsburg: P&R, 2006).

Philip Yancey, *Where Is God When It Hurts?* (Grand Rapids: Zondervan, 1990).

WEEK EIGHT:

Ann Voskamp, *One Thousand Gifts: A Dare to Live Fully Right Where You Are* (Grand Rapids: Zondervan, 1996).

Timothy Keller and Katherine L. Alsdorf, *Every Good Endeavor: Connecting Your Work to God's Work* (New York: Dutton, 2012).

Eugene H. Peterson, *Christ Plays in Ten Thousand Places: A Conversation in Spiritual Theology* (Grand Rapids: W.B. Eerdmans, 2005).

A. W. Pink, *The Sovereignty of God* (Radford, VA: Wilder Publications, 2009).

Victor Hugo, *Les Misérables* (London: Penguin Classics, 2012).

Rosaria Butterfield, *The Secret Thoughts of an Unlikely Convert: An English Professor's Journey into Christian Faith* (Pittsburgh: Crown & Covenant, 2012).

R. C. Sproul, *The Holiness of God* (Wheaton: Tyndale House, 1985).

Jonathan Edwards, *The Religious Affections* (Edinburgh: Banner of Truth Trust, 1986).

Edward T. Welch, *Running Scared: Fear, Worry, and the God of Rest* (Greensboro: New Growth Press, 2007).

Jerry Bridges, *Trusting God* (Colorado Springs: NavPress, 2017).

WEEK NINE:

Timothy Keller, and Katherine L. Alsdorf, *Every Good Endeavor: Connecting Your Work to God's Work* (New York: Dutton, 2012).

Mark Batterson, *Whisper: How to Hear the Voice of God* (Colorado Springs: Multnomah, 2017).

Luder G. Whitlock, *The Spiritual Quest: Pursuing Christian Maturity* (Grand Rapids: Baker Books, 2000).

R. C. Sproul, *The Holiness of God* (Wheaton: Tyndale House, 1985).

John Calvin, *Institutes of the Christian Religion* (Peabody: Hendrickson Publishers, 2008).

Robert Capon (@Robert_F_Capon), "The world is to God as wine and chocolate are to us," Twitter, November 20, 2014, www.twitter.com/robert_f_capon/status/535499126222237967

Elizabeth Barrett Browning, "Aurora Leigh," *The Oxford Book of English Mystical Verse* eds. D. H. S. Nicholson and A. H. E. Lee (New York: Bartleby.com, 2000).

Michelangelo as quoted in Emilie Barnes, *Keep It Simple for Busy Women: Inspiring Ideas to Reduce Stress and Enjoy Life More* (Eugene, OR: Harvest House, 2002).

John Calvin as quoted, www.christianitytoday.com/history/issues/issue-28/1536-john-calvin-publishes-institutes-of-christian-religion.html, accessed June 27, 2018.

A. W. Tozer, *The Knowledge of the Holy: The Attributes of God, Their Meaning in the Christian Life* (San Francisco: Harper & Row, 1978).

WEEK TEN:

Francis A. Schaeffer, *Escape from Reason* (Downers Grove: InterVarsity Press, 2014).

Philip Yancey, *Reaching for the Invisible God* (Grand Rapids: Zondervan, 2002).

Rankin Wilbourne, *Union with Christ: The Way to Know and Enjoy God* (Colorado Springs, CO: David C Cook, 2016).

Carolyn Custis James, *The Gospel of Ruth: Loving God Enough to Break the Rules* (Grand Rapids: Zondervan, 2008).

R. C. Sproul, *The Holiness of God* (Wheaton: Tyndale House, 1985).

C. S. Lewis, *The Lion, the Witch, and the Wardrobe* (New York: HarperCollins, 2008).

Francis Schaeffer, *Death in the City* (Wheaton: Crossway, 2002).

Sally Lloyd-Jones, *Baby's Hug-a-Bible* (New York. Harper Collins. 2010).

Richard L. Pratt, *Designed for Dignity: What God Has Made it Possible for You to Be* (Phillipsburg: P&R, 1993).

John Donne, "First Prebend Sermon." Sermon at St. Paul's, London, England, May 8, 1625.

WEEK ELEVEN:

Eugene H. Peterson, *The Jesus Way: A Conversation On the Ways That Jesus Is the Way* (Grand Rapids: William B. Eerdmans, 2007).

Shawn D Wright, *Our Sovereign Refuge: The Pastoral Theology of Theodore Beza* (Eugene, OR: Wipf & Stock, 2006).

Heidelberg Catechism

J. R. R. Tolkien, *The Hobbit* (New York: Houghton Mifflin Harcourt, 2012).

Paul D. Tripp, *Broken-Down House: Living Productively in a World Gone Bad* (Wapwallopen, PA: Shepherd Press, 2009).

Charles H. Spurgeon, "The Unconquerable King," from Metropolitan Tabernacle Pulpit, Vol. 16 Sermon No. 949, delivered Sept. 4, 1870. For more info, visit www.spurgeon.org/resource-library/sermons/the-unconquerable-king

The Metropolitan Pulpit, Vol. XI (London: Passmore & Alabaster, 1871).

A. W. Pink, *The Attributes of God* (Grand Rapids: Baker Book House, 1975).

Joni Eareckson Tada and Steve Estes, *A Step Further* (Grand Rapids: Zondervan, 1978).

Thomas Reade, *Christian Retirement or Spiritual Exercises of the Heart* (New York: Robert Carter, 1848).

WEEK TWELVE:

R. C. Sproul, *Truths We Confess: A Layman's Guide to the Westminster Confession of Faith* (Phillipsburg: P&R, 2006).

Friedrich W. Nietzsche and Helen Zimmern, *Beyond Good and Evil: Prelude to a Philosophy of the Future* (Mineola: Dover Publications, 1997).

Sinclair B. Ferguson, *The Whole Christ: Legalism, Antinomianism, and Gospel Assurance: Why the Marrow Controversy Still Matters* (Wheaton: Crossway, 2016).

Henry Miller, *The Wisdom of the Heart* (New York: New Directions, 1960).

Sidney Greidanus, *Preaching Christ from Genesis: Foundations for Expository Sermons* (Grand Rapids: William B. Eerdmans, 2007).

John Milton, *First Six Books of Milton's Paradise Lost, Rendered into Grammatical Construction* Found Gale ECCO, 2018.

R. C. Sproul, *Truths We Confess: A Layman's Guide to the Westminster Confession of Faith* (Phillipsburg: P&R, 2006).

Lord Byron, *Manfred* (London: John Murray, 1817).

Arthur Pink, *The Divine Covenants* (Grand Rapids: Baker Book House, 1973).

Blaise Pascal, *Pensees* (London: Penguin Books, 1993).

WEEK THIRTEEN

Elyse Fitzpatrick, *Good News for Weary Women: Escaping the Bondage of To-Do Lists, Steps, and Bad Advice* (Carol Stream, IL: Tyndale, 2014).

Richard Sibbes, *The Bruised Reed* (Carlisle, PA: Puritan Paperbacks, 1998).

David Kinnaman, *Good Faith: Being a Christian When Society Thinks You're Irrelevant and Extreme* (Grand Rapids: Baker Books, 2016).

Augustine, *The Confessions of Augustine in Modern English*. ed. Sherwood E. Wirt (Grand Rapids: Zondervan, 1977).

Ann Voskamp, *One Thousand Gifts: A Dare to Live Fully Right Where You Are* (Grand Rapids: Zondervan, 1996).

H. C. G. Moule, *Charles Simeon* (London: Methuen & Co. 1892).

Francis A. Schaeffer, *How Should We Then Live? The Rise and Decline of Western Thought and Culture* (Wheaton: Crossway, 2005).

Francis A. Schaeffer, *How Should We Then Live? The Rise and Decline of Western Thought and Culture* (Wheaton: Crossway, 2005).

Jack Miller, *1994 Sonship Course Notebook* (Philadelphia: World Harvest Mission, 2013).

Philip Freeman, *St. Patrick of Ireland: A Biography* (New York: Simon & Schuster, 2004).

George Swinnock, https://puritanquoter.wordpress.com/2010/09/13/sin-goes-in-a-disguise/, accessed April 2, 2018.

WEEK FOURTEEN

Ron Julian, *Righteous Sinner: The Believer's Struggle With Faith, Grace, and Works* (Colorado Springs: NavPress, 1998).

John R. Stott, *Basic Christianity* (Grand Rapids: Eerdmans, 1971).

R. C. Sproul, *The Holiness of God* (Wheaton: Tyndale House, 1985).

Cornelius Plantinga, *Not The Way It's Supposed to Be: A Breviary of Sin* (Grand Rapids: Eerdmans Apollos, 1995).

Jen Wilkin, *Sermon on the Mount* (Nashville: LifeWay, 2014).

Rankin Wilbourne, *Union with Christ: The Way to Know and Enjoy God* (Colorado Springs: David C Cook, 2016).

Dick Keyes, *Beyond Identity: Finding Your Self in the Image and Character of God* (Carlisle, PA: Paternoster Press, 1998).

A. W. Tozer, *The Knowledge of the Holy: The Attributes of God, Their Meaning in the Christian Life* (San Francisco: Harper & Row, 1978).

Horatius Bonar, http://www.gracegems.org/book4/43.htm, accessed May 6, 2018.

David F. Wells, *Above All Earthly Pow'rs: Christ In a Postmodern World* (Grand Rapids: Eerdmans, 2006).

WEEK FIFTEEN

Richard Sibbes, *The Bruised Reed* (Carlisle, PA: Puritan Paperbacks, 1998).

Thomas Manton, *An Exposition of the Epistle of Jude* (Lafayette: Sovereign Grace Publishers, 2001).

Attributed to William Temple

Luther, Martin. *On Christian Liberty,* http://www.quotissimo.com /quote/christ-grace-love-sin-martin-luther-1432/, accessed April 11, 2018.

Francis A. Schaeffer, *The Complete Works of Francis A. Schaeffer: A Christian Worldview* (Westchester: Crossway, 1985).

Paul D. Tripp, *Dangerous Calling: Confronting the Unique Challenges of Pastoral Ministry* (Wheaton: Crossway, 2012).

Thomas Merton, *No Man Is an Island* (New York: Harcourt, 1955).

Ann Voskamp, *One Thousand Gifts: A Dare to Live Fully Right Where You Are* (Grand Rapids: Zondervan, 1996).

Richard M. Weaver, *Ideas Have Consequences* (Chicago: University of Chicago Press, 2013).

Jen Wilkin, *None Like Him: 10 Ways God is Different From Us (And Why That's a Good Thing)* (Wheaton, Illinois: Crossway, 2016).

WEEK SIXTEEN

John Calvin, *Institutes of the Christian Religion, Vol 1.* (Philadelphia: Westminster Press, 1960).

John Eldredge, *Wild at Heart: Discovering the Secret of a Man's Soul* (Nashville: Thomas Nelson, 2001).

Francis A. Schaeffer, *The Complete Works of Francis A. Schaeffer: A Christian Worldview* (Westchester: Crossway, 1985).

Thomas Watson, *A Divine Cordial* (Grand Rapids: Baker Book House, 1980).

Kevin DeYoung, *The Biggest Story: How the Snake Crusher Brings Us Back to the Garden* (Wheaton: Crossway, 2015).

Samuel Bolton, *The True Bounds of Christian Freedom* (Edinburgh: Banner of Truth Trust, 1978).

Jonathan Edwards, *The Works of Jonathan Edwards, A.M* (Edinburgh: Banner of Truth, 1979).

Alister E. McGrath, *Studies in Doctrine* (Grand Rapids: Zondervan, 1997).

Matt Chandler and Jared C. Wilson, *The Explicit Gospel* (Wheaton: Crossway, 2012).

John Calvin, *Institutes of the Christian Religion* (Peabody, MA: Hendrickson, 2008).

WEEK SEVENTEEN

Leif Enger, *Peace Like a River* (New York: Atlantic Monthly Press, 2002).

John Preston, *The Fullness of Christ: A 21st Century Edition.* ed. James T. O'Brien (Simpsonville, SC: New Puritan Press, 2012).

John R. Stott, *Basic Christianity* (Grand Rapids: Eerdmans, 1971).

Matt Chandler and Jared C. Wilson, *The Explicit Gospel* (Wheaton: Crossway, 2012).

Brennan Manning, *The Ragamuffin Gospel* (Sisters, OR: Multnomah Publishers, 2005).

Paul D. Tripp, *Broken-Down House: Living Productively in a World Gone Bad* (Wapwallopen, PA: Shepherd Press, 2009).

Elyse Fitzpatrick, *Good News for Weary Women: Escaping the Bondage of To-Do Lists, Steps, and Bad Advice* (Carol Stream, IL: Tyndale House, 2014).

A. A. Bonar, *Memoirs and Remains of R.M. McCheyne* (Simpsonville, SC: Christian Classics Foundation, 1997).

James Buchanan and J. I. Packer, *The Doctrine of Justification: An Outline of its History in the Church and of its Exposition from Scripture* (Edinburgh: The Banner of Truth Trust, 2016).

Betsy Gómez, "Our Longing to be Free from Guilt" from *Gentle Leading Advent Devotional,* Abbey Wedgeworth, editor (December 16, 2018).

Richard Sibbes, *The Bruised Reed* (Simpsonville, SC: Puritan Paperbacks, 1998).

WEEK EIGHTEEN

A. W. Tozer, *The Knowledge of the Holy: The Attributes of God, Their Meaning in the Christian Life* (San Francisco: Harper & Row, 1978).

Harry Blamires, *Recovering the Christian Mind: Meeting the Challenge of Secularism* (Downers Grove: Inter-Varsity Press, 1988).

Victor Hugo, *Les Misérables* (London: Penguin Classics, 2012).

Charles M. Schulz. *Peanuts* BrainyQuote.com, BrainyMedia Inc, 2019. https://www.brainyquote.com/quotes/charles_m_schulz_393098, accessed February 5, 2019.

Jeremiah Burroughs, *An Exposition of the Prophecy of Hosea* (Edinburgh: James Nisbet & Co. 1865).

Harold L. Senkbeil, *Dying to Live: The Power of Forgiveness* (St. Louis: CPH, 1994).

Paul D. Tripp, *Broken-Down House: Living Productively in a World Gone Bad* (Wapwallopen, PA: Shepherd Press, 2009).

Cornelius Plantinga, *Not The Way It's Supposed to Be: A Breviary of Sin* (Grand Rapids: Eerdmans Apollos, 1995).

Donald Miller, *Searching For God Knows What* (Nashville: Thomas Nelson, 2004).

WEEK NINETEEN

Victor Hugo, *Les Misérables* (London: Penguin Classics, 2012).

John R. Stott, *Basic Christianity* (Grand Rapids: Eerdmans, 1971).

John Flavel, *The Christian Treasury* (Edinburgh: Johnstone, Hunter and Co., 1886).

Donald Miller, *Searching For God Knows What* (Nashville: Thomas Nelson, 2004).

Jared C. Wilson, *Gospel Wakefulness* (Wheaton: Crossway, 2011).

R. C. Sproul, *The Holiness of God* (Wheaton: Tyndale, 1985).

A. W. Tozer, *The Knowledge of the Holy: The Attributes of God, Their Meaning in the Christian Life* (San Francisco: Harper & Row, 1978).

R. C. Sproul, *The Holiness of God* (Wheaton: Tyndale, 1985).

Pirates of the Caribbean, The Curse of the Black Pearl. Directed by Gore Verbinski (Los Angeles: Disney Studios, 2003), DVD.

John Owen, *Temptation & Sin* (Lafayette, IN: Sovereign Grace Publishers, Inc., 2001).

WEEK TWENTY

Thabiti M. Anyabwile, *Captivated: Beholding the Mystery of Jesus' Death and Resurrection* (Grand Rapids: Reformation Heritage Books, 2014).

Joe Thorn, *Note to Self: The Discipline of Preaching to Yourself* (Wheaton: Crossway, 2011).

Sinclair B. Ferguson, *The Whole Christ: Legalism, Antinomianism, and Gospel Assurance: Why the Marrow Controversy Still Matters* (Wheaton: Crossway, 2016).

Frederick Buechner, *The Alphabet of Grace* (New York: Harper & Row, 1989).

Kevin DeYoung, *The Biggest Story: How the Snake Crusher Brings Us Back to the Garden* (Wheaton: Crossway, 2015).

Francine Rivers, *Redeeming Love* (Chicago: Multnomah, 1997).

Isaac Watts, "I'll Praise My Maker," *Baptist Hymnal* (Nashville: Convention Press, 1991).

J. I. Packer, *Knowing God* (Downers Grove: InterVarsity Press, 1973).

Bonar, Horatius, https://gracequotes.org/author-quote/horatius-bonar, accessed May 27, 2018.

Brennan Manning, *The Furious Longing of God* (Colorado Springs: David C. Cook, 2009).

C. S. Lewis, *Mere Christianity* (New York: Harper Collins, 2001).

WEEK TWENTY-ONE

C. S. Lewis, *Mere Christianity* (New York: Harper Collins, 2001).

Gerald R. McDermott, *The Great Theologians: A Brief Guide* (Downers Grove: IVP Academic, 2010).

John R. Stott, *Basic Christianity* (Grand Rapids: Eerdmans, 1971).

Richard F. Lovelace, *Dynamics of Spiritual Life: An Evangelical Theology of Renewal* (Downers Grove: Inter-Varsity Press, 1979).

Nancy Guthrie, *Praying Through the Bible for Your Kids* (Carol Stream, IL: Tyndale, 2016).

Bob George, *Classic Christianity: Life's Too Short to Miss the Real Thing* (Eugene, OR: Harvest House, 1989).

Philip Yancey, *Where Is God When It Hurts?* (Grand Rapids: Zondervan, 1990).

Iain H. Murray, *The Forgotten Spurgeon* (Edinburgh: Banner of Truth Trust, 2009).

Blaise Pascal, *Pensées and Other Writings.* Translated by Honor Levi and Anthony Levi (Oxford: Oxford Press, 1999).

WEEK TWENTY-TWO

Frederick Buechner, *Wishful Thinking: A Seeker's ABC* (New York: HarperOne, 1993).

Blaise Pascal, *Thoughts, Letters & Minor Works, The Five Foot Shelf of Classics, Vol. XLVIII* (New York: Cosimo, 2009).

Max Lucado, *God Came Near: Chronicles of the Christ* (Portland: Multnomah Press, 1987).

Stephen W. Brown, *Overcoming Setbacks* (Colorado Springs: NavPress, 1992).

Dorothy Sayers, *Creed or Chaos* (Manchester, NH: Sophia Institute Press, 1995).

William Blake and Alicia Ostriker, *The Complete Poems [of] William Blake* (New York: Penguin, 1977).

Richard Selzer, *Mortal Lessons: Notes on the Art of Surgery* (San Diego: Harcourt Brace, 1996).

W. P. Keller, *A Shepherd Looks at Psalm 23* (Grand Rapids: Zondervan, 2007).

WEEK TWENTY-THREE

Augustine, et al. *Nicene and Post-Nicene Fathers* (New York: Cosimo Classics, 2007).

Martin Bucer, *In Sacra Quatuor Evangelia, Enerrationes* (Basel, Switzerland: Hervagius, 1536).

Anthony Carter, https://www.ligonier.org/blog/jesus-christ-our-prophet-priest-and-king/, accessed April 11, 2018.

Matthew Richard, "Jesus Christ: Prophet, Priest, King," https://corechristianity.com/resource -library/articles/how-is-jesus-our-prophet-priest-and-king, accessed November 29, 2018.

John Newton, "How Sweet the Name of Jesus Sounds," *The Trinity Hymnal* (Suwanee, GA: Great Commission Publications, 1990) 647.

William Ames and John D. Eusden, *The Marrow of Theology* (Grand Rapids: Baker Books, 1997).

Kevin DeYoung, *The Good News We Almost Forgot: Rediscovering the Gospel in a 16th Century Catechism* (Chicago: Moody Publishers, 2010).

Ashbel Green, *Lectures on the Shorter Catechism in Two Volumes, Vol. 1* (Philadelphia: Presbyterian Board of Publication, 1841).

Kim Riddlebarger, https://graceonlinelibrary.org/doctrine-theology/christology/the-triple-cure -jesus-christ-our-prophet-priest-and-king-by-kim-riddlebarger/, accessed April 10, 2018.

François Turrettini, George M. Giger, and James T. Dennison, *Institutes of Elenctic Theology* (Phillipsburg, N.J: P & R Pub, 1992).

WEEK TWENTY-FOUR

A. A. Hodge, *Popular Lectures on Theological Themes* (Princeton: 1887), https://www .monergism.com/popular-lectures-theological-themes-ebook

Jean Calvin and Ford L. Battles, *Calvin: Institutes of the Christian religion* (Louisville: Westminster John Knox Press, 2001).

Richard Sibbes, *The Bruised Reed* (Edinburgh: Banner of Truth Trust, 1998).

R. C. Sproul, *Essential Truths of the Christian Faith* (Wheaton: Tyndale House, 1998).

J. I. Packer, *Knowing God* (Downers Grove: InterVarsity Press, 1973).

J. I. Packer, *Concise Theology: A Guide to Historic Christian Beliefs* (Wheaton: Tyndale House, 1993).

Thomas Watson, *A Body of Divinity: Contained in Sermons Upon the Westminster Assembly's Catechism* (London: Banner of Truth Trust, 1965).

Walter A. Elwell, *Entry for 'Prophet, Christ as'. Evangelical Dictionary of Biblical Theology* (Grand Rapids: Baker Books, 1996) https://www.studylight.org/dictionaries/bed/p/prophet-christ -as.html. 1996.

Timothy Keller, "Christ Our Prophet." Sermon, Redeemer Presbyterian Church, Manhattan, NY, July 16, 1989.

Joel Beeke, "Christ Alone," *Tabletalk*, November 1, 2012, https://www.ligonier.org/learn/articles/ christ-alone/

WEEK TWENTY-FIVE

Attributed to John Flavel

Joe Thorn, *Note to Self: The Discipline of Preaching to Yourself* (Wheaton: Crossway, 2011).

Richard Sibbes, *The Bruised Reed* (Edinburgh: Banner of Truth Trust, 1998).

Joel Beeke, "Christ Alone," *Tabletalk*, November 1, 2012, https://www.ligonier.org/learn/articles /christ-alone/

Benjamin Warfield, *Perfectionism, Part One, vol. 7 of The Works of Benjamin B. Warfield* (New York: Oxford University Press, 1932).

Attributed to Jonathan Edwards

Attributed to Robert Murray McCheyne. www.mcheyne.info/quotes.php

Gerald Strauss, *Law, Resistance, and the State: The Opposition to Roman Law in Reformation Germany* (Princeton: Princeton University Press, 1986).

Clayton Kraby, "Jesus Christ: Our Great High Priest," https://reasonabletheology.org/jesus-christ -our-great-high-priest-2/

Martin Luther, *Commentary on Galatians* (Grand Rapids: Fleming H. Revell, 1988).

WEEK TWENTY-SIX

Paul D. Tripp, *New Morning Mercies: A Daily Gospel Devotional* (Wheaton: Crossway, 2014).

C. S. Lewis, *Mere Christianity* (New York: Harper Collins, 2001).

J. C. Philpot, *Meditations on the Sacred Humanity of the Blessed Redeemer* (Harpenden, Herts., England: Gospel Standard Strict Baptist Trust, 1978).

Richard Sibbes, *The Bruised Reed* (Edinburgh: Banner of Truth Trust, 1998).

R. C. Sproul, *Truths We Confess: A Layman's Guide to the Westminster Confession of Faith, in three volumes* (Phillipsburg: P&R, 2006).

William Shakespeare, *The Tragedy of Richard II.* ed. Barbara A. Mowat and Paul Werstein (New York: Washington Square Press, 1996).

David K. Naugle, *Reordered Love, Reordered Lives: Learning the Deep Meaning of Happiness* (Grand Rapids: William B. Eerdmans Pub, 2008).

John Calvin, *Calvin's Commentaries, Vol XVIs* (Grand Rapids: Baker, 1979).

Timothy Keller, *Jesus the King: Understanding the Life and Death of the Son of God* (New York: Riverhead Books, 2013).

Edward Perronet, "All Hail the Power of Jesus' Name," *The Trinity Hymnal* (Suwanee, GA: Great Commission Publications, 2001.) 296.

WEEK TWENTY-SEVEN

Frederick Buechner, *The Faces of Jesus: A Life Story* (Brewster: Paraclete Press, 2014).

Attributed to Augustine

Timothy Keller, *The Reason for God: Belief in an Age of Skepticism* (New York: Dutton, 2008).

Nancy Guthrie, *Come, Thou Long Expected Jesus: Experiencing the Peace and Promise of Christmas* (Wheaton: Crossway Books, 2008).

J. C. Ryle, *Expository Thoughts on the Gospels: St. Matthew* (New York: Robert Carter & Brothers, 1860).

Frederick S. Leahy *The Cross He Bore: Meditations on the Sufferings of the Redeemer* (Edinburgh: Banner of Truth Trust, 1996).

John R. Stott, *Basic Christianity* (Grand Rapids: Eerdmans, 1971).

Rowan Williams, *The Wound of Knowledge: Christian Spirituality from the New Testament to St. John of the Cross* (Cambridge: Cowley Publications, 1991).

Thomas Traherne and Bertram Dobell, *Centuries of Meditations* (New York: Cosimo Classics, 2009).

John L. Dagg, *Manual of Theology* (Berryville, VA: Hess, 1998).

WEEK TWENTY-EIGHT

Timothy Keller, *Jesus the King: Understanding the Life and Death of the Son of God* (New York: Riverhead Books, 2013).

Joe Thorn, *Note to Self: The Discipline of Preaching to Yourself* (Wheaton: Crossway, 2011).

Anne Riley, *Voyage to the Star Kingdom* (Scotts Valley, CA: CreateSpace Ind. Publishing, 2016).

Edward T. Welch, *Running Scared: Fear, Worry, and the God of Rest* (Greensboro: New Growth Press, 2007).

Timothy Keller, *Jesus the King: Understanding the Life and Death of the Son of God* (New York: Riverhead Books, 2013).

Andrew Peterson *On the Dark Sea of Darkness* (New York: Waterbrook, 2008).

Attributed to Charles Spurgeon, James C. Galvin, editor, *Faith Alone: A Daily Devotional* (Grand Rapids: Zondervan, 2005).

Emily Brontë as quoted in George Grant and Gregory Wilbur, *The Christian Almanac: A Book of Days Celebrating History's Most Significant People & Events* (Nashville: Cumberland House, 2004).

WEEK TWENTY-NINE

Attributed to Robert Farrar Capon

Richard Sibbes, *The Bruised Reed* (Edinburgh: Banner of Truth Trust, 1998).

Karen Hodge, "From life-taker to life-giver," The Journeywomen Podcast, interview with Hunter Beless, July 30, 2018.

Charles Spurgeon, *Morning & Evening* (New Kensington: Whitaker House, 2001).

Thomas Watson, *All Things for Good* (Edinburgh: Banner of Truth Trust, 1986).

C. S. Lewis, *Mere Christianity* (New York: Harper Collins, 2001).

J. W. Alexander, *The Life of Archibald Alexander* (Berryville, VA: Hess Publications, 1999).

Robert Murray McCheyne and Andrew A. Bonar, editor, *Memoir and Remains of Robert Murray M'Cheyne* (Edinburgh: Banner of Truth Trust, 1973).

Marilynne Robinson, *Gilead: A Novel* (New York: Picador, 2004).

John R. Stott, *Basic Christianity* (Grand Rapids: Eerdmans, 1971).

Blaise Pascal, *Pensees*, ed. A. J. Krailsheimer (New York: Penguin Books, 1995).

WEEK THIRTY

Paul D. Tripp, *Dangerous Calling: Confronting the Unique Challenges of Pastoral Ministry* (Wheaton: Crossway, 2012).

C. S. Lewis, *Mere Christianity* (New York: Harper Collins, 2001).

Geerhardus Vos and Richard B. Gaffin, editor, *Redemptive History and Biblical Interpretation: The Shorter Writings of Geerhardus Vos* (Phillipsburg, N.J: P&R, 2001).

Dan B. Allender, *How Children Raise Parents: The Art of Listening to Your Family* (Colorado Springs: Waterbrook Press, 2005).

J. C. Ryle, *Expository Thoughts on the Gospels, St. John Vol. 1* (Cambridge: James Clark & Co. 1969).

Isaac Watts, "Psalm 130" *The Baptist Hymnal*. (Nashville: Convention Press, 1991).

Benjamin Breckenridge Warfield, *Perfectionism, Part One, vol. 7 of The Works of Benjamin B. Warfield* (New York: Oxford University Press, 1932; repr., Grand Rapids: Baker, 2000).

John Owen as quoted in Johanna Tooke, *When Stuff's Not Enough: A Christian Perspective on Decluttering Your Life* (Citrus Heights, CA: Umbach, 2012).

Robert Farrar Capon, *The Astonished Heart: Reclaiming the Good News from the Lost-and-Found of Church History* (Grand Rapids: William B. Eerdmans Publishing Company, 1996).

Richard Sibbes, *The Bruised Reed* (Edinburgh: Banner of Truth Trust, 1998).

WEEK THIRTY-ONE

Paul D. Tripp, *Broken-Down House: Living Productively in A World Gone Bad* (Wapwallopen, PA: Shepherd Press, 2009).

Jean Calvin and Ford L. Battles, *Calvin: Institutes of the Christian Religion* (Louisville: Westminster John Knox Press, 2001).

Hannah Anderson, *Humble Roots: How Humility Grounds and Nourishes Your Soul* (Chicago: Moody Publishers, 2016).

Lawrence J. Crabb, *Men and Women: Enjoying the Difference* (Grand Rapids: Zondervan, 2013).

Michael Horton, *Putting Amazing Back into Grace* (Grand Rapids: Baker Book House, 1994).

Loraine Boettner, *The Reformed Doctrine of Predestination* (Grand Rapids: William B. Eerdmans Publishing Co, 1932).

Thomas Brooks, *Precious Remedies Against Satan's Devices* (London: Banner of Truth Trust, 1968).

WEEK THIRTY-TWO

Paul D. Tripp, *Dangerous Calling: Confronting the Unique Challenges of Pastoral Ministry* (Wheaton: Crossway, 2012).

Bryan Chapell, *Holiness by Grace: Delighting in the Joy That Is Our Strength* (Wheaton: Crossway, 2003).

J. C. Ryle, *Holiness: Its Nature, Hindrances, Difficulties, and Roots* (Chicago: Moody Publishers, 2010).

Stephen Charnock, *The Chief Sinners Objects of the Choicest Mercy* (Geanies House: Solus Christus, 2011).

John R. Stott, *Basic Christianity* (Grand Rapids: Eerdmans, 1971).

Hannah Anderson, *Humble Roots: How Humility Grounds and Nourishes Your Soul* (Chicago: Moody Publishers, 2016).

William Cowper and Charles J. Doe, *William Cowper's Olney Hymns and Other Sacred Works* (Minneapolis: Curiosmith, 2010).

Thomas Brooks, *Precious Remedies Against Satan's Devices* (London: Banner of Truth Trust, 1968).

Martin Luther as quoted in William C. Placher and Derek R. Nelson, *Readings In the History of Christian Theology* (Louisville, KY: Westminster John Knox Press, 2015).

WEEK THIRTY-THREE

David M. Lloyd-Jones, *The Life of Peace: An Exposition of Philippians 3 and 4* (Grand Rapids: Baker Book House, 1992).

Hugh Latimer, *The Works of Hugh Latimer*, Vol. 2 (Cambridge: Cambridge University Press, 1845).

Nancy Guthrie, *Praying Through the Bible for Your Kids* (Carol Stream: Tyndale, 2016).

John Flavel, *Method of Grace In the Holy Spirit's Applying to the Souls of Men the Eternal Redemption ... Contrived By the Father and Accomplished By the Son* (London: Forgotten Books, 2015).

Various, *Apostolic Fathers* Michael W. Holmes, editor (Ingersoll, ON: Devoted Publishing, 2018).

Elyse Fitzpatrick, *Good News for Weary Women: Escaping the Bondage of To-Do Lists, Steps, and Bad Advice* (Carol Stream: Tyndale, 2014).

Robert Murray McCheyne as quoted in Andrew A. Bonar, *Robert Murray McCheyne: A Biography* (Grand Rapids: Zondervan, 1983).

WEEK THIRTY-FOUR

Marilynne Robinson, *Gilead: A Novel* (New York: Picador, 2004).

Rosemarie Miller, *1994 Sonship Course Notebook* (Philadelphia: World Harvest Mission, 2013).

Sinclair Ferguson, *Children of the Living God* (Edinburgh: Banner of Truth Trust, 1989).

Frederick Buechner, *Telling Secrets* (New York: Harper Collins, 1991).

Sinclair B. Ferguson, *Devoted to God: Blueprint for Sanctification* (Edinburgh: Banner of Truth Trust, 2016).

J.L. Girardeau, *Discussions of Theological Questions* (Richmond: Presbyterian Committee of Publications, 1900).

J. I. Packer, *Knowing God* (Downers Grove: InterVarsity Press, 1993).

Jonathan Edwards, Sereno E. Dwight, and Edward Hickman, *The Works of Jonathan Edwards* (Edinburgh: Banner of Truth Trust, 1990).

C. H. Spurgeon as quoted in Bryan Chapell, *Holiness by Grace: Delighting in the Joy That Is Our Strength* (Wheaton: Crossway, 2003).

WEEK THIRTY-FIVE

Rob Lister, *God is Impassible and Impassioned: Toward a Theology of Divine Emotion* (Wheaton: Crossway, 2013).

Sinclair B. Ferguson, *Devoted to God: Blueprint for Sanctification* (Edinburgh: Banner of Truth Trust, 2016).

Flannery O'Connor and Sally Fitzgerald. *The Habit of Being: Letters* (New York: Farrar, Straus, Giroux, 1979).

C S. Storms, *Pleasures Evermore: The Life-Changing Power of Enjoying God* (Colorado Springs: NavPress, 2000).

Bryan Chapell, *Holiness by Grace: Delighting in the Joy That Is Our Strength* (Wheaton: Crossway, 2003).

Elyse Fitzpatrick and Dennis Johnson, *Counsel from the Cross: Connecting Broken People to the Love of Christ* (Wheaton: Crossway, 2012).

Jerry Bridges, *The Gospel for Real Life: Turn to the Liberating Power of the Cross . . . Every Day* (Colorado Springs: NavPress, 2003).

David Powlison, *Making All Things New: Restoring Joy to the Sexually Broken* (Wheaton: Crossway, 2017).

Jen Wilkin, "The Will of God," The Journeywomen Podcast, interview with Hunter Beless, October 22, 2018.

John R. Stott, *Basic Christianity* (Grand Rapids: Eerdmans, 1971).

WEEK THIRTY-SIX

Rankin Wilbourne, *Union with Christ: The Way to Know and Enjoy God* (Colorado Springs: David C. Cook, 2016).

Max Lucado, *A Gentle Thunder: Hearing God Through the Storm* (Nashville: Thomas Nelson, 2012).

John Piper, *Future Grace: The Purifying Power of the Promises of God* (Colorado Springs: Multnomah Books, 2012).

John R. Stott, *Basic Christianity* (Downers Grove: IVP Books, 2006).

Larry Crabb, *Shattered Dreams: God's Unexpected Path to Joy* (Colorado Springs: Waterbrook Press, 2010).

C. S. Lewis, *Mere Christianity* (New York: Harper Collins, 2001).

Mark Batterson, *Whisper: How to Hear the Voice of God* (Colorado Springs: Multnomah, 2017).

John Calvin, *Institutes of the Christian Religion, Vol 1* (Philadelphia: Westminster Press, 1960).

WEEK THIRTY-SEVEN

John Owen as quoted by John M. Drescher, www.sermonillustrations.com/a-z/l/last_words.htm

George Herbert as quoted in Douglas Wilson, *Writers to Read: Nine Names that Belong On Your Bookshelf.* (Wheaton: Crossway, 2015).

Susan Hunt, "Passing Your Experience to the Next Generation," interview by Leslie Basham, *Revive Our Hearts,* August 31, 2018, https://www.reviveourhearts.com/radio/revive-our-hearts/passing-your-experience-next-generation/

Edward T. Welch, *Running Scared: Fear, Worry, and the God of Rest* (Greensboro: New Growth Press, 2007).

R. C. Sproul, *Truths We Confess: A Layman's Guide to the Westminster Confession of Faith, in Three Volumes* (Phillipsburg: P&R, 2006).

Fanny Crosby, https://www.google.com/url?q=https://www christianitytoday.com/history/people/poets/fanny-crosby.html&sa=D&ust=1553945293104000&usg=AFQjCNH3Jc1SXUrnZe_n_7XXBqwaKNsfLw, accessed November 5, 2018.

Bryan Chapell, *Christ-Centered Preaching: Redeeming the Expository Sermon* (Grand Rapids: Baker Academic, 2005).

Richard Baxter and John T. Wilkinson, *The Saints' Everlasting Rest* (Vancouver: Regent College Pub, 2004).

Philip H. Eveson, *The Great Exchange: Justification by Faith Alone in the Light of Recent Research* (Bromley, Kent: Day One Publications, 1996).

Thomas Brooks, *Precious Remedies Against Satan's Devices* (London: Banner of Truth Trust, 1968).

WEEK THIRTY-EIGHT

Elisabeth Elliot, *Keep A Quiet Heart* (Grand Rapids: Fleming H. Revell, 2004).

Geerhardus Vos, *The Pauline Eschatology* (Phillipsburg: P&R, 1930).

Matt Redmond, "Memories of the Future Past" (2016).

J. R. R. Tolkien, *The Return of the King: Being the Third Part of The Lord of the Rings* (Boston: Houghton Mifflin Co, 1965).

Timothy Keller, *The Reason for God: Belief in an Age of Skepticism* (New York: Dutton, 2008).

Beth Moore (@BethMooreLPM), "One day all of us in Christ will sit," Twitter, November 21, 2018, 6:46 am, https://twitter.com/BethMooreLPM/status/1065224943347089408

Marilynne Robinson, *Gilead: A Novel* (New York: Picador, 2004).

Bryan Chapell, *Standing Your Ground: A Call to Courage in an Age of Compromise: Messages from Daniel* (Grand Rapids: Baker Book House, 1989).

Richard Baxter and John T. Wilkinson, *The Saints' Everlasting Rest* (Vancouver: Regent College Pub, 2004).

WEEK THIRTY-NINE

Jen Wilkin, *Women of the Word: How to Study the Bible with Both Our Hearts and Our Minds* (Wheaton: Crossway, 2014).

Dallas Willard, *The Great Omission: Rediscovering Jesus's Essential Teachings on Discipleship* (New York: HarperCollins e-books, 2006).

Julian of Norwich as quoted in A. W. Tozer, *The Knowledge of the Holy: The Attributes of God, Their Meaning in the Christian Life* (San Francisco: Harper & Row, 1978).

W. Somerset Maugham, *The Painted Veil* (New York: Vintage Books, 2006).

Lawrence J. Crabb, *Men and Women: Enjoying the Difference* (Grand Rapids: Zondervan, 2013).

Dietrich Bonhoeffer, *The Cost of Discipleship* (New York: Touchstone, 1995).

Dan B. Allender, *How Children Raise Parents: The Art of Listening to Your Family* (Colorado Springs: Waterbrook Press, 2005).

Hugh Latimer, http://www.winwisdom.com/quotes/author/hugh-latimer.aspx, accessed April 10, 2018.

Coelestius as quoted in John Owen, *Theomachia Autexousiastike: Or, A Display of Arminianism. Being a Discovery of the Old* (Gale ECCO, Print Editions, 2010).

Paul D. Tripp, *Broken-Down House: Living Productively in a World Gone Bad* (Wapwallopen, Pa: Shepherd Press, 2009).

WEEK FORTY

J. A. Motyer, *The Message of Exodus: The Days of Our Pilgrimage* (Downers Grove: InterVarsity Press, 2005).

Jen Wilkin, *Women of the Word: How to Study the Bible with Both Our Hearts and Our Minds* (Wheaton: Crossway, 2014).

Martin Luther as quoted in Gerald L. Bray, *Galatians, Ephesians* (Downers Grove: IVP Academic, 2011).

Kevin DeYoung, *The Biggest Story: How the Snake Crusher Brings Us Back to the Garden* (Wheaton: Crossway, 2015).

Matthew Henry, *Matthew Henry's Concise Commentary on the Whole Bible* (Nashville: Thomas Nelson, Inc, 1997).

Isaac Watts et al., *The Psalms, Hymns, and Spiritual Songs of the Rev. Isaac Watts* (Frisco: Doxology & Theology Press, 2016).

Sinclair B. Ferguson, *The Whole Christ: Legalism, Antinomianism, and Gospel Assurance: Why the Marrow Controversy Still Matters* (Wheaton: Crossway, 2016).

Samuel Bolton, *The True Bounds of Christian Freedom* (Carlisle: Banner of Truth, 2001).

Carolyn Custis James, *The Gospel of Ruth: Loving God Enough to Break the Rules* (Grand Rapids: Zondervan, 2008).

C. S. Lewis, *Mere Christianity* (New York: Harper Collins, 2001).

WEEK FORTY-ONE

R. C. Sproul, *The Holiness of God* (Wheaton: Tyndale, 1985).

Philip Eveson, *Great Exchange: Justification by Faith Alone* (Leominster, Herefordshire: Day One, 1998).

Ralph Erskine, *The Poetical Works of the Late Reverend and Learned Mr. Ralph Erskine* (Falkirk: Patrick Mair, 1797). Found on https://books.google.com

J. A. Motyer, *The Message of Exodus: The Days of Our Pilgrimage* (Downers Grove: InterVarsity Press, 2005).

Ann Voskamp, *The Greatest Gift: Unwrapping the Full Love Story of Christmas* (Carol Stream: Tyndale. 2013).

Sinclair B. Ferguson, *The Whole Christ: Legalism, Antinomianism, and Gospel Assurance: Why the Marrow Controversy Still Matters* (Wheaton: Crossway, 2016).

Sinclair B. Ferguson, *The Whole Christ: Legalism, Antinomianism, and Gospel Assurance: Why the Marrow Controversy Still Matters* (Wheaton: Crossway, 2016).

Ann Voskamp, *The Greatest Gift: Unwrapping the Full Love Story of Christmas* (Carol Stream, IL: Tyndale. 2013).

Lancelot Andrewes, *The Devotions of Bishop Andrewes* (London: Christian Classics Ethereal Library. 1876).

Elyse Fitzpatrick and Dennis Johnson, *Counsel from the Cross* (Wheaton: Crossway, 2012).

WEEK FORTY-TWO

Jared C. Wilson, *Gospel Wakefulness* (Wheaton: Crossway, 2011).

Hannah Anderson, *Humble Roots: How Humility Grounds and Nourishes Your Soul* (Chicago: Moody Publishers, 2016).

Paul D. Tripp, *Dangerous Calling: Confronting the Unique Challenges of Pastoral Ministry* (Wheaton: Crossway, 2012).

Gloria Furman, "God isn't testing you: An invitation to radical dependence," Kindled podcast, interview with Haley Williams, April 16, 2008.

Emily P. Freeman, *Grace for the Good Girl: Letting Go of the Try-Hard Life* (Grand Rapids: Revell, 2011).

J. I. Packer, *Knowing God* (Downers Grove: InterVarsity Press, 1993).

Sally Lloyd-Jones, *The Jesus Storybook Bible: Every Story Whispers His Name* (Grand Rapids: Zonderkidz, 2007).

Attributed to Michael Horton

Gerald L. Bray, *The Doctrine of God* (Downers Grove: InterVarsity Press, 1993).

WEEK FORTY-THREE

Martin Luther, *Luther: Letters of Spiritual Counsel*, Theodore G. Tappert, ed. (Philadelphia: Library of Christian Classics, 1955).

Dorothy L. Sayers, *Creed or Chaos?: Why Christians Must Choose Either Dogma or Disaster* (Manchester, NH: Sophia Institute, 1995).

Nancy Guthrie, *Praying Through the Bible for Your Kids* (Carol Stream, IL: Tyndale, 2016).

Vern S. Poythress, *The Shadow of Christ in the Law of Moses* (Phillipsburg, NJ: P&R, 2018).

John Murray, *Collected Writings of John Murray: Lectures in Systematic Theology* (Edinburgh: Banner of Truth, 1991).

Scotty Smith and Michael Card, *Unveiled Hope* (Nashville: Thomas Nelson, 1997).

Thomas Reade, *Christian Retirement or Spiritual Exercises of the Heart* (New York: Robert Carter, 1848).

Timothy Keller (@timkellernyc) Twitter, April 24, 2018, 11:23 a.m., https://twitter.com/timkellernyc/status/988845793892237314?lang=en

Nancy Guthrie, *Praying Through the Bible for Your Kids* (Carol Stream, IL: Tyndale, 2016).

Kevin DeYoung, *The Biggest Story: How the Snake Crusher Brings Us Back to the Garden* (Wheaton: Crossway, 2015).

WEEK FORTY-FOUR

Francis Schaeffer, *True Spirituality* (Wheaton: Tyndale, 2012).

Richard Sibbes, *The Bruised Reed* (Carlisle, PA: Puritan Paperbacks, 1998).

John H. Gerstner, *Theology for Everyman* (Orlando: Soli Deo Gloria Publications, 1997).

Attributed to John Calvin

Tim Keller, *Church Planter's Manual* (New York: Redeemer PC, 2002).

Michael Horton, "Union With Christ: The Double Cure," *Modern Reformation*, Vol. 15, Number 4, July/August 2006.

Brennan Manning, *The Ragamuffin Gospel* (Sisters, OR: Multnomah Publishers, 2005).

Joe Thorn, *Note to Self: The Discipline of Preaching to Yourself* (Wheaton: Crossway, 2011).

Octavious Winslow, "Go to Jesus," http://www.gracegems.org/03/take.html, accessed December 5, 2018.

WEEK FORTY-FIVE

Attributed to John Calvin

Thabiti M. Anyabwile, *Captivated: Beholding the Mystery of Jesus' Death and Resurrection* (Grand Rapids: Reformation Heritage Books, 2014).

Leo Tolstoy, George Grant, and Gregory Wilbur, *The Christian Almanac: A Book of Days Celebrating History's Most Significant People & Events* (Nashville: Cumberland House, 2004).

Charles Spurgeon, *Morning and Evening* (Fearn: Christian Focus, 1994).

Emily Dickinson, "Letters from Dickinson to Otis Phillips Lord" (April 30, 1882). www.archive.emilydickinson.org/correspondence/lord/1750.html

Oswald Chambers, *My Utmost for His Highest* (Grand Rapids: Discovery House, 2017).

"Phoebe Palmer: Mother of the Holiness Movement," *Christianity Today.* www.christianitytoday.com/history/people/moversandshakers/phoebe-palmer.html

Brennan Manning, *The Ragamuffin Gospel* (Sisters, OR: Multnomah Publishers, 1990).

Nancy Guthrie, *Hearing Jesus Speak Into Your Sorrow* (Carol Stream, IL: Tyndale House, 2009).

Henri Nouwen, *Bread for the Journey: A Daybook of Wisdom and Faith* (San Francisco: Harper, 1997).

J. Gresham Machen, *What is Faith?* (Grand Rapids: Eerdmans, 2005).

Attributed to Charles H. Spurgeon, www.cross-points.org/100-best-charles-spurgeon-quotes/

WEEK FORTY-SIX

Bryan Chapell, *Unlimited Grace: The Heart Chemistry That Frees from Sin and Fuels the Christian Life* (Chicago: Crossway, 2016).

Archibald Alexander, *Thoughts on Religious Experience* (Carlisle, PA: Banner of Truth Trust, 1989).

Victor Hugo, *Les Misérables* (New York: Signet Classic, 1987).

Steve Brown, *Born Free* (Grand Rapids: Raven's Ridge Books, 1993).

James Henley Thornwell, "National Sins: Fast-Day Sermon," Preached in the Presbyterian Church, Columbia, S. C., Wednesday, November 21, 1860. (Columbia: Southern Guardian Steam-Power Press, 1860).

David Hansen, *The Art of Pastoring: Ministry Without All the Answers* (Downers Grove: InterVarsity Press, 1994).

Lawrence J. Crabb, *Men and Women: Enjoying the Difference* (Grand Rapids: Zondervan, 2013).

Andrew Bonar, *Memoir and Remains of R.M. M'Cheyne* (Edinburgh: Banner of Truth Trust, 1966).

Bryan Chapell, *Holiness by Grace* (Wheaton: Crossway, 2001).

Donald Miller, *Searching For God Knows What* (Nashville: Thomas Nelson, 2004).

WEEK FORTY-SEVEN

J. C. Ryle, *Holiness: Its Nature, Hindrances, Difficulties, and Roots* (Peabody: Hendrickson Publishers, 2007).

Sinclair B. Ferguson, *Grow in Grace* (London: Marshalls, 1981).

Richard G. Kyle, *God's Watchman: John Knox's Faith and Vocation* (Eugene: Pickwick Publications, 2014).

John Calvin, *Institutes of the Christian Religion* (Peabody, MA: Hendrickson Publishers, 2008).

Eugene H. Peterson, *Leap Over a Wall: Earthy Spirituality for Everyday Christians* (New York: HarperCollins, 1997).

Richard Sibbes, *The Bruised Reed* (Carlisle, PA: Puritan Paperbacks, 1998).

Richard J. Foster, *Celebration of Discipline: The Path to Spiritual Growth* (San Francisco: Harper & Row, 1988).

David Mathis, *Habits of Grace: Enjoying Jesus Through the Spiritual Disciplines* (Wheaton: Crossway, 2016).

Attributed to Charles H. Spurgeon, www.cross-points.org/100-best-charles-spurgeon-quotes/

WEEK FORTY-EIGHT

Sheldon Vanauken, *A Severe Mercy: A Story of Faith, Tragedy, and Triumph* (San Francisco: Harper, 1977).

Conrad Mbewe, "The African Import of Charismatic Chaos," (sermon, Grace Community Church, Sun Valley, CA, Oct 16, 2013).

R. C. Sproul, *The Prayer of the Lord* (Orlando: Reformation Trust, 2009).

Eugene H. Peterson, *Eat This Book: A Conversation in the Art of Spiritual Reading* (Grand Rapids: William B. Eerdmans, 2006).

Dennis Johnson, "The Rules of the Road." *Tabletalk*, February 1999, 10.

Elyse Fitzpatrick and Dennis Johnson, *Counsel from the Cross* (Wheaton: Crossway, 2012).

Luder G. Whitlock, *The Spiritual Quest: Pursuing Christian Maturity* (Grand Rapids: Baker Books, 2000).

John White, *The Fight: A Practical Handbook for Christian Living* (Downers Grove: InterVarsity Press, 1976).

Walter Marshall and Bruce H. McRae, *Gospel Mystery of Sanctification: Growing in Holiness by Living in Union With Christ* (Eugene: Wipf & Stock, 2005).

Jackie Hill Perry (@JackieHillPerry), "Mind renewal is a slow, active work" Twitter, November 29, 2017, 7:43 pm, https://twitter.com/JackieHillPerry/status/936078209879220224

WEEK FORTY-NINE

John Piper, *When I Don't Desire God: How to Fight for Joy* (Wheaton: Crossway, 2004).

Thomas Brooks, *Precious Remedies Against Satan's Devices* (London: Banner of Truth Trust, 1968).

Walter Marshall and Bruce H. McRae, *Gospel Mystery of Sanctification: Growing in Holiness by Living in Union With Christ* (Eugene: Wipf & Stock, 2005).

John Newton by Direction of His Executors, *The Posthumous Works of the Late Rev. John Newton* (Philadelphia: W.W. Woodward, 1809). https://books.google.com

Michael R. Emlet, *CrossTalk: Where Life & Scripture Meet* (Greensboro: New Growth Press, 2009).

David Calhoun, *Habakkuk: Covenant Theological Seminary Tape of the Month* (St. Louis: Covenant Theological, 2001).

Attributed to Thomas Watson, www.christianquotes.info/quotes-by-author/thomas-watson -quotes/

J. I. Packer, *Knowing God* (Downers Grove: InterVarsity Press, 1973).

C S. Storms, *Pleasures Evermore: The Life-Changing Power of Enjoying God* (Colorado Springs: NavPress, 2000).

WEEK FIFTY

Kevin DeYoung, *The Good News We Almost Forgot: Rediscovering the Gospel in a 16th Century Catechism* (Chicago: Moody Publishers, 2010).

Elizabeth Harwell, *The Good Shepherd's Pasture: A Story of Your Baptism* (Lawrenceville, GA: Committee for Discipleship Ministries, 2019).

Michael Horton *A Better Way: Rediscovering the Drama of God-Centered Worship* (Grand Rapids: Baker, 2002).

Timothy Keller, *Counterfeit Gods: The Empty Promises of Money, Sex, and Power, and the Only Hope That Matters* (New York: Riverhead Books, 2011).

R. C. Sproul, *A Taste of Heaven: Worship in the Light of Eternity* (Orlando: Reformation Trust Publishing, 2006).

Marilynne Robinson, *Gilead: A Novel* (New York: Picador, 2004).

Edmund P. Clowney and Gerald L. Bray, *The Church* (Downers Grove: InterVarsity Press, 1995).

WEEK FIFTY-ONE

John Owen quoted in John Nevin and J. Philip Horne, *The Mystical Presence: A Vindication of the Reformed or Calvinistic Doctrine of the Holy Eucharist* (Scotts Valley, CA: CreateSpace, 2012).

Michael Horton, *Putting Amazing Back into Grace* (Grand Rapids: Baker Book House, 1994).

J. Knox Chamberlin, *Paul and the Self: Apostolic Teaching for Personal Wholeness* (Eugene: Wipf & Stock, 2011).

Thomas Watson, *The Thomas Watson Collection* (Scotts Valley, CA: Create Space, 2014).

Augustine, *Confessions*, ed. Henry Chadwick (Oxford: Oxford University Press, 1998).

Harold L. Senkbeil, *Dying to Live: The Power of Forgiveness* (St. Louis: CPH, 1994).

Eugene H. Peterson, *The Jesus Way: A Conversation on the Ways That Jesus Is the Way* (Grand Rapids: William B. Eerdmans, 2011).

J. Todd Billings, *Remembrance, Communion, and Hope: Rediscovering the Gospel at the Lord's Table* (Grand Rapids: William B. Eerdmans, 2018).

Shauna Niequist, *Bread & Wine: A Love Letter to Life Around the Table* (Grand Rapids: Zondervan, 2013).

WEEK FIFTY-TWO

Brennan Manning, *The Furious Longing of God* (Colorado Spring: David C. Cook, 2009).

Iain H. Murray, *Revival and Revivalism* (Carlisle, PA: Banner of Truth, 1994).

Eugene H. Peterson, *Tell It Slant: A Conversation on the Language of Jesus in His Stories and Prayers* (Grand Rapids: William B. Eerdmans, 2012).

Harvie M. Conn, *Evangelism: Doing Justice and Preaching Grace* (Phillipsburg, PA: P&R, 1992).

Donald S. Whitney, *Spiritual Disciplines for the Christian Life* (Colorado Springs: NavPress, 1991).

E. M. Bounds, *The Complete Works of E. M. Bounds on Prayer* (Grand Rapids: Baker Book House, 1990).

D. Martyn Lloyd-Jones, *Studies in the Sermon on the Mount, Volume Two* (Grand Rapids: William B. Eerdmans Publishing Company, 1967).

Paul E. Miller, *A Praying Life: Connecting With God in a Distracting World* (Colorado Springs: NavPress, 2009).

John Piper, *Desiring God: Meditations of a Christian Hedonist* (Sisters, OR: Multnomah, 2011).

Fanny J. Crosby as quoted in *Prayers for You* (Nashville: Thomas Nelson, 2019).